Effective DevOps with AWS
Second Edition

Implement continuous delivery and integration in the
AWS environment

Yogesh Raheja
Giuseppe Borgese
Nathaniel Felsen

BIRMINGHAM - MUMBAI

Effective DevOps with AWS
Second Edition

Commissioning Editor: Gebin George
Acquisition Editor: Heramb Bhavsar
Content Development Editor: Abhijit Sreedharan
Technical Editor: Swathy Mohan
Copy Editor: Safis Editing
Project Coordinator: Jagdish Prabhu
Proofreader: Safis Editing
Indexer: Priyanka Dhadke
Graphics: Tom Scaria
Production Coordinator: Aparna Bhagat

First published: July 2017
Second edition: September 2018

Production reference: 1280918

Published by Packt Publishing Ltd.
Livery Place
35 Livery Street
Birmingham
B3 2PB, UK.

ISBN 978-1-78953-997-4

www.packtpub.com

`mapt.io`

Mapt is an online digital library that gives you full access to over 5,000 books and videos, as well as industry leading tools to help you plan your personal development and advance your career. For more information, please visit our website.

Why subscribe?

- Spend less time learning and more time coding with practical eBooks and Videos from over 4,000 industry professionals

- Improve your learning with Skill Plans built especially for you

- Get a free eBook or video every month

- Mapt is fully searchable

- Copy and paste, print, and bookmark content

Packt.com

Did you know that Packt offers eBook versions of every book published, with PDF and ePub files available? You can upgrade to the eBook version at `www.packt.com` and as a print book customer, you are entitled to a discount on the eBook copy. Get in touch with us at `customercare@packtpub.com` for more details.

At `www.packt.com`, you can also read a collection of free technical articles, sign up for a range of free newsletters, and receive exclusive discounts and offers on Packt books and eBooks.

Contributors

About the authors

Yogesh Raheja is a certified DevOps and cloud expert with a decade of IT experience. He has expertise in technologies such as OS, source code management, build and release tools, continuous integration/deployment/delivery tools, containers, configuration management tools, monitoring, logging tools, and public and private clouds. He loves to share his technical expertise with audience worldwide at various forums, conferences, webinars, blogs, and LinkedIn. He has written *Automation with Puppet 5* and *Automation with Ansible* and has published his online courses on Udemy. He has also reviewed multiple books for Packt like *Implementing Splunk 7, Third Edition* and *Splunk Operational Intelligence Cookbook, Third Edition*.

A big thanks to God who made me capable of sharing my knowledge with the world. Many thanks go to the great team at Packt for their outstanding work for this project. I would like to thank my mother Sudesh Rani and wife Divya Vohra Raheja for their love, endless support, patience, and help to chase my dreams. They makes everything possible for me. Finally, a special thanks to Gagandeep Singh, Kulbhushan Mayer and the great team of Thinknyx Technologies who inspired and motivated me to write this book.

Giuseppe Borgese is currently working as a DevOps AWS Specialist for Siemens. He possesses a master's degree in Internet Technology and is a certified AWS DevOps Engineer Professional holding 4 certifications. His contributions to the AWS community include a Youtube channel featuring a series of AWS Tutorials and numerous articles for renowned blogs such as LinuxAcademy. He also holds VMware and Cisco certifications. This is his second book and the first book published with Packt. In this book, the chapters, *Scaling Your Infrastructure* and *Hardening the Security of Your AWS Environment* have been contributed by him.

Nathaniel Felsen is a DevOps engineer who started working on DevOps engineering concepts over 10 years ago, before the term was even coined. He worked in several companies ranging from small start-ups to enterprises, including Qualys, Square, and more recently, Medium.

Outside of work, Nathaniel lives a fabulous life where he enjoys running after his very active kids and spending a fortune on occasional date nights with his wife. Although Nathaniel is French, he prefers exploring local stout beers with friends than drinking wine. He holds a MS degree in system, network, and security from Ecole Pour l'Informatique et les Techniques Avancées (EPITA), a top CS engineering school in France.

About the reviewer

Hai Dam is working as DevOps Engineer in Netcompany, Denmark. His DevOps toolchain: Jenkins, CircleCI, ELK, AWS, Docker.

Packt is searching for authors like you

If you're interested in becoming an author for Packt, please visit `authors.packtpub.com` and apply today. We have worked with thousands of developers and tech professionals, just like you, to help them share their insight with the global tech community. You can make a general application, apply for a specific hot topic that we are recruiting an author for, or submit your own idea.

Table of Contents

Preface

The DevOps movement has transformed the way modern tech companies work. Amazon Web Services (AWS), which has been at the forefront of the cloud computing revolution, has also been a key contributor to the DevOps movement, creating a huge range of managed services that help you implement DevOps principles.

In this book, you'll understand how the most successful tech start-ups launch and scale their services on AWS, and learn how you can do the same, too. This book explains how to treat infrastructure as code, meaning you can bring resources online and offline as easily as you control your software. You will also build a continuous integration and continuous deployment pipeline to keep your app up to date.

Once you have got to grips will all this, you'll move on to learning how to scale your applications to offer maximum performance to users even when traffic spikes, by using the latest technologies such as containers. In addition to this, you'll get insights into monitoring and alerting, so you can make sure your users have the best experience when using your service. In the concluding chapters, you'll cover inbuilt AWS tools such as CodeDeploy and CloudFormation, which are used by many AWS administrators to perform DevOps.

By the end of this book, you'll have learned how to ensure the security of your platform and data using the latest and most prominent AWS tools.

Who this book is for

This book is for you if you are a developer, DevOps engineer, or you work in a team which wants to build and use AWS for software infrastructure. Basic computer science knowledge is required to get the most out of this book.

What this book covers

Chapter 1, *The Cloud and DevOps Revolution*, this chapter will set the foundation to anyone about the need of DevOps and Cloud Journey. An in depth understanding of DevOps culture, DevOps Terminology and AWS ecosystem will be gained to start and prepare the roadmap for future chapters.

Chapter 2, *Deploying Your First Web Application*, this chapter will demonstrate AWS infrastructure provisioning in simplest form with some of the best AWS authentication practices. We will create a simple web application and understand how to host the application on AWS in the easiest form and finally will terminate the instance. This whole process will be implemented using AWS cli utility and will be automated in further chapter to understand how manual tasks can be automated using different available AWS and other famous services and products.

Chapter 3, *Treating Your Infrastructure as Code*, this chapter will focus on Automating Provisioning using AWS native utility CloudFormation and the techniques used to create CloudFormation templates. Then we will introduce a Configuration Management system to automate application deployments with Ansible.

Chapter 4, *Infrastructure as Code with Terraform*, this chapter will focus on understanding the fundamentals of Terraform. We will provision our first AWS instance using Terraform templates and then extend the power of Terraform to deploy the application using another Terraform Template. Finally we will understand AWS provisioning using Terraform by integrate it with Ansible automation for application deployments.

Chapter 5, *Adding Continuous Integration and Continuous Deployment*, this chapter will focus on building CI/CD pipelines using AWS DevOps services with Automated Testing Framework. We will prepare a technology framework using multiple tools like Version Control, Continuous Integration, Automated Testing tools, AWS native DevOps tools and Infrastructure Automation tools to understand how fail fast and fail often lead to an robust production environment.

Chapter 6, *Scaling Your Infrastructure*, this chapter will introduce other useful cost effective AWS services to build scalable AWS infrastructure with performance oriented vision. AWS services like Elastic Cache, CloudFront, SQS, Kinesis and so on will be used to build our application Framework.

Chapter 7, *Running Containers in AWS,* this chapter will introduce one of the most niche technologies in the market Docker. We will get started with the understanding of container using Docker with all of the essential concepts. Here we will build AWS container environment with ECS and build a complete framework of ECS for our application. At last we will build a complete CI/CD pipeline to deploy AWS ECS services using AWS DevOps tool set.

Chapter 8, *Hardening the Security of Your AWS Environment*, this chapter will focus on identifying and securing your AWS environment using AWS auditing services, AWS IAM services for managing and providing limited access as per roles, strengthening AWS VPC model and finally protecting against ransomware and other vulnerabilities.

Chapter 9, *Monitoring and Alerting,* this chapter will focus on building a monitoring framework for your AWS environment using AWS CloudWatch service. We will use some of the famous dashboard tools for visualization of logs. Finally a notification framework will be created using AWS SNS services to notify the users about the health of your AWS environment to take corrective actions. For this chapter refer to `https://www.packtpub.com/sites/default/files/downloads/Monitoring_and_Alerting.pdf`.

To get the most out of this book

The software required for this book are as follows:

- AWS Management Console
- AWS compute services
- AWS IAM
- AWS CLI setup
- JavaScript for the web application

Download the example code files

You can download the example code files for this book from your account at `www.packt.com`. If you purchased this book elsewhere, you can visit `www.packt.com/support` and register to have the files emailed directly to you.

You can download the code files by following these steps:

1. Log in or register at `www.packt.com`.
2. Select the **SUPPORT** tab.
3. Click on **Code Downloads & Errata**.
4. Enter the name of the book in the **Search** box and follow the onscreen instructions.

Once the file is downloaded, please make sure that you unzip or extract the folder using the latest version of:

- WinRAR/7-Zip for Windows
- Zipeg/iZip/UnRarX for Mac
- 7-Zip/PeaZip for Linux

The code bundle for the book is also hosted on GitHub at `https://github.com/PacktPublishing/Effective-DevOps-with-AWS-Second-Edition`. In case there's an update to the code, it will be updated on the existing GitHub repository.

We also have other code bundles from our rich catalog of books and videos available at `https://github.com/PacktPublishing/`. Check them out!

The codes can also be found at following repositories:

- `https://github.com/yogeshraheja/Effective-DevOps-with-AWS`
- `https://github.com/giuseppeborgese/effective_devops_with_aws__second_edition`

Download the color images

We also provide a PDF file that has color images of the screenshots/diagrams used in this book. You can download it here: `https://www.packtpub.com/sites/default/files/downloads/9781789539974_ColorImages.pdf`.

Conventions used

There are a number of text conventions used throughout this book.

`CodeInText`: Indicates code words in text, database table names, folder names, filenames, file extensions, pathnames, dummy URLs, user input, and Twitter handles. Here is an example: "Click on the start button and search for `settings` option."

A block of code is set as follows:

```
var http = require("http") http.createServer(function (request, response) {
// Send the HTTP header
// HTTP Status: 200 : OK
// Content Type: text/plain
response.writeHead(200, {'Content-Type': 'text/plain'})
// Send the response body as "Hello World" response.end('Hello World\n')
}).listen(3000)

// Console will print the message console.log('Server running')
```

When we wish to draw your attention to a particular part of a code block, the relevant lines or items are set in bold:

```
$ aws ec2 describe-instance-status --instance-ids i-057e8deb1a4c3f35d --
output text| grep -i SystemStatus

SYSTEMSTATUS ok
```

Any command-line input or output is written as follows:

```
$ aws ec2 authorize-security-group-ingress \
    --group-name HelloWorld \
    --protocol tcp \
    --port 3000 \
    --cidr 0.0.0.0/0
```

Bold: Indicates a new term, an important word, or words that you see onscreen. For example, words in menus or dialog boxes appear in the text like this. Here is an example: "In this menu, find the feature called **Windows Subsystem for Linux (Beta).**"

Warnings or important notes appear like this.

Tips and tricks appear like this.

Get in touch

Feedback from our readers is always welcome.

General feedback: If you have questions about any aspect of this book, mention the book title in the subject of your message and email us at customercare@packtpub.com.

Errata: Although we have taken every care to ensure the accuracy of our content, mistakes do happen. If you have found a mistake in this book, we would be grateful if you would report this to us. Please visit www.packt.com/submit-errata, selecting your book, clicking on the Errata Submission Form link, and entering the details.

Piracy: If you come across any illegal copies of our works in any form on the Internet, we would be grateful if you would provide us with the location address or website name. Please contact us at copyright@packt.com with a link to the material.

If you are interested in becoming an author: If there is a topic that you have expertise in and you are interested in either writing or contributing to a book, please visit authors.packtpub.com.

Reviews

Please leave a review. Once you have read and used this book, why not leave a review on the site that you purchased it from? Potential readers can then see and use your unbiased opinion to make purchase decisions, we at Packt can understand what you think about our products, and our authors can see your feedback on their book. Thank you!

For more information about Packt, please visit packt.com.

The Cloud and DevOps Revolution

1

The technological industry is constantly changing. Although the internet was born only a quarter of a century ago, it has already transformed the way that we live. Every day, over a billion people visit Facebook; every minute, approximately 300 hours of video footage are uploaded on YouTube; and every second, Google processes approximately 40,000 search queries. Being able to handle such a staggering scale isn't easy. However, this book will provide you with a practical guide for deployment philosophy, tooling, or using the best practices of the companies. Through the use of **Amazon Web Services (AWS)**, you will be able to build the key elements required to efficiently manage and scale your infrastructure, your engineering processes, and your applications, with minimal cost and effort. This first chapter will explain the new paradigms of the following topics:

- Thinking in terms of the cloud, and not infrastructure
- Adopting a DevOps culture
- Deploying in AWS

Thinking in terms of the cloud, and not infrastructure

We will now describe a real incident that took place in a datacenter in late December, 2011, when dozens of alerts were received from our live monitoring system. This was a result of losing connectivity to the datacenter. In response to this, administrator rushed to the **Network Operations Center** (**NOC**), hoping that it was only a small glitch in the monitoring system. With so much redundancy, we may wonder how everything *can go offline*. Unfortunately, the big monitoring screens in the NOC room were all red, which is not a good sign. This was the beginning of a very long nightmare.

As it happens, this was caused by an electrician who was working in the datacenter and mistakenly triggered the fire alarm. Within seconds of this occurring, the fire suppression system set off and released its aragonite on top of the server racks. Unfortunately, this kind of fire suppression system made so much noise when it released its gas that sound waves instantly killed hundreds of hard drives, effectively shutting down the data center facility. It took months to recover from this.

Deploying your own hardware versus in the cloud

It wasn't long ago that tech companies, small and large, had to have a proper technical operations team, able to build infrastructures. The process went a little bit like this:

1. Fly to the location where you want to set up your infrastructure. Here, take a tour of different datacenters and their facilities. Observe the floor considerations, power considerations, **Heating, Ventilation, and Air Conditioning** (**HVAC**), fire prevention systems, physical security, and so on.
2. Shop for an internet service provider. Ultimately, you are considering servers and a lot more bandwidth, but the process is the same—you want to acquire internet connectivity for your servers.
3. Once this is done, it's time to buy your hardware. Make the right decisions here, because you will probably spend a big portion of your company's money on selecting and buying servers, switches, routers, firewalls, storage, UPS (for when you have a power outage), KVM, network cables, labeling (which is dear to every system administrator's heart), and a bunch of spare parts, hard drives, raid controllers, memory, power cables, and so on.

4. At this point, once the hardware has been purchased and shipped to the data center location, you can rack everything, wire all the servers, and power everything on. Your network team can kick in and establish connectivity to the new datacenter using various links, configuring the edge routers, switches, top of the rack switches, KVM, and firewalls (sometimes). Your storage team is next, and will provide the much-needed **Network Attached Storage** (**NAS**) or **Storage Area Network** (**SAN**). Next comes your sysops team, which will image the servers, upgrade the BIOS (sometimes), configure the hardware raid, and finally, put an OS on the servers.

Not only is this a full-time job for a big team, but it also takes a lot of time and money to even get there. As you will see in this book, getting new servers up and running with AWS only takes us a few minutes. In fact, you will soon see how to deploy and run multiple services in a few minutes, and just when you need it, with the *pay-what-you-use* model.

Cost analysis

From the perspective of cost, deploying services and applications in a cloud infrastructure such as AWS usually ends up being a lot cheaper than buying your own hardware. If you want to deploy your own hardware, you have to pay for all of the hardware mentioned previously (servers, network equipment, storage, and so on) upfront as well as licensed software, in some cases. In a cloud environment, *you pay as you go*. You can add or remove servers in no time, and will only be charged for the duration in which the servers were running. Also, if you take advantage of PaaS and SaaS applications, you will usually end up saving even more money by lowering your operating costs, as you won't need as many administrators to administrate your servers, database, storage, and so on. Most cloud providers (AWS included) also offer tiered pricing and volume discounts. As your service grows, you will end up paying less for each unit of storage, bandwidth, and so on.

Just-in-time infrastructure

As you just saw, when deploying in the cloud, you only pay for the resources that you are provided with. Most cloud companies use this to their advantage, in order to scale their infrastructure up or down as the traffic to their site changes. This ability to add or remove new servers and services in no time and on demand is one of the main differentiators of an effective cloud infrastructure.

In the following example, you can see the amount of traffic at `https://www.amazon.com/` during the month of November. Thanks to Black Friday and Cyber Monday, the traffic triples at the end of the month:

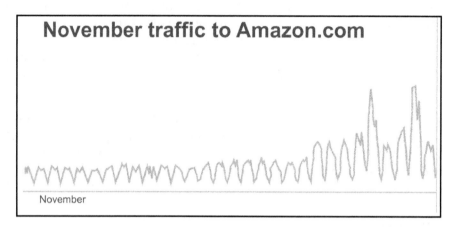

If the company were hosting their service in an old-fashioned way, they would need to have enough servers provisioned to handle this traffic, so that only 24% of their infrastructure would be used during the month, on average:

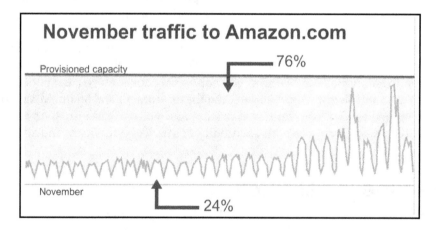

However, thanks to being able to scale dynamically, they can provide only what they really need, and then dynamically absorb the spikes in traffic that Black Friday and Cyber Monday trigger:

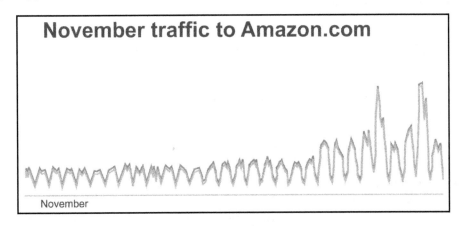

You can also see the benefits of having fast auto-scaling capabilities on a very regular basis, across multiple organizations using the cloud. This is again a real case study taken by the company *medium, very often*. Here, stories become viral, and the amount of traffic going on drastically changes. On January 21, 2015, the White House posted a transcript of the State of the Union minutes before President Obama began his speech: http://bit.ly/2sDvseP. As you can see in the following graph, thanks to being in the cloud and having auto-scaling capabilities, the platform was able to absorb five times the instant spike of traffic that the announcement made, by doubling the number of servers that the front service used. Later, as the traffic started to drain naturally, you automatically removed some hosts from your fleet:

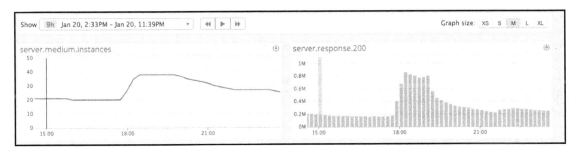

The different layers of a cloud

Cloud computing is often broken down into three different types of services, generally called **service models**, as follows:

- **Infrastructure as a Service** (**IaaS**): This is the fundamental building block, on top of which everything related to the cloud is built. IaaS is usually a computing resource in a virtualized environment. This offers a combination of processing power, memory, storage, and network. The most common IaaS entities that you will find are **Virtual Machines** (**VMs**) and network equipment, such as load balancers or virtual Ethernet interfaces, and storage, such as block devices. This layer is very close to the hardware, and offers the full flexibility that you would get when deploying your software outside of a cloud. If you have any experience with datacenters, it will also apply mostly to this layer.

- **Platform as a Service** (**PaaS**): This layer is where things start to get really interesting with the cloud. When building an application, you will likely need a certain number of common components, such as a data store and a queue. The PaaS layer provides a number of ready-to-use applications, to help you build your own services without worrying about administrating and operating third-party services, such as database servers.

- **Software as a Service** (**SaaS**): This layer is the icing on the cake. Similar to the PaaS layer, you get access to managed services, but this time, these services are a complete solution dedicated to certain purposes, such as management or monitoring tools.

We would suggest that you go through the *National Institute of Standard and Technology (NIST) Definition of Cloud Computing* at https://nvlpubs.nist.gov/nistpubs/legacy/sp/nistspecialpublication800-145.pdf and the *NIST Cloud Computing Standards Roadmap* at https://www.nist.gov/sites/default/files/documents/itl/cloud/NIST_SP-500-291_Version-2_2013_June18_FINAL.pdf. This book covers a fair amount of services of the PaaS and SaaS types. While building an application, relying on these services makes a big difference, in comparison to the more traditional environment outside of the cloud. Another key element to success when deploying or migrating to a new infrastructure is adopting a DevOps mindset.

Adopting a DevOps culture

Running a company with a DevOps culture is all about adopting the right culture to allow developers and the operations team to work together. A DevOps culture advocates the implementation of several engineering best practices, by relying on tools and technologies that you will discover throughout this book.

The origin of DevOps

DevOps is a new movement that officially started in Belgium in 2009, when a group of people met at the first DevOpsdays conference, organized by Patrick Debois, to discuss how to apply some agile concepts to infrastructure. Agile methodologies transformed the way software is developed. In a traditional waterfall model, the product team would come up with specifications; the design team would then create and define a certain user experience and user interface; the engineering team would then start to implement the requested product or feature, and would then hand off the code to the QA team, who would test and ensure that the code behaved correctly, according to the design specifications. Once all the bugs were fixed, a release team would package the final code, which would be handed off to the technical operations team, to deploy the code and monitor the services over time:

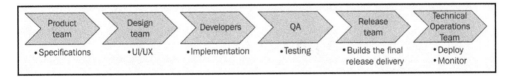

The increasing complexity of developing certain software and technologies showed some limitations with this traditional waterfall pipeline. The agile transformation addressed some of these issues, allowing for more interaction between the designers, developers, and testers. This change increased the overall quality of the product, as these teams now had the opportunity to iterate more on product development. However, apart from this, you would still be in a very classical waterfall pipeline, as follows:

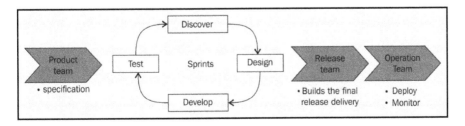

All of the agility added by this new process didn't extend past the QA cycles, and it was time to modernize this aspect of the software development life cycle. This foundational change with the agile process which allows for more collaboration between the designers, developers, and QA teams, is what DevOps was initially after, but very quickly, the DevOps movement started to rethink how developers and operations teams could work together.

The developers versus operations dilemma

In a non-DevOps culture, developers are in charge of developing new products and features and maintaining the existing code, but ultimately, they are rewarded when their code is shipped. The incentive is to deliver as quickly as possible. On the other hand, the operations team, in general, is responsible for maintaining the uptime of the production environment. For these teams, change is a negative thing. New features and services increase the risk of having an outage, and therefore, it is important to move with caution. To minimize the risk of outages, operations teams usually have to schedule any deployments ahead of time, so that they can stage and test any production deployment and maximize their chances of success. It is also very common for enterprise software companies to schedule maintenance windows, and, in these cases, production changes can only be made a few times a quarter, half-yearly, or once a year. Unfortunately, many times, deployments won't succeed, and there are many possible reasons for that.

Too much code changing at once

There is a correlation that can be made between the size of the change and the risk of introducing critical bugs into the product, as follows:

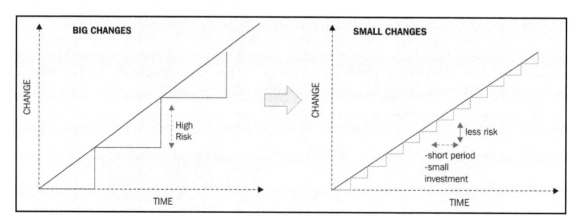

Differences in the production environment

It is often the case that the code produced by developers works fine in a development environment, but not in production. A lot of the time, this is because the production environment is very different from other environments, and some unforeseen errors occur. The common mistakes involve the development environment, because services are collocated on the same servers, or there isn't the same level of security. As a consequence, services can communicate with one another in development, but not in production. Another issue is that the development environment might not run the same versions of a certain library/software, and therefore, the interface to communicate with them might differ. The development environment may be running a newer version of a service, which has new features that the production doesn't have yet; or it could be simply a question of scale. Perhaps the dataset used in development isn't as big as that of production, and scaling issues will crop up once the new code is out in production.

Communication

One of the biggest dilemmas in information technology is miscommunication.

The following is according to Conway's Law:

> *"Organizations which design systems are constrained to produce designs which are copies of the communication structures of these organizations."*
>
> *—Melvin Conway*

In other words, the product that you are building reflects the communication of your organization. A lot of the time, problems don't come from the technology, but from the people and organizations surrounding the technology. If there is dysfunction among your developers and operations team in the organization, this will show. In a DevOps culture, developers and operations have a different mindset. They help to break down the silos that surround those teams, by sharing responsibilities and adopting similar methodologies to improve productivity. Together, they try to automate whatever is possible (not everything, as not everything can be automated in a single go) and use metrics to measure their success.

Key characteristics of a DevOps culture

As we have noted, a DevOps culture relies on a certain number of principles. These principles are to source control (version control) everything, automate whatever is possible, and measure everything.

Source control everything

Revision control software has been around for many decades now, but too often, only the product code is checked. When practicing DevOps, not only is the application code checked, but configurations, tests, documentation, and all of the infrastructure automation needed to deploy the application in all environments, are also checked. Everything goes through the regular review process by the **Source Code Manager** (**SCM**).

Automating testing

Automated software testing predates the history of DevOps, but it is a good starting point. Too often, developers focus on implementing features and forget to add a test to their code. In a DevOps environment, developers are responsible for adding proper testing to their code. QA teams can still exist; however, similar to other engineering teams, they work on building automation around testing.

This topic could fill its own book, but in a nutshell, when developing code, keep in mind that there are four levels of testing automation to focus on, in order to successfully implement DevOps:

- **Unit testing**: This is to test the functionality of each code block and function.
- **Integration testing**: This is to make sure that services and components work together.
- **User interface testing**: This is often the most challenging component to successfully implement.
- **System testing**: This is end-to-end testing. For example, in a photo- sharing application, the end-to-end testing could be to open the home page, sign in, upload a photo, add a caption, publish the photo, and then sign out.

Automating infrastructure provisioning and configuration

In the last few decades, the size of the average infrastructure and the complexity of the stack have skyrocketed. Managing infrastructure on an ad-hoc basis, as was once possible, is very error-prone. In a DevOps culture, the provisioning and configuration of servers, networks, and services in general, are performed through automation. Configuration management is often what the DevOps movement is known for. However, as you know, this is just a small piece of a big puzzle.

Automating deployment

As you now, it is easier to write software in small chunks and deploy the new chunks as soon as possible, to make sure that they are working. To get there, companies practicing DevOps rely on continuous integration and continuous deployment pipelines. Whenever a new chunk of code is ready, the continuous integration pipeline kicks off. Through an automated testing system, the new code is run through all of the relevant, available tests. If the new code shows no obvious regression, it is considered valid and can be merged to the main code base. At that point, without further involvement from the developer, a new version of the service (or application) that includes those new changes will be created and handed off to a system called a **continuous deployment system**. The continuous deployment system will take the new builds and automatically deploy them to the different environments that are available. Depending on the complexity of the deployment pipeline, this might include a staging environment, an integration environment, and sometimes, a pre-production environment. Ultimately, if everything goes as planned (without any manual intervention), this new build will get deployed to production.

One aspect about practicing continuous integration and continuous deployment that often gets misunderstood is that new features don't have to be accessible to users as soon as they are developed. In this paradigm, developers heavily rely on feature flagging and dark launches. Essentially, whenever you develop new code and want to hide it from the end users, you set a flag in your service configuration to describe who gets access to the new feature, and how. At the engineering level, by dark launching a new feature this way, you can send production traffic to the service, but hide it from the UI, to see the impact it has on your database or on performance, for example. At the product level, you can decide to enable the new feature for only a small percentage of your users, to see if the new feature is working correctly and if the users who have access to the new feature are more engaged than the control group, for example.

Measuring everything

Measuring everything is the last major principle that DevOps-driven companies adopt. As Edwards Deming said, *you can't improve what you can't measure.* DevOps is an ever-evolving process and methodology that feeds off those metrics to assess and improve the overall quality of the product and the team working on it. From a tooling and operating standpoint, the following are some of the metrics most organizations look at:

- How many builds are pushed to production a day
- How often you need to roll back production in your production environment (this is indicated when your testing didn't catch an important issue)
- The percentage of code coverage
- The frequency of alerts resulting in paging the on-call engineers for immediate attention
- The frequency of outages
- Application performance
- The **Mean Time to Resolution** (**MTTR**), which is the speed at which an outage or a performance issue can be fixed

At the organizational level, it is also interesting to measure the impact of shifting to a DevOps culture. While this is a lot harder to measure, you can consider the following points:

- The amount of collaboration across teams
- Team autonomy
- Cross-functional work and team efforts
- Fluidity in the product
- How often Dev and Ops communicate
- Happiness among engineers
- Attitudes towards automation
- Obsession with metrics

As you just learned, having a DevOps culture means, first of all, changing the traditional mindset that developers and operations are two separate silos, and making the teams collaborate more, during all phases of the software development life cycle.

In addition to a new mindset, DevOps culture requires a specific set of tools geared toward automation, deployment, and monitoring:

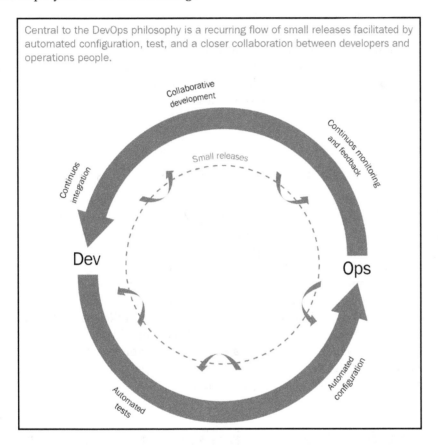

Central to the DevOps philosophy is a recurring flow of small releases facilitated by automated configuration, test, and a closer collaboration between developers and operations people.

With AWS, Amazon offers a number of services of the PaaS and SaaS types that will let us do just that.

Deploying in AWS

AWS is at the forefront of cloud providers. Launched in 2006, with SQS and EC2, Amazon quickly became the biggest IaaS provider. They have the biggest infrastructure and ecosystem, with constant additions of new features and services. In 2018, they passed more than a million active customers. Over the last few years, they have managed to change peoples mindsets about the cloud, and deploying new services to this is now the norm. Using AWS's managed tools and services is a way to drastically improve your productivity and keep your team lean. Amazon continually listens to its customer's feedback and looks at the market trends. Therefore, as the DevOps movement started to get established, Amazon released a number of new services tailored toward implementing some DevOps best practices. In this book, you will see how these services synergize with the DevOps culture.

How to take advantage of the AWS ecosystem?

Amazon services are like Lego pieces. If you can picture your final product, then you can explore the different services and start combining them, in order to build the stack needed to quickly and efficiently build your product. Of course, in this case, the *if* is a big if, and, unlike Lego, understanding what each piece can do is a lot less visual and colorful. That is why this book is written in a very practical way; throughout the different chapters, we are going to take a web application and deploy it like it's our core product. You will see how to scale the infrastructure supporting it, so that millions of people can use it, and also so that you can make it more secure. And, of course, we will do this following DevOps best practices. By going through that exercise, you will learn how AWS provides a number of managed services and systems to perform a number of common tasks, such as computing, networking, load balancing, storing data, monitoring, programmatically managing infrastructure and deployment, caching, and queuing.

How does AWS synergize with a DevOps culture?

As you saw earlier in this chapter, having a DevOps culture is about rethinking how engineering teams work together, by breaking the development and operations silos and bringing a new set of tools, in order to implement the best practices. AWS helps to accomplish this in many different ways. For some developers, the world of operations can be scary and confusing, but if you want better cooperation between engineers, it is important to expose every aspect of running a service to the entire engineering organization.

As an operations engineer, you can't have a gatekeeper mentality towards developers. Instead, it's better to make them comfortable by accessing production and working on the different components of the platform. A good way to get started with this is in the AWS console, as follows:

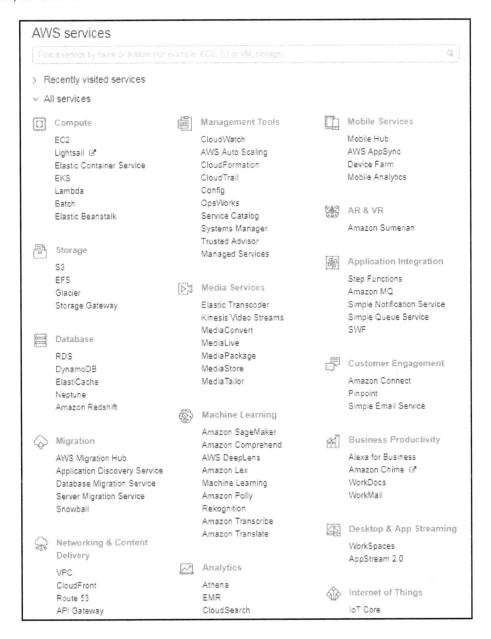

While a bit overwhelming, this is still a much better experience for people who are unfamiliar with navigating this web interface, rather than referring to constantly out-of-date documentation, using SSH and random plays in order to discover the topology and configuration of the service. Of course, as your expertise grows and your application becomes more complex, the need to operate it faster increases, and the web interface starts to show some weaknesses. To get around this issue, AWS provides a very DevOps-friendly alternative. An API is accessible through a command-line tool and a number of SDKs (including Java, JavaScript, Python, .NET, PHP, Ruby Go, and C++). These SDKs let you administrate and use the managed services. Finally, as you saw in the previous section, AWS offers a number of services that fit DevOps methodologies and will ultimately allow us to implement complex solutions in no time.

Some of the major services that you will use, at the computing level are Amazon **Elastic Compute Cloud** (EC2), the service to create virtual servers. Later, as you start to look into how to scale the infrastructure, you will discover Amazon EC2 Auto Scaling, a service that lets you scale pools on EC2 instances, in order to handle traffic spikes and host failures. You will also explore the concept of containers with Docker, through Amazon **Elastic Container Service** (ECS). In addition to this, you will create and deploy your application using AWS Elastic Beanstalk, with which you retain full control over the AWS resources powering your application; you can access the underlying resources at any time. Lastly, you will create serverless functions through AWS Lambda, to run custom code without having to host it on our servers. To implement your continuous integration and continuous deployment system, you will rely on the following four services:

- **AWS Simple Storage Service** (**S3**): This is the object store service that will allow us to store our artifacts
- **AWS CodeBuild:** This will let us test our code
- **AWS CodeDeploy:** This will let us deploy artifacts to our EC2 instances
- **AWS CodePipeline:** This will let us orchestrate how our code is built, tested, and deployed across environments

To monitor and measure everything, you will rely on **AWS CloudWatch,** and later, on **ElasticSearch/Kibana**, to collect, index, and visualize metrics and logs. To stream some of our data to these services, you will rely on **AWS Kinesis**. To send email and SMS alerts, you will use the **Amazon SNS** service. For infrastructure management, you will heavily rely on **AWS CloudFormation**, which provides the ability to create templates of infrastructures. In the end, as you explore ways to better secure our infrastructure, you will encounter **Amazon Inspector** and **AWS Trusted Advisor**, and you will explore the IAM and the VPC services in more detail.

Summary

In this chapter, you learned that adopting a DevOps culture means changing the way that traditional engineering and operations teams operate. Instead of two isolated teams with opposing goals and responsibilities, companies with a DevOps culture take advantage of complementary domains of expertise to better collaborate through converging processes and using a new set of tools. These new processes and tools include not only automating whatever possible, from testing and deployment through to infrastructure management, but also measuring everything, so that you can improve each process over time. When it comes to cloud services, AWS is leading the catalogue with more services than any other cloud provider. All of these services are usable through APIs and SDKs, which is good for automation. In addition, AWS has tools and services for each key characteristic of the DevOps culture.

In Chapter 2, *Deploying Your First Web Application*, we will finally gets our hands dirty and start to use AWS. The final goal of the chapter will be to have a Hello World application, accessible to anyone on the internet.

Questions

1. What is DevOps?
2. What is DevOps – IaC?
3. List the key characteristics of a DevOps culture.
4. What are the three major service models in the cloud?
5. What is the AWS cloud?

Further reading

You can explore more about AWS services at https://aws.amazon.com/products/.

2
Deploying Your First Web Application

In the previous chapter, we covered a general introduction to the cloud, its benefits, and what having a DevOps philosophy means. AWS offers a number of services that are all easily accessible through the web interface, command-line interface, various SDKs, and APIs. In this chapter, we will take advantage of the web interface and command-line interface to create and configure our account and create a web server to host a simple Hello World application, all in a matter of minutes.

In this chapter, we will go through the following topics:

- Creating and configuring your account
- Spinning up your first web server

Technical requirements

The technologies and services used in this chapter are as follows:

- AWS Management Console
- AWS compute services
- AWS IAM
- AWS CLI setup
- JavaScript for the web application
- GitHub for ready made code

The GitHub links for the code are as follows:

- https://raw.githubusercontent.com/yogeshraheja/Effective-DevOps-with-AWS/master/Chapter02/helloworld.js
- https://raw.githubusercontent.com/yogeshraheja/Effective-DevOps-with-AWS/master/Chapter02/helloworld.conf

Creating and configuring your account

If you haven't signed up for AWS yet, it is time to do so.

Signing up

This step is, of course, fairly simple and self-explanatory. In order to sign up (if you haven't done so yet), open https://portal.aws.amazon.com in your browser, click on the **Create a new AWS account** button, and follow the steps. You will need an email address and your credit card information.

The two exceptions to this process are as follows:

- If you plan to deploy servers in China, then you need to create your account in the AWS China region at https://www.amazonaws.cn/.
- AWS has a special facility called **GovCloud** for specific regulatory needs of United States federal, state, and local agencies. To sign up for this, go to the following link at https://aws.amazon.com/govcloud-us/contact/.

 In this book, we will use servers located in Northern Virginia so you will need to sign up using the standard registration process.

Amazon runs a free-tier program for new users. This is designed to help you to discover AWS services free of cost. Amazon gives free credit on most services. It is likely that over time the offer will change, so this book isn't going to cover the specifics of this offer, but the details are available at https://aws.amazon.com/free/.

Once you're done with the sign-up process, you will be on the AWS Management Console landing page. This screen can be a bit overwhelming as Amazon now has a lot of services, but you will quickly get used to it. If you are a fan of bookmarks, this page is definitely a prime candidate:

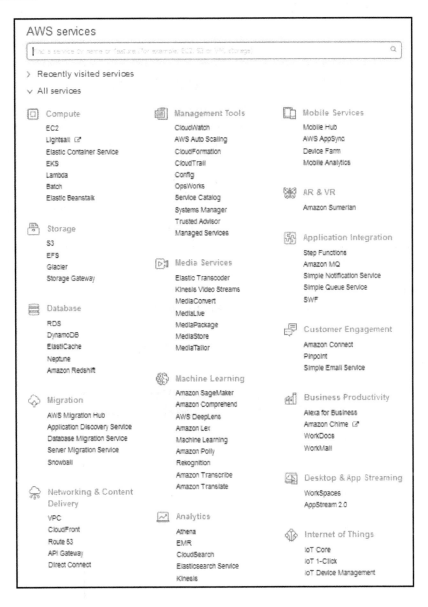

The account you just created is called a **root** account. This account will always have full access to all resources. Because of this, make sure that you keep your password in a safe place. The best practice is to use the root account only to create the initial user through the IAM service that we will discover shortly. In addition, it is strongly recommended to switch to **multi-factor authentication** (**MFA**) and use the identity service **IAM**—to manage user accounts, so pick a relatively complex password.

Enabling MFA on the root account

In order to avoid any kind of issues, the first thing we need to do once we sign up is enable MFA. In case you haven't seen or heard of this before, MFA is a security system that requires more than one method of authentication from independent categories of credentials. These are used to verify the user's identity in order to log in. In practice, once enabled, you will need the password previously set when you signed up in order to login. However, you will also need another code provided from a different source. That second source can be provided through a physical device such as the SafeNet IDProve, which is available at `http://amzn.to/2u4K1rR`, through an SMS on your phone, or through an application installed on your smartphone. We will use the third option—an application installed on your smartphone, which is completely free:

1. Go to your App Store, Google Play Store, or App Marketplace and install an application called **Google Authenticator** (or any other equivalent, such as **Authy**).

2. In the AWS Management Console, open the **My Security Credentials** page in the top-right corner:

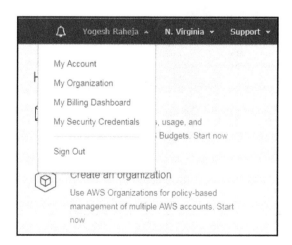

3. If prompted to create and use AWS **Identity and Access Management (IAM)**, users with limited permissions, click on the **Continue to Security Credentials** button. We will explore the IAM system in Chapter 3, *Treating Your Infrastructure as Code.* Expand the **Multi-factor authentication (MFA)** section on the page.

4. Pick virtual MFA and follow the instructions to sync Google authentication with your root account (note that the scan QR code option is the easiest one to pair the device).

From this point on, you will need your password and the token displayed on the MFA application in order to log in as root in the AWS console.

Two general tips for managing your passwords and MFA are as follows:

- There are a number of good applications to manage passwords, such as **1Password** at https://agilebits.com/onepassword or **Dashlane** at https://www.dashlane.com.
- For MFA, you can also try using **Authy** at https://www.authy.com. This works like Google Authenticator but also has a centralized server allowing it to work across multiple devices (including desktop applications), so if you lose your phone, you won't lose access to AWS.

As we have seen earlier, the root account usage should be limited to a bare minimum. So, in order to create virtual servers, configure services, and so on, we will rely on the IAM service which will let us have granular control over permissions for each user.

Creating a new user in IAM

In this section, we will create and configure accounts for different individuals who need access to AWS. For now, we will keep things simple and only create an account for ourselves, as follows:

1. Navigate to the **IAM** menu in the AWS console (`https://console.aws.amazon.com/iam/`) or go to the **Services** drop-down list on the top left corner of the AWS console page and search for `IAM`:

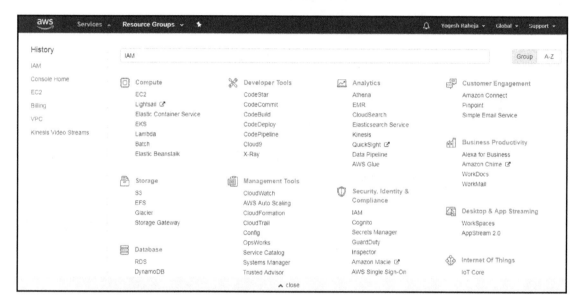

2. Choose the **Users** option from the navigation pane.
3. Create a new user by clicking on the **Add user** button, and make sure that you tick the **Programmatic access** option to generate an access key ID and a secret access key for the user.
4. Select the default options for now and create a user. Don't forget to download credentials.
5. Back in the **Users** menu, click on your username to access the details page.

6. In the **Permissions** tab, click on the **Add permissions** button and select the **Attach existing policies directly** option. Click on **AdministratorAccess** to provide full access to AWS services and resources to our newly created user.

7. Select the checkbox next to the **AdministratorAccess** option to provide full access to AWS services and resource to our newly created user. You will be left with a screen that looks like this:

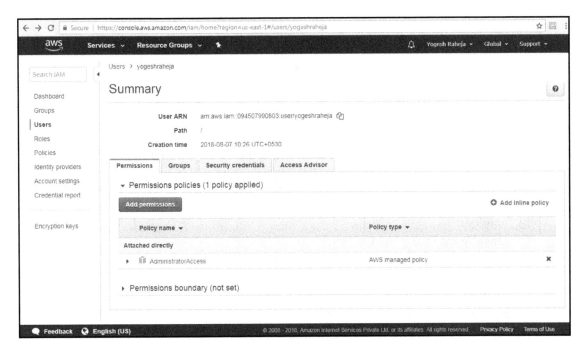

The last thing we need to do is add a password and turn on MFA for this account. This can be done as follows:

8. Click on the **Security credentials** tab.

9. Now click on the **Console password** option and enable the password for the newly created user. Set the password of your choice and click on the **Apply** button.

10. Once you're done with adding a password, click on the **Assigned MFA device** option.

11. Select **A virtual MFA device** option and follow the remaining instructions in order to turn on MFA in your newly created account. You will get a message stating that **The MFA device was successfully associated with your account,** as shown in the following screenshot:

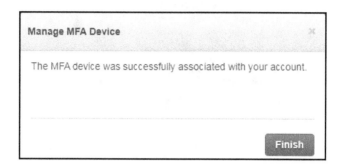

12. At this point, you are ready to start using the newly created user account. The important thing to note here is that signing in with an IAM user account is different from the root account. The main difference is that you sign in using a different URL.

13. Navigate to `https://console.aws.amazon.com/iam/home#home` or click on the **Dashboard** in the **IAM** menu.

14. You will see your unique sign-in URL under **IAM users sign-in link**. Feel free to also customize the link. Save this new URL in your bookmarks, and, from now on, use this link to sign into the AWS console.

15. Sign out from the root account.

16. Sign back in, but this time use your IAM user account at `https://AWS-account-ID` or `alias.signin.aws.amazon.com/console.`

Do not share your access key and secret key. By going through those steps, we enforced the use of MFA to access the AWS Console with our IAM user. We now need two factors (the password and the MFA token) to access the console. That said, we also created an access key which is far less secure. Anyone in possession of the secret key and access key (both present in the `credentials.csv`) will have full administrative access to the AWS account. Make sure to never share these credentials online. In Chapter 8, *Hardening the Security of Your AWS Environment*, we will make a few changes to better protect this key and require the use of MFA to gain administrator privileges.

The next step in configuring our account is to configure our computers to interact with AWS using the command-line interface.

Installing and configuring the command-line interface (CLI)

Using Amazon's web interface is usually a great way to explore new services. The problem is that when you want to go fast, create more repeatable steps, or create good documentation, having simple commands to execute becomes more efficient. Amazon provides a great and easy-to-use CLI. The tool is written in Python and therefore is cross-platform (Windows, Mac, and Linux).

We will install the tool on our laptop/desktop so that we can interact with AWS using bash commands. Linux and macOS X come natively with bash. If you use one of these operating systems, you can skip the next section. On Windows, we first need to install a feature called **Windows Subsystem for Linux** (**WSL**), which will give us the ability to run Bash commands that are very similar to what you get on Ubuntu Linux.

Installing WSL (Windows only)

Nowadays, Linux and macOS X are among the most predominant OS used by developers. Windows recently released a partnership with Canonical, the company behind one of the most popular Linux distributions, support for Bash, and most of the common Linux packages. By installing this tool on Windows, we will be able to interact with our servers more efficiently, which will also run Linux:

1. Click on the Start button and search for settings, and then open the **Settings** application:

2. This will lead you to the following window, where you have to search for `Windows Update settings`. Open the **Windows Update settings** menu:

3. In the left-hand side menu of **Windows Update settings**, click on the **For developers** sub-menu and turn on the **Developer mode** option.

4. Once your developer mode is turned on, search in the search bar on the left-hand-side menu for the `Control Panel` option:

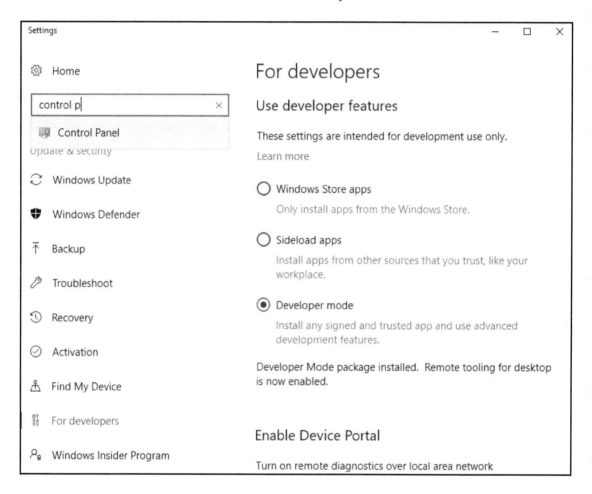

5. In the **Control Panel** dashboard, select the **Category** option from the **View by** drop-down, and click on the **Programs** option. Then, under **Programs and Features**, click on the **Turn Windows features on or off** option:

Adjust your computer's settings   View by: Category ▼

System and Security
Review your computer's status
Save backup copies of your files with File History
Backup and Restore (Windows 7)

User Accounts
Change account type

Network and Internet
View network status and tasks
Choose homegroup and sharing options

Appearance and Personalization

Hardware and Sound
View devices and printers
Add a device
Adjust commonly used mobility settings

Clock, Language, and Region
Add a language
Change input methods
Change date, time, or number formats

Programs
Uninstall a program
Get programs

Ease of Access
Let Windows suggest settings
Optimize visual display

Programs and Features
Uninstall a program | 🛡 Turn Windows features on or off | View installed updates
Run programs made for previous versions of Windows | How to install a program

Default Programs
Change default settings for media or devices | Make a file type always open in a specific program
Set your default programs

Java

6. In this menu, find the feature called **Windows Subsystem for Linux (Beta)**, and click on the **OK** button:

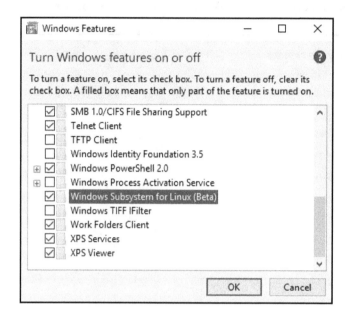

This will install the feature and ask you to restart your computer.

7. Once you are back in Windows, click on the Start button again, search for `bash`, and start the Bash on Ubuntu on the Windows application:

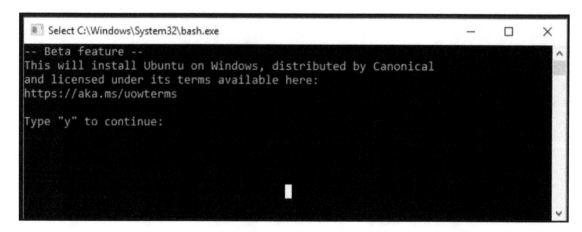

8. After a few initialization steps, you will be able to use Bash on Windows in the same way you would on Linux.

From that point on, use the Bash application to run the commands present in the book.

Installing the AWS CLI package

The AWS CLI utility is written in Python. While there are several ways to install it, we will use **PyPA**, the Python package manager, to install this tool.

To install PyPA, depending on your OS, you will need to run the following commands:

- On Windows:

    ```
    $ sudo apt install python-pip
    ```

- On macOS X:

    ```
    $ sudo easy_install pip
    ```

- On Debian-based Linux distributions:

    ```
    $ sudo apt-get install python-pip python-dev build-essential
    ```

- On Red Hat/CentOS-based Linux distributions:

    ```
    $ sudo yum -y install python-pip
    ```

Once PyPA is installed, you will get access to the `pip` command.

Lastly, to install the AWS CLI using the `pip` command, you simply need to run the following command:

```
$ sudo pip install --upgrade --user awscli
```

If you get an output to upgrade your `pip` version to the latest available level, execute `pip install --upgrade pip`.

 We have demonstrated all of the outputs from CentOS-based Linux distribution but the process is equally applicable on all of the mentioned supported platforms.

Configuring the AWS CLI

To do this, you will need to extract the AWS access key ID and secret access key from the file downloaded in step 4 of the *Creating a new user in IAM* section:

```
$ more credentials.csv
User Name,Access Key Id,Secret Access Key "yogeshraheja",
AKIAII55DTLEV3X4ETAQ, mL2dEC8/ryuZ7fu6UI6kOm7PTlfROCZpai07Gy6T
```

We will run the following command to configure our AWS account:

```
$ aws configure
AWS Access Key ID [None]: AKIAII55DTLEV3X4ETAQ
AWS Secret Access Key [None]: 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
Default region name [None]: us-east-1
Default output format [None]:
```

At this point, we are ready to start using the CLI. We can quickly verify that everything is working by listing the user accounts, as follows:

```
$ aws iam list-users
{
    "Users": [
        {
            "UserName": "yogeshraheja",
            "PasswordLastUsed": "2018-08-07T09:57:53Z",
            "CreateDate": "2018-08-07T04:56:03Z",
            "UserId": "AIDAIN22VCQLK43UVWLMK",
            "Path": "/",
            "Arn": "arn:aws:iam::094507990803:user/yogeshraheja"
        }
    ]
}
```

AWS aws-shell

Amazon has a second CLI tool called `aws-shell`. This tool is more interactive than the classic `awscli` command, as it offers out-of-the-box auto-completion and a split-screen view that lets you access the documentation as you type your commands. If you are a new AWS user, give it a shot (`pip install aws-shell`).

Creating our first web server

Now that we have our environment set up, we are finally ready to launch our first EC2 instance. There are a couple of ways to do that. Since we just installed and configured `awscli` and we want to see effective ways of managing infrastructures, we will demonstrate how to do this using the CLI.

Launching a virtual server requires having a certain amount of information ahead of time. We will use the `aws ec2 run-instances` command, but we need to supply it with the following:

- An AMI ID
- An instance type
- A security group
- An SSH key-pair

Amazon Machine Images (AMIs)

An AMI is a package that contains, among other things, the root file system with the operating system (for example, Linux, UNIX, or Windows) as well as additional software required to start up the system. To find the proper AMI, we will use the `aws ec2 describe-images` command. By default, the `describe-images` command will list all available public AMIs, which is way over 3 million by now. To get the best out of that command, it is important to combine it with the filter option to only include the AMI we would like to use. In our case, we want to use the following to filter our AMIs:

- We want the name to be Amazon Linux AMI, which designates the Linux distribution officially supported by AWS. Amazon Linux is based off Red Hat/CentOS but includes a few extra packages to make the integration with other AWS services easy to do. You can read more about AWS Linux at http://amzn.to/2uFT13F.
- We want to use the x84_64 bits version of Linux to match the architecture we will use.
- The virtualization type should be HVM, which stands for hardware virtual machine. This is the newest and best-performing type of virtualization.
- We want GP2 support, which will let us use the newest generation of instances that don't come with *instance store,* meaning that the servers that power our instances will be different from the servers that store our data.

In addition, we will sort the output by age and only look at the most recently released AMI:

```
$ aws ec2 describe-images --filters "Name=description,Values=Amazon Linux
AMI * x86_64 HVM GP2" --query 'Images[*].[CreationDate, Description,
ImageId]' --output text | sort -k 1 | tail
```

The output of running the preceding command can be shown as follows:

```
packt1@DESKTOP-0NTP3SR:/mnt/c/Windows/System32$  aws ec2 describe-images --filters "Name=description,V
alues=Amazon Linux AMI * x86_64 HVM GP2"     --query 'Images[*].[CreationDate, Description, ImageId]' -
-output text | sort -k 1 | tail
2018-01-08T18:43:48.000Z        Amazon Linux AMI 2017.09.1.20180108 x86_64 HVM GP2        ami-cb9ec1b1
2018-01-10T18:55:00.000Z        Amazon Linux AMI 2017.09.1.20180108 x86_64 HVM GP2        ami-ca1c47b0
2018-01-15T19:14:50.000Z        Amazon Linux AMI 2017.09.1.20180115 x86_64 HVM GP2        ami-97785bed
2018-01-18T23:05:02.000Z        Amazon Linux AMI 2017.09.1.20171120 x86_64 HVM GP2        ami-1ac9e760
2018-03-07T06:59:59.000Z        Amazon Linux AMI 2017.09.1.20180307 x86_64 HVM GP2        ami-1853ac65
2018-03-07T07:00:50.000Z        Amazon Linux AMI 2017.09.1-testlongids.20180307 x86_64 HVM GP2  ami-07
fc3cb791f32513e
2018-04-13T00:32:59.000Z        Amazon Linux AMI 2018.03.0.20180412 x86_64 HVM GP2        ami-467ca739
2018-05-08T18:06:53.000Z        Amazon Linux AMI 2018.03.0.20180508 x86_64 HVM GP2        ami-14c5486b
2018-06-22T22:26:53.000Z        Amazon Linux AMI 2018.03.0.20180622 x86_64 HVM GP2        ami-cfe4b2b0
```

As you can see, at this time, the most recent AMI ID is `ami-cfe4b2b0`. This might differ by the time you execute the same command, as the Amazon vendors included regularly update their OS.

When using the `aws cli --query` option, the output can be very consequential for certain commands. Taking the preceding example, if we only care about a subset of information, we can supplement the commands with the `--query` option to filter the information we want only. This option uses the **JMESPath** query language.

Instance types

In this section, we will select the virtual hardware to use for our virtual server. AWS provides a number of options best described in their documentation at `https://aws.amazon.com/ec2/instance-types/`. We will talk about instance types in more detail in `Chapter 6`, *Scaling Your Infrastructure*.

For now, we will select the `t2.micro` instance type as it is eligible for the AWS free usage tier.

Security groups

Security groups work a bit like firewalls. All EC2 instances have a set of security groups assigned to them, and each security group contains rules to allow traffic to flow inbound (**ingress**) and/or outbound (**egress**).

For this exercise, we will create a small web application running on port `tcp/3000`. In addition, we want to be able to SSH into the instance, so we also need to allow inbound traffic to port `tcp/22`. We will create a simple security group to allow this, by performing the following steps:

1. First, we need to find out our default **virtual private cloud** (**VPC**) ID. Despite being in a cloud environment, where the physical resources are shared by all AWS customers, there is still a strong emphasis on security. AWS segmented their virtual infrastructure using the concept of VPC. You can imagine this as being a virtual datacenter with its own network. The security groups that protect our EC2 instances are tied with subnets that in turn are tied to the network that the VPC provides:

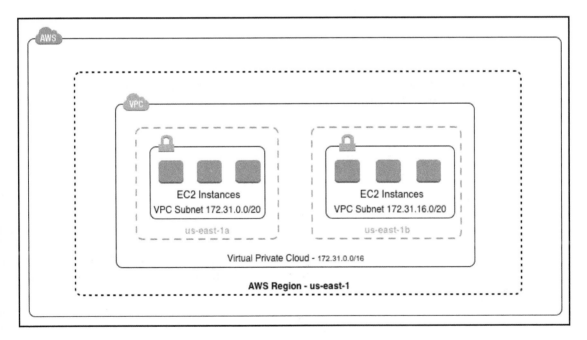

To identify our VPC ID, we can run the following command:

```
$ aws ec2 describe-vpcs

{
    "Vpcs": [
        {
            "VpcId": "vpc-4cddce2a",
            "InstanceTenancy": "default",
            "CidrBlockAssociationSet": [
                {
                    "AssociationId": "vpc-cidr-assoc-3c313154",
                    "CidrBlock": "172.31.0.0/16",
                    "CidrBlockState": {
                        "State": "associated"
                    }
                }
            ],
            "State": "available",
            "DhcpOptionsId": "dopt-c0be5fa6",
            "CidrBlock": "172.31.0.0/16",
            "IsDefault": true
        }
    ]
}
```

2. Now that we know the VPC ID (yours will be different), we can create our new security group, as follows:

```
$ aws ec2 create-security-group \
    --group-name HelloWorld \
    --description "Hello World Demo" \
    --vpc-id vpc-4cddce2a

{
    "GroupId": "sg-01864b4c"
}
```

3. By default, security groups allow all outbound traffic from the instance. We just need to open up SSH (tcp/22) and tcp/3000 for inbound traffic. We then need to input the following:

```
$ aws ec2 authorize-security-group-ingress \
    --group-name HelloWorld \
    --protocol tcp \
    --port 22 \
    --cidr 0.0.0.0/0
$ aws ec2 authorize-security-group-ingress \
```

```
--group-name HelloWorld \
--protocol tcp \
--port 3000 \
--cidr 0.0.0.0/0
```

4. We can now verify the change made using the following code, as the previous commands aren't verbose:

```
$ aws ec2 describe-security-groups \
    --group-names HelloWorld \
    --output text
```

```
SECURITYGROUPS   Hello World Demo    sg-01864b4c     HelloWorld
094507990803     vpc-4cddce2a
IPPERMISSIONS    22        tcp       22
IPRANGES         0.0.0.0/0
IPPERMISSIONS    3000      tcp       3000
IPRANGES         0.0.0.0/0
IPPERMISSIONSEGRESS        -1
IPRANGES         0.0.0.0/0
```

As expected, we opened up the traffic to the proper ports. If you know how to find your public IP, you can improve the SSH rule by replacing 0.0.0.0/0 with your IP/32 so that only you can try to SSH into that EC2 instance.

Using the aws cli --output option

By default, most of the commands will return a JSON output. AWS has a a certain number of options globally available. You can see them used a bit in this chapter. The first option is --output [json | text | table]:

```
root@yogesh# aws ec2 describe-subnets --output text
SUBNETS  False  us-east-1d  4091  172.31.32.0/20  True  True  available  subnet-e67190bc vpc-4cddce2a
SUBNETS  False  us-east-1b  4090  172.31.64.0/20  True  True  available  subnet-658b6149 vpc-4cddce2a
SUBNETS  False  us-east-1e  4091  172.31.48.0/20  True  True  available  subnet-d890d3e4 vpc-4cddce2a
SUBNETS  False  us-east-1c  4090  172.31.16.0/20  True  True  available  subnet-6fdd7927 vpc-4cddce2a
SUBNETS  False  us-east-1a  4091  172.31.0.0/20   True  True  available  subnet-4c99c229 vpc-4cddce2a
SUBNETS  False  us-east-1f  4091  172.31.80.0/20  True  True  available  subnet-b03baebc vpc-4cddce2a
```

Generating your SSH keys

By default, Amazon EC2 uses SSH key pairs to give you SSH access to your EC2 instances. You can either generate a key pair in EC2 and download the private key or generate a key yourself using a third-party tool such as OpenSSL, importing the public key in EC2. We will use the first method to create EC2 SSH keys.

Here, ensure that you set read only permissions on your newly generated private (`.pem`) key file:

```
$ aws ec2 create-key-pair --key-name EffectiveDevOpsAWS --query
'KeyMaterial' --output text > ~/.ssh/EffectiveDevOpsAWS.pem
$ aws ec2 describe-key-pairs --key-name EffectiveDevOpsAWS
{
    "KeyPairs": [
        {
            "KeyName": "EffectiveDevOpsAWS",
            "KeyFingerprint":
            "27:83:5d:9b:4c:88:f6:15:c7:39:df:23:4f:29:21:3b:3d:49:e6:af"
        }
    ]
}
$ cat ~/.ssh/EffectiveDevOpsAWS.pem
-----BEGIN RSA PRIVATE KEY-----
MIIEpAIBAAKCAQEAiZLtUMnO2OKnHvTJOiIP26fThdsU0YRdlKI60in85x9aFZXSrZsKwOh
WPpMtnUMJKeGvVQut+gJ1I1PNNjPqS2Dy60jH55hntUhr/ArpaL2ISDX4BgRAP1jcukBqS6
+pL+mTp6OUNTToUt7LvAZoeo+10SYbzHF1ZMQLLs96fCMNvnbJdUCa904dJjJs7t/G2ou9R
iNMRx8midrWcmmuGKOb1s6FgrxJ5OAMYegeccFVfGOjqPk3f+6QTPOTMNgNQ8ANKOMA9Ytc
Ica/75QGUPifusTqUT4Fqtv3rbUYPvacAnYL9eCthtn1XMG7Oo/mR5MrU60wib2QcPipmrG
NbwIDAQABAoIBABSyqkmxUxGGaCZcJbo9Ta16fnRxFZzAEWQ/VCIydv4+1UrSE7RS0zdavT
8E3aP/Ze2LKtncu/wVSpJaFVHGVcWpfGKxvIG3iELZ9oUhDyTW/x3+IKanFRNyxyKudk+Uy
huPRMu/7JhksV9mbbiILkfiPzSMSzpjB4p1hEkypfbvBnrbB+sRycx+jK51209rNDukkJVv
yFCnqPiH0wmvKRqHTNOMGWmM6CPOU+VpuMX+dIlrSeId7j6hqMjA0rGncnxYi035v2zicvI
sEKHZ9MZCnkiRb3kJ9PhueTwwUQmoBYfV5E+1Wu34UmdsmALQEX3xniaR6xf9iWhQ2Nh8La
ECgYEAzXHOZDPAUzXitO735KBUaiBp9NMv2gzE862Yf2rmDkFM4Y5RE3DKHrKfeOkrYqlG1
1On0m44GHBk/g4eqqIEaBjVp6i/Lk74tpQU6Kn1HT3w9lbXEFsCWjYZnev5oHP6PdedtRYN
zZsCSNUdlw0kOG5WZZJ4E7mPZyrvK5pq+rMCgYEAq22KT0nD3d59V+LVVZfMzJuUBDeJeD1
39mmVbzAq9u5Hr4MkurmcIj8Q6jJIQaiC8XC1gBVEl08ZN2oY1+CBE+Gesi7mGOQ2ovDmoT
fYRgScKKHv7WwR+N5/N7o26x+ZaoeaBe43Vjp6twaTpKkBOIuT50tvb25v9+UVMpGKcFUC
gYEAoOFjJ3KjREYpT1jnROEM2cKiVrdefJmNTel+RyF2IGmgg+1Hrjqf/OQSH8QwVmWK9So
sfIwVX4X8gDqcZzDS1JXGEjIB7IipGYjiysP1D74myTF93u/16qD89H8LD0xjBTSo6lrn2j
9tzY0eS+Bdodc9zvKhF4kzNC4Z9wJIjiMCgYAOtqstXP5zt5n4hh6bZxkL4rqUlhO1f0khn
DRYQ8EcSp1agh4P7Mhq5BDWmRQ81nMOuAbMBIdLmV1ntTKGrN1HUJEnaAEV19icqaKR6dIl
SFYC4stODH2KZ8ZxiQkXqzGmxBbDNYwIWaKYvPbFJkBVkx1Rt9bLsKXpl/72xSkltQKBgQC
YEjUVp4dPzZL1CFryOwV72PMMX3FjOflTgAWr8TJBq/OLujzgwYsTy6cdD3AqnMQ2BlU7Gk
4mmDZCVVsMqHFbIHEa5Y4e5qIQhamedl3IgmnMpdyuDYaT/Uh4tw0JxIJabqm+sQZv4s1Ot
gh00JlGrgFs+0D39Fy8qszqr6J04w==
-----END RSA PRIVATE KEY-----

$ chmod 400 ~/.ssh/EffectiveDevOpsAWS.pem
```

Launching an EC2 instance

We now have all the information required to launch our instance. Let's finally launch it as follows:

```
$ aws ec2 run-instances \
    --instance-type t2.micro \
    --key-name EffectiveDevOpsAWS \
    --security-group-ids sg-01864b4c \
    --image-id ami-cfe4b2b0
{
    "Instances": [
        {
            "Monitoring": {
                "State": "disabled"
            },
            "PublicDnsName": "",
            "StateReason": {
                "Message": "pending",
                "Code": "pending"
            },
            "State": {
                "Code": 0,
                "Name": "pending"
            },
            "EbsOptimized": false,
            "LaunchTime": "2018-08-08T06:38:43.000Z",
            "PrivateIpAddress": "172.31.22.52",
            "ProductCodes": [],
            "VpcId": "vpc-4cddce2a",
            "CpuOptions": {
                "CoreCount": 1,
                "ThreadsPerCore": 1
            },
            "StateTransitionReason": "",
            "InstanceId": "i-057e8deb1a4c3f35d",
            "ImageId": "ami-cfe4b2b0",
            "PrivateDnsName": "ip-172-31-22-52.ec2.internal",
            "KeyName": "EffectiveDevOpsAWS",
            "SecurityGroups": [
                {
                    "GroupName": "HelloWorld",
                    "GroupId": "sg-01864b4c"
                }
            ],
            "ClientToken": "",
            "SubnetId": "subnet-6fdd7927",
            "InstanceType": "t2.micro",
```

```
            "NetworkInterfaces": [
                {
                    "Status": "in-use",
                    "MacAddress": "0a:d0:b9:db:7b:38",
                    "SourceDestCheck": true,
                    "VpcId": "vpc-4cddce2a",
                    "Description": "",
                    "NetworkInterfaceId": "eni-001aaa6b5c7f92b9f",
                    "PrivateIpAddresses": [
                        {
                            "PrivateDnsName": "ip-172-31-22-
                            52.ec2.internal",
                            "Primary": true,
                            "PrivateIpAddress": "172.31.22.52"
                        }
                    ],
                    "PrivateDnsName": "ip-172-31-22-52.ec2.internal",
                    "Attachment": {
                        "Status": "attaching",
                        "DeviceIndex": 0,
                        "DeleteOnTermination": true,
                        "AttachmentId": "eni-attach-0428b549373b9f864",
                        "AttachTime": "2018-08-08T06:38:43.000Z"
                    },
                    "Groups": [
                        {
                            "GroupName": "HelloWorld",
                            "GroupId": "sg-01864b4c"
                        }
                    ],
                    "Ipv6Addresses": [],
                    "OwnerId": "094507990803",
                    "SubnetId": "subnet-6fdd7927",
                    "PrivateIpAddress": "172.31.22.52"
                }
            ],
            "SourceDestCheck": true,
            "Placement": {
                "Tenancy": "default",
                "GroupName": "",
                "AvailabilityZone": "us-east-1c"
            },
            "Hypervisor": "xen",
            "BlockDeviceMappings": [],
            "Architecture": "x86_64",
            "RootDeviceType": "ebs",
            "RootDeviceName": "/dev/xvda",
            "VirtualizationType": "hvm",
```

```
                "AmiLaunchIndex": 0
            }
        ],
        "ReservationId": "r-09a637b7a3be11d8b",
        "Groups": [],
        "OwnerId": "094507990803"
    }
```

You can track the progress of the instance creation. To do that, get the instance ID provided in the output of the `aws ec2 run-instances` command and run the following command:

```
$ aws ec2 describe-instance-status --instance-ids i-057e8deb1a4c3f35d
{
    "InstanceStatuses": [
        {
            "InstanceId": "i-057e8deb1a4c3f35d",
            "InstanceState": {
                "Code": 16,
                "Name": "running"
            },
            "AvailabilityZone": "us-east-1c",
            "SystemStatus": {
                "Status": "initializing",
                "Details": [
                    {
                        "Status": "initializing",
                        "Name": "reachability"
                    }
                ]
            },
            "InstanceStatus": {
                "Status": "initializing",
                "Details": [
                    {
                        "Status": "initializing",
                        "Name": "reachability"
                    }
                ]
            }
        }
    ]
}
```

The instance will be ready once the status under `SystemStatus` changes from `initializing` to `ok`:

```
$ aws ec2 describe-instance-status --instance-ids i-057e8deb1a4c3f35d --
output text| grep -i SystemStatus

SYSTEMSTATUS ok
```

Connecting to the EC2 instance using SSH

The main goal of this chapter is to create a simple `Hello World` web application. Since we are starting with a Vanilla OS, we need to connect to the host to make the necessary changes to turn our standard server into a web server. In order to SSH our instance, we need to find the DNS name of our running instance, as follows:

```
$ aws ec2 describe-instances \
    --instance-ids i-057e8deb1a4c3f35d \
    --query "Reservations[*].Instances[*].PublicDnsName"

[
    [
        "ec2-34-201-101-26.compute-1.amazonaws.com"
    ]
]
```

We now have the public DNS name of our instance and the private key to SSH into it. The last thing to know is that, for the OS that we selected while choosing our AMI in Amazon Linux, the default user account is called `ec2-user`:

```
$ ssh -i ~/.ssh/EffectiveDevOpsAWS.pem ec2-user@
ec2-34-201-101-26.compute-1.amazonaws.com

The authenticity of host 'ec2-34-201-101-26.compute-1.amazonaws.com
(172.31.22.52)' can't be established.

ECDSA key fingerprint is
SHA256:V4kdXmwb5ckyU3hw/E7wkWqbnzX5DQR5zwP1xJXezPU.

ECDSA key fingerprint is
MD5:25:49:46:75:85:f1:9d:f5:c0:44:f2:31:cd:e7:55:9f.

Are you sure you want to continue connecting (yes/no)? yes
Warning: Permanently added
'ec2-34-201-101-26.compute-1.amazonaws.com,172.31.22.52' (ECDSA) to the
list of known hosts.
```

```
  __|  __|_  )
  _|  (  /  Amazon Linux AMI
  ___|\___|___|
```

```
https://aws.amazon.com/amazon-linux-ami/2018.03-release-notes/

1 package(s) needed for security, out of 2 available

Run "sudo yum update" to apply all updates.
[ec2-user@ip-172-31-22-52 ~]$
```

If you experience any issues, add the –vvv option in your SSH command to troubleshoot it.

Creating a simple Hello World web application

Now that we are connected to our EC2 instance, we are ready to start playing around with it. In this book, we will focus on the most common use case for AWS in tech companies: hosting an application. In terms of languages, we will use JavaScript, which is one of the most popular languages on GitHub. That said, this application is aimed more at giving support in order to demonstrate how to best use AWS using the DevOps principles. Having any kind of knowledge about JavaScript isn't required in order to understand this book:

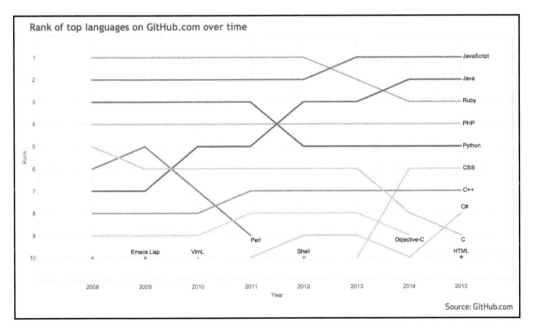

Some of the main advantages that JavaScript offers with regards to this book include the fact that:

- It is fairly easy to write and read, even for beginners
- It doesn't need to be compiled
- It can be run server side thanks to Node.js (`https://nodejs.org`)
- It is officially supported by AWS and therefore the AWS SDK for JavaScript is a *first-class citizen*

For the rest of the chapter, all the commands and code are to be run on our instance through SSH.

Installing Node.js

The first thing we need to do is install Node.js. Amazon Linux is based on **Red Hat Enterprise Linux** (**RHEL**) and uses the `yum` utility to manage and install packages. The OS comes with **Extra Packages for Enterprise Linux** (**EPEL**) preconfigured in it. As we would expect, Node.js is present in EPEL:

```
[ec2-user@ip-172-31-22-52 ~]$ sudo yum install --enablerepo=epel -y nodejs
[ec2-user@ip-172-31-22-52 ~]$ node -v
v0.10.48
```

This is definitely an old version of the node but it's going to be good enough for what we need.

Running a Node.js Hello World application

Now that the node is installed, we can create a simple Hello World application. Here is the code for creating this:

```
var http = require("http") http.createServer(function (request, response) {
// Send the HTTP header
// HTTP Status: 200 : OK
// Content Type: text/plain
response.writeHead(200, {'Content-Type': 'text/plain'})
// Send the response body as "Hello World" response.end('Hello World\n')
}).listen(3000)

// Console will print the message console.log('Server running')
```

Feel free to copy this into a file. Alternatively, if you want to save time, download this from GitHub:

```
[ec2-user@ip-172-31-22-52 ~]$
wget
https://raw.githubusercontent.com/yogeshraheja/Effective-DevOps-with-AWS/ma
ster/Chapter02/helloworld.js -O /home/ec2-user/helloworld.js
--2018-08-19 13:06:42--
https://raw.githubusercontent.com/yogeshraheja/Effective-DevOps-with-AWS/ma
ster/Chapter02/helloworld.js
Resolving raw.githubusercontent.com (raw.githubusercontent.com)...
151.101.200.133
Connecting to raw.githubusercontent.com
(raw.githubusercontent.com)|151.101.200.133|:443... connected.
HTTP request sent, awaiting response... 200 OK
Length: 384 [text/plain]
Saving to: '/home/ec2-user/helloworld.js'

/home/ec2-user/helloworld.js
100%[=====================================================================
===============>] 384 --.-KB/s in 0s

2018-08-19 13:06:42 (37.9 MB/s) - '/home/ec2-user/helloworld.js' saved
[384/384]


[ec2-user@ip-172-31-22-52 ~]$
```

In order to run the Hello World application, we are now simply going to run the following code:

```
[ec2-user@ip-172-31-22-52 ~]$ node helloworld.js
Server running
```

If everything goes well, you will now be able to open this in your browser at the following link: http://your-public-dns-name:3000. Or in my case, this will be found here: http://ec2-34-201-101-26.compute-1.amazonaws.com:3000. You will then be able to see the result, as follows:

We will now stop the execution of the Hello World web application with *Ctrl + C* in your Terminal window.

Turning our simple code into a service using upstart

Since we started the node application manually in the Terminal, closing the SSH connection or hitting *Ctrl + C* on the keyboard will stop the node process, and therefore our Hello World application will not work anymore. Amazon Linux, unlike a standard Red Hat-based distribution, comes with a system called **upstart**.

This is fairly easy to use and provides a couple of extra features that traditional **System-V bootup** scripts don't have, such as the ability to respawn a process that died unexpectedly. To add an upstart configuration, you need to create a file inside /etc/init on the EC2 instance.

Here is the code to insert it in /etc/init/helloworld.conf:

```
description "Hello world Daemon"

# Start when the system is ready to do networking. Start on started
elastic-network-interfaces

# Stop when the system is on its way down. Stop on shutdown

respawn script
exec su --session-command="/usr/bin/node /home/ec2-user/helloworld.js" ec2-
user
end script
```

 Why start on elastic network interfaces? If you are familiar with upstart outside of AWS, you might have used start on run level [345]. In AWS, the problem with that is that your network comes from **Elastic Network Interface** (ENI), and if your application starts before this service, it might not be able to connect to the network correctly.

```
[ec2-user@ip-172-31-22-52 ~]$
sudo wget
https://raw.githubusercontent.com/yogeshraheja/Effective-DevOps-with-AWS/ma
ster/Chapter02/helloworld.conf -O /etc/init/helloworld.conf
--2018-08-19 13:09:39--
https://raw.githubusercontent.com/yogeshraheja/Effective-DevOps-with-AWS/ma
ster/Chapter02/helloworld.conf
Resolving raw.githubusercontent.com (raw.githubusercontent.com)...
151.101.200.133
Connecting to raw.githubusercontent.com
```

```
(raw.githubusercontent.com)|151.101.200.133|:443... connected.
HTTP request sent, awaiting response... 200 OK
Length: 301 [text/plain]
Saving to: '/etc/init/helloworld.conf'

/etc/init/helloworld.conf
100%[=====================================================================
===============>] 301  --.-KB/s in 0s

2018-08-19 13:09:39 (54.0 MB/s) - '/etc/init/helloworld.conf' saved
[301/301]


[ec2-user@ip-172-31-22-52 ~]$
```

We can now simply start our application, as follows:

```
[ec2-user@ip-172-31-22-52 ~]$ sudo start helloworld
helloworld start/running, process 2872
[ec2-user@ip-172-31-22-52 ~]$
```

As expected, `http://your-public-dns-name:3000` still works, and this time we can safely close our SSH connection.

Terminating our EC2 instance

As with most Hello World exercises, once the `helloworld` message is displayed, the goal is reached. It is now time to think about shutting down our server. Since we only pay for what we consume in AWS, freeing up unnecessary resources such as this server is a good strategy for making AWS very cost effective.

We can do a clean shutdown of the Hello World service using the `stop` command. We can then exit the virtual server and terminate our instance, as follows:

```
[ec2-user@ip-172-31-22-52 ~]$ sudo stop helloworld
helloworld stop/waiting
[ec2-user@ip-172-31-22-52 ~]$ ec2-metadata --instance-id
instance-id: i-057e8deb1a4c3f35d
[ec2-user@ip-172-31-22-52 ~]$ exit
logout
$ aws ec2 terminate-instances --instance-ids i-057e8deb1a4c3f35d
{
    "TerminatingInstances": [
        {
            "InstanceId": "i-057e8deb1a4c3f35d",
            "CurrentState": {
```

```
            "Code": 32,
            "Name": "shutting-down"
        },
        "PreviousState": {
            "Code": 16,
            "Name": "running"
        }
    }
  ]
}
```

Summary

This chapter was a quick and simple introduction to AWS and its most notorious service, EC2. After signing up for AWS, we configured our environment in such a way that we could create a virtual server using the command-line interface. Leading to this, we selected our first AMI, created our first security group, and generated our SSH keys, which we will reuse throughout the book. After launching an EC2 instance, we manually deployed a simple Node.js application to display Hello World.

While the process wasn't very fastidious thanks to the AWS CLI, it still required going through numerous steps, which aren't very repeatable. We also deployed the application without any automation or validation. Furthermore, the only way we can check if the application is running is by manually checking the endpoint. In the remainder of the book, we will revisit the process of creating and managing web applications and infrastructure, but, this time, we will follow the DevOps principles and incorporate their best practices.

In Chapter 3, *Treating Your Infrastructure as Code*, we will address one of the first issues we encountered: managing our infrastructure with automation. To do that, we will write code to manage our infrastructure.

Questions

Please answer the following questions:

1. How do you create a free-tier AWS account?
2. How do you create your first AWS cloud instance using the AWS Console portal?
3. How do you create your first AWS cloud instance using the AWS CLI utility?
4. How do you deploy a simple Hello World web application on your newly created AWS instance?
5. How do you destroy your created AWS instance to complete this exercise?

Further reading

Refer to the following links for for more information on AWS and AWS CLI:

- **AWS Free Tier**: https://aws.amazon.com/free/
- **AWS Command Line Interface**: https://aws.amazon.com/cli/

3
Treating Your Infrastructure as Code

In the previous chapter, we familiarized ourselves with AWS. We also created an EC2 instance and deployed a Hello World web application onto it. However, to get there, we had to go through a number of steps to configure the instance and its security groups. Because we did that in a very manual fashion using the command-line interface, the steps that we went through will not be reusable or auditable, as you may recall from the first chapter when implementing DevOps best practices. Two key concepts that you should rely on as often as possible are source control (version control) and automation. In this chapter, we will explore how to apply those principles to our infrastructure.

In a cloud environment, where almost everything is abstracted and served through the intermediary of virtual resources, it is easy to imagine that code can describe the topology of a network and the configuration of a system. To go through that transformation, we will learn about two key concepts in an effective DevOps organization. The first one is commonly called **Infrastructure as Code** (**IAC**). This is the process of describing all your virtual resources in the form of codes. These resources may include virtual servers, load balancers, storage, the network layer, and so on. The second concept, which is very close to IAC, focuses further on system configuration and is called **configuration management**. Through configuration management systems, developers and system administrators have the ability to automate operating system configuration, package installation, and even application deployment.

Going through that transformation is a crucial step for any DevOps-focused organization. By having the code to describe the different resources and their configurations, we will be able to use the same tools and processes as we do when developing applications. We will be able to use source control and make smaller changes to individual branches, as well as submitting pull requests, following standard review processes, and finally, testing changes before they are applied to our production environment. This will give us better clarity, accountability, and auditability for infrastructure changes. Because of that, we will also be able to manage a much bigger fleet of resources without necessarily needing more engineers or without spending a lot more time operating all the resources. This will also open up the door to further automation, as we will see with continuous deployment in Chapter 5, *Adding Continuous Integration and Continuous Deployment*. In this chapter, we will cover the following topics:

- Managing your infrastructure with CloudFormation
- Adding a configuration management system

Technical requirements

The technical requirements for this chapter are as follows:

- AWS Console
- AWS CloudFormation
- AWS CloudFormation Designer
- CloudFormer
- Troposphere
- Git
- GitHub
- Ansible

The GitHub links to find the codes in this chapter are as follows:

- https://raw.githubusercontent.com/yogeshraheja/Effective-DevOps-with-AWS/master/Chapter03/EffectiveDevOpsTemplates/helloworld-cf-template-part-1.py
- https://raw.githubusercontent.com/yogeshraheja/Effective-DevOps-with-AWS/master/Chapter03/EffectiveDevOpsTemplates/helloworld-cf-template.py
- https://github.com/yogeshraheja/Automation-with-Ansible-By-Yogesh-Raheja

- https://github.com/yogeshraheja/Effective-DevOps-with-AWS/blob/master/Chapter03/ansible/roles/nodejs/tasks/main.yml
- https://github.com/yogeshraheja/Effective-DevOps-with-AWS/blob/master/Chapter03/ansible/roles/helloworld/tasks/main.yml
- https://github.com/yogeshraheja/Effective-DevOps-with-AWS/blob/master/Chapter03/ansible/roles/helloworld/meta/main.yml
- https://github.com/yogeshraheja/Effective-DevOps-with-AWS/tree/master/Chapter03/ansible
- https://github.com/yogeshraheja/EffectiveDevOpsTemplates/blob/master/ansiblebase-cf-template.py

Managing your infrastructure with CloudFormation

CloudFormation introduces a new way to manage services and their configurations. Through the creation of JSON or YAML files, CloudFormation lets you describe the AWS architecture you would like to build. Once your files are created, you can simply upload them to CloudFormation, which will execute them, and automatically create or update your AWS resources. Most AWS-managed tools and services are supported. You can get the full list at http://amzn.to/1Odslix. In this chapter, we will only look at the infrastructure we have built so far, but we will add more resources in the following chapters. After a brief overview of how CloudFormation is structured, we will create a minimal list stack to recreate the Hello World web application from Chapter 2, *Deploying Your First Web Application*. After that, we will see two more options to create CloudFormation templates—the designer, which lets you visually edit your template in a Web GUI, and CloudFormer, a tool to generate templates from existing infrastructure.

Getting started with CloudFormation

As you would expect, you can access CloudFormation through the AWS console at https://console.aws.amazon.com/cloudformation, or by using the following command line:

```
$ aws cloudformation help # for the list of options
```

The service is organized around the concept of stacks. Each stack typically describes a set of AWS resources and their configuration in order to start an application. When working with CloudFormation, most of your time is spent editing those templates. There are different ways to get started with the actual editing of the templates. One of the easiest ways is to edit existing templates. AWS has a number of well-written examples available at `http://amzn.to/27cHmrb`. At the highest level, templates are structured as follows:

```
{
"AWSTemplateFormatVersion" : "version date", "Description" : "Description",
"Resources" : { },
"Parameters" : { },
"Mappings" : { },
"Conditions" : { },
"Metadata" : { },
"Outputs" : { }
}
```

The `AWSTemplateFormatVersion` section is currently always `2010-09-09` and this represents the version of the template language used. This version is currently the only valid value. The `Description` section is there for you to summarize what the template does. The `Resources` section describes which AWS services will be instantiated and what their configurations are. When you launch a template, you have the ability to provide some extra information to CloudFormation, such as which SSH key-pair to use. For example, if you want to give SSH access to your EC2 instances, this kind of information goes into the `Parameters` section. The `Mappings` section is useful when you try to create a more generic template.

You can, for example, define which **Amazon Machine Image** (**AMI**) to use for a given region, so that the same template can be used to start an application in that AWS region. The `Conditions` section allows you to add conditional logic to your other sections (if statements, logical operators, and so on), while the `Metadata` section lets you add more arbitrary information to your resources. Finally, the `Outputs` section lets you extract and print out useful information based on the execution of your template, such as the IP address of the EC2 server created, for example. In addition to those examples, AWS also provides a couple of tools and services around CloudFormation template creation. The first tool you can use to create your templates is called CloudFormation Designer.

AWS CloudFormation Designer

AWS CloudFormation Designer is a tool that lets you create and edit CloudFormation templates using a graphic user interface. Designer hides a lot of the complexity of editing a CloudFormation template using a standard text editor. You can access this directly at `https://console.aws.amazon.com/cloudformation/designer`, or in the CloudFormation dashboard after you click on the **Create Stack** button, as shown here:

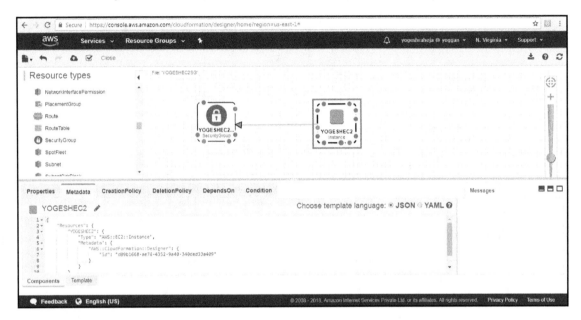

The workflow is fairly simple. You simply drag and drop resources from the left-hand side menu into a canvas.

Once your resources are added, you can then connect them to other resources using the small dots surrounding each resource icon. In the preceding example, we are connecting an EC2 instance to its security group. There are a number of hidden gems that can help you when designing your template. You can right-click on resources and directly access the documentation for the CloudFormation resource as follows:

When dragging a dot to connect two resources, a designer will highlight resources that are compatible with that connection. The editor on the bottom section of the designer supports auto completion using *Ctrl* + Spacebar:

```
YOGESHEC2SG  ✎

31 ▾     "Resources": {
32 ▾        "YOGESHEC2": {
33              "Type": "AWS::EC2::Instance",
34              "Properties": {},
35 ▾            "Metadata": {  KeyName
36 ▾                "AWS::Clou  AdditionalInfo
37                    "id":     AvailabilityZone
38                }             BlockDeviceMappings
39            }                 CreditSpecification
40         }                    DisableApiTermination
   Components    Template       EbsOptimized
                                ElasticGpuSpecifications
```

Once your template is complete, you can simply click on a button and go from designing your stack to launching it. The next tool we will look at is called **CloudFormer**.

CloudFormer

CloudFormer is a tool that lets you create CloudFormation templates by looking at pre-existing resources. If you have a set of resources that you have already created on an ad hoc basis, as we have done so far in the book, then you can use CloudFormer to group them under a new CloudFormation template. You can then later customize the template that CloudFormer generates using a text editor or even CloudFormation designer, making it fit your needs. Unlike most AWS tools and services, CloudFormer isn't completely managed by AWS; it's a self-hosted tool that you can instantiate on demand using CloudFormation. To do so, follow the given steps:

1. Open `https://console.aws.amazon.com/cloudformation` in your browser.
2. Now, scroll down the AWS console screen, select **Create a Template from your Existing Resources** option, and click on the **Launch CloudFormer** button.
3. In the **Select a sample template** drop-down menu, choose the **CloudFormer** option and click on the **Next** button, as shown in the following screenshot:

4. On that screen, at the top, you can provide a stack name (feel free to keep the default name, `AWSCloudFormer`) and in the bottom part, you are asked to provide three additional parameters, a **Username**, a **Password** and **VPC Selection**. This username and password will be used later to log into CloudFormer. Pick a username and a password, select the **Default** VPC, and click on the **Next** button.

5. On the next screen, you can provide extra tags and more advanced options, but we will simply continue by clicking on the **Next** button.

6. This brings us to the review page, where we will check the checkbox to acknowledge that this will cause AWS CloudFormation to create IAM resources. Click on the **Create** button.

7. This will bring us back to the main screen of the CloudFormation console, where we can see our AWS CloudFormer stack being created . Once the **Status** column goes from **CREATE_IN_PROGRESS** to **CREATE_COMPLETE**, select it and click on the **Outputs** tab at the bottom. At that point, you have created the resources needed to use CloudFormer. In order to create a stack with it, do the following: in the **Outputs** tab (which illustrates the **Outputs** section of CloudFormation), click on the website URL link. This will open up the CloudFormer tool. Log in using the username and password provided in the fourth step of the previous set of instructions, and you should see something like the following:

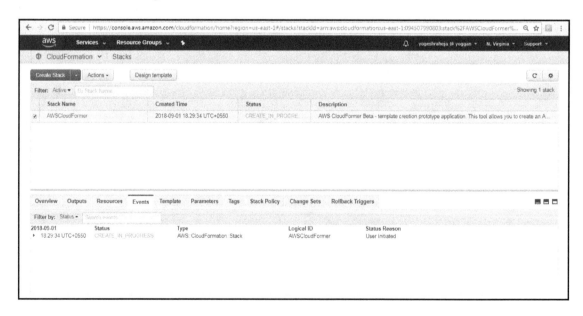

8. Select the AWS region where you want to create the template and then click on the **Create Template** button. The following screen will then appear:

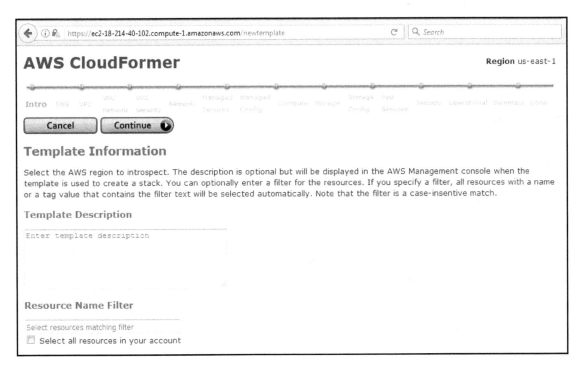

9. Follow the workflow proposed by the tool to select the different resources that you want for your CloudFormation template, as far as the last step.
10. In the end, you will be able to download the generated template or save it directly in S3.

The CloudFormation template generated by CloudFormer will usually need a bit of editing, as you will often want to create a more flexible stack with input parameters and an **Outputs** section.

Recreating our Hello World example with CloudFormation

Designer and CloudFormer are two very useful tools when you are in the process of architecting your infrastructure and trying to add source control to your design. That said, whenever you wear your DevOps hat, it's a different story. Using those tools markedly reduces the added value that CloudFormation provides by using the JSON format. If you got a chance to read some of the templates available, or tried to use CloudFormer on your existing infrastructure, you probably noticed that raw CloudFormation templates tend to be fairly long and not **Don't Repeat Yourself** (**DRY**).

From a DevOps perspective, one of the most powerful aspects of CloudFormation is the ability to write code to dynamically generate those templates. To illustrate that point, we are going to turn to Python, and a library called `troposphere`, to generate our Hello World CloudFormation template.

There are also a number of more advanced tools to assist with the creation of CloudFormation templates. If you plan on using other third-party services in addition to AWS, you can take a look at Terraform from Hashicorp (available at `https://www.terraform.io`), for example, which handles a number of other cloud providers and services in addition to CloudFormation.

Using Troposphere to create a Python script for our template

We will first install the `troposphere` library. Again, we are demonstrating all of the outputs from a CentOS 7.x-based Linux distribution, but the process applies equally to all of the supported platforms mentioned. The following is the command to install the `troposphere` library:

```
$ pip install troposphere
```

One known issue with the Troposphere is the upgraded version of `setuptools`. If you come across the following issue, then the solution is to upgrade `setuptools` using the `pip install -U setuptools` command.

Once you have run the preceding command, you may encounter the following error:

```
....
setuptools_scm.version.SetuptoolsOutdatedWarning: your setuptools is too
old (<12)
------------------------------------
Command "python setup.py egg_info" failed with error code 1 in /tmp/pip-
install-pW4aV4/cfn-flip/
```

In order to fix the error, you can run the following command:

```
$ pip install -U setuptools

Collecting setuptools
    Downloading
https://files.pythonhosted.org/packages/ff/f4/385715ccc461885f3cedf57a41ae3
c12b5fec3f35cce4c8706b1a112a133/setuptools-40.0.0-py2.py3-none-any.whl
(567kB)
        100% |████████████████████████████████| 573kB
22.2MB/s
Installing collected packages: setuptools
    Found existing installation: setuptools 0.9.8
        Uninstalling setuptools-0.9.8:
            Successfully uninstalled setuptools-0.9.8
Successfully installed setuptools-40.0.0
```

Once the installation is complete, you can then create a new file called `helloworld-cf-template.py`.

We will start our file by importing a number of definitions from the `troposphere` module as follows:

```
"""Generating CloudFormation template."""

from troposphere import (
    Base64,
    ec2,
    GetAtt,
    Join,
    Output,
    Parameter,
    Ref,
    Template,
)
```

We are also going to define a first variable that will make editing the code easier for the remainder of the book. This is because we will create new scripts by building on this initial template:

```
ApplicationPort = "3000"
```

From a code standpoint, the first thing we will do is initialize a `Template` variable. By the end of our script, the template will contain the entire description of our infrastructure and we will be able to simply print its output to get our CloudFormation template:

```
t = Template()
```

Throughout this book, we will create and run several CloudFormation templates concurrently. To help us identify what's in a given stack, we have the ability to provide a description. After the creation of the template, add the description as follows:

```
add_description("Effective DevOps in AWS: HelloWorld web application")
```

When we launched EC2 instances using the web command-line interface, we selected which key-pair to use in order to gain SSH access to the host. In order to not lose this ability, the first thing our template will have is a parameter to offer the CloudFormation user the ability to select which key-pair to use when launching the EC2 instance. To do that, we are going to create a `Parameter` object and initialize it by providing an identifier, a description, a parameter type, a description of the parameter type, and a constraint description to help make the right decision when we launch the stack. In order for this parameter to exist in our final template, we will also use the `add_parameter()` function defined in the template class:

```
t.add_parameter(Parameter(
    "KeyPair",
    Description="Name of an existing EC2 KeyPair to SSH",
    Type="AWS::EC2::KeyPair::KeyName",
    ConstraintDescription="must be the name of an existing EC2 KeyPair.",
))
```

The next thing we will look at is the security group. We will proceed exactly as we did for our `KeyPair` parameter. We want to open up `SSH/22` and `TCP/3000` to the world. Port `3000` was defined in the `ApplicationPort` variable declared earlier. In addition, this time, the information defined isn't a parameter like before, but a resource. Consequently, we will add that new resource using the `add_resource()` function as follows:

```
t.add_resource(ec2.SecurityGroup(
    "SecurityGroup",
    GroupDescription="Allow SSH and TCP/{} access".format(ApplicationPort),
    SecurityGroupIngress=[
```

```
            ec2.SecurityGroupRule(
                IpProtocol="tcp",
                FromPort="22",
                ToPort="22",
                CidrIp="0.0.0.0/0",
            ),
            ec2.SecurityGroupRule(
                IpProtocol="tcp",
                FromPort=ApplicationPort,
                ToPort=ApplicationPort,
                CidrIp="0.0.0.0/0",
            ),
        ],
    ))
```

In our next section, we will replace the need to log on to our EC2 instance and install the `helloworld.js` file and its `init` scripts by hand. To do so, we will take advantage of the `UserData` features that EC2 offers. When you create an EC2 instance, the `UserData` optional parameter gives you the ability to provide a set of commands to run once the virtual machine has spawned up (you can read more on this topic at http://amzn.to/1VU5b3s). One of the constraints of the `UserData` parameter is that the script must be base64-encoded in order to be added to our API call.

We are going to create a small script to reproduce the steps that we went through in Chapter 2, *Deploying Your First Web Application*. Here, we will encode, deploy our first web application deployment step in base-64 and store it in a variable called ud. Note that installing the application in the `home` directory of `ec2-user` isn't very clean. For now, we are trying to stay consistent with what we did in Chapter 2, *Deploying Your First Web Application*. We will fix that in Chapter 5, *Adding Continuous Integration and Continuous Deployment*, as we improve our deployment system:

```
ud = Base64(Join('\n', [
    "#!/bin/bash",
    "sudo yum install --enablerepo=epel -y nodejs",
    "wget http://bit.ly/2vESNuc -O /home/ec2-user/helloworld.js",
    "wget http://bit.ly/2vVvT18 -O /etc/init/helloworld.conf",
    "start helloworld"
]))
```

We will now focus on the main resource of our template, which is our EC2 instance. The creation of the instance requires providing a name for identifying the resource, an image ID, an instance type, a security group, the key-pair to use for the SSH access, and the user data. In order to keep things simple, we will hardcode the AMI ID (`ami-cfe4b2b0`) and instance type (`t2.micro`).

The remaining pieces of information needed to create our EC2 instances are the security group information and the `KeyPair` name, which we collected previously by defining a parameter and a resource. In CloudFormation, you can refer to pre-existing subsections of your template by using the `Ref` keyword. In Troposphere, this is done by calling the `Ref()` function. As before, we will add the resulting output to our template with the help of the `add_resource` function:

```
...
t.add_resource(ec2.Instance(
    "instance",
    ImageId="ami-cfe4b2b0",
    InstanceType="t2.micro",
    SecurityGroups=[Ref("SecurityGroup")],
    KeyName=Ref("KeyPair"),
    UserData=ud,
))
...
```

In the last section of our script, we will focus on producing the `Outputs` section of the template that gets populated when CloudFormation creates a stack. This selection allows you to print out useful information that was computed during the launch of the stack. In our case, there are two useful pieces of information—the URL to access our web application, and the public IP address of the instance, so that we can SSH into it if we want to. In order to retrieve such information, CloudFormation uses the `Fn::GetAtt` function. In Troposphere, this is translated into the `GetAtt()` function:

```
...
t.add_output(Output(
    "InstancePublicIp",
    Description="Public IP of our instance.",
    Value=GetAtt("instance", "PublicIp"),
))

t.add_output(Output(
    "WebUrl",
    Description="Application endpoint",
    Value=Join("", [
        "http://", GetAtt("instance", "PublicDnsName"),
        ":", ApplicationPort
    ]),
))
...
```

At that point, we can make our script output the final result of the template we generated:

```
print t.to_json()
```

The script is now complete. We can save this and quit our editor. The file created should look like the file at the following link: `https://raw.githubusercontent.com/yogeshraheja/Effective-DevOps-with-AWS/master/Chapter03/EffectiveDevOpsTemplates/helloworld-cf-template-part-1.py`.

We can now run our script, giving it the proper permissions and generating the CloudFormation template by saving the output of our script in a file as follows:

```
$ python helloworld-cf-template.py > helloworld-cf.template
```

 `cloud-init` is a set of Python scripts compatible with most Linux distributions and cloud providers. This complements the `UserData` field by moving most standard operations, such as installing packages, creating files, and running commands into different sections of the template. This book doesn't cover that tool, but if your CloudFormation templates rely heavily on the `UserData` field, take a look at it. You can get its documentation at `http://bit.ly/1W6s96M`.

Creating the stack in the CloudFormation console

At this point, we can launch our template using the following steps:

1. Open the CloudFormation web console in your browser with the following link: `https://console.aws.amazon.com/cloudformation`. Click on the **Create Stack** button.
2. On the next screen, we will upload our newly generated template, `helloworld-cf.template`, by selecting **Upload a template to Amazon S3**, and then browsing to select our `helloworld-cf.template` file.
3. We will then pick a stack name, such as `HelloWorld`.
4. After the stack name, we can see the **Parameters** section of our template in action. CloudFormation lets us pick which SSH key-pair to use. Select your key-pair using the drop-down menu.
5. On the next screen, we have to ability the add optional tags to our resources; in the **Advanced** section, we can see how we can potentially integrate CloudFormation and SNS, make decisions on what to do when a failure or a timeout occurs, and even add a stack policy that lets you control who can edit the stack, for example. For now, we will simply click on the **Next** button.

6. This leads us to the review screen where we can verify the information selected and even estimate how much it will cost to run that stack. Click on the **Create** button.

7. This will bring us to the main CloudFormation console. On that screen, we are able to see how our resources are created in the **Events** tab.

8. When the creation of the template is complete, click on the **Outputs** tabs, which will reveal the information we generated through the **Outputs** section of our template, as shown here:

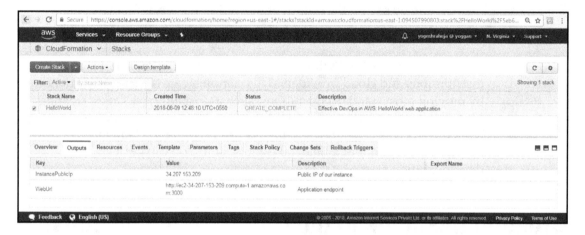

9. Click on the link in the value of the **WebUrl** key, which will open our Hello World page.

Adding our template to a source control system

Now that we have tested our template and know it's working, we are going to commit it to our source control system. This will allow us to keep track of changes, making it possible to treat our infrastructure code at the same standard as our application code (more on this in `Chapter 5`, *Adding Continuous Integration and Continuous Deployment*).

To do that, we will rely on Git. AWS has a service called AWS CodeCommit (`http://amzn.to/2tKUj0n`), which lets you manage Git repositories easily. However, because this service is a lot less popular than GitHub (`https://github.com`), we will instead use the latter. If you don't have an account for GitHub yet, start by signing up for the service—it's completely free.

Once logged into GitHub, create a new repository for the CloudFormation template:

1. In your browser, open `https://github.com/new`.
2. Call the new repository the following: `EffectiveDevOpsTemplates`.
3. Check the **Initialize this repository with a README** checkbox.
4. Finally, click on the **Create repository** button, as shown here:

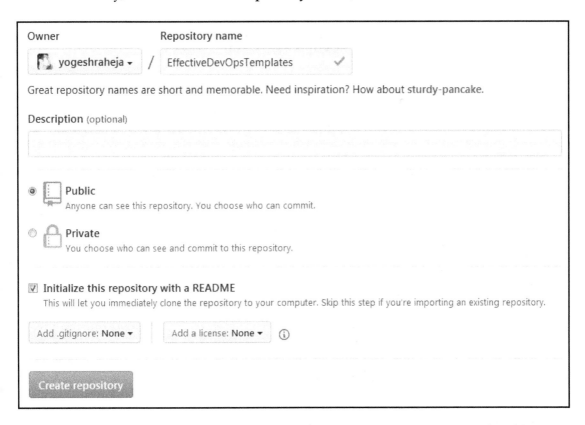

5. Once your repository is created, you will want to clone it into your computer. For that, you need to have Git installed (search on Google for instructions on how to install Git for your operating system if you don't have it yet). For CentOS, you just need to run `yum -y install git`, as the Git package is a part of Linux distribution now:

   ```
   $ git clone
   https://github.com/<your_github_username>/EffectiveDevOpsTempla
   tes
   ```

6. Now that the repository is cloned, we will go into it and copy the template previously created in the new GitHub repository:

```
$ cd EffectiveDevOpsTemplates
$ cp <path_to_helloworld_template>/helloworld-cf-template.py .
```

7. Finally, we will add and commit that new file to our project and push it to GitHub as follows:

```
$ git add helloworld-cf-template.py
$ git commit -m "Adding helloworld Troposphere template"
$ git push
```

Monorepo versus multirepo: When managing your code, there are two common approaches to organizing your code repositories. You can create one repository for each project you have, or decide to put your entire organization code under a single repository. We will choose the simplest option for this book, which is one repository per project, but with the recent releases of several open source projects, such as Bazel from Google, Buck from Facebook, or Pants from Twitter, using a monorepo becomes a very compelling option as it avoids juggling between multiple repositories when making big changes to your infrastructure and services simultaneously.

Updating our CloudFormation stack

One of the biggest benefits of using the CloudFormation template to manage our resources is that the resources created from CloudFormation are tightly coupled to our stack. If we want to make a change to our stack, we can update the template and apply the change to our existing CloudFormation stack. Let's see how that works.

Updating our Python script

Our `helloworld-cf-template.py` script is fairly basic. At this point, we are only taking advantage of Python as far as using the `troposphere` library to easily generate JSON output in a more pleasant way than if we had to write it by hand. Of course, you might already realize that we are barely scratching the surface of what we can do when we have the ability to write scripts to create and manage infrastructures. The following section is a simple example that will let us write a couple more lines of Python and illustrate the concept of updating a CloudFormation stack, while taking advantage of more services and external resources.

The security groups we created in our previous example open up two ports to the world: 22 (SSH) and 3000 (the web application port). We could try to harden one aspect of our security by only allowing our own IP to use SSH. This means changing the **Classless Inter-Domain Routing (CIDR)** IP information in our Python script on the security group that handles the port 22 traffic. There are a number of free services online that will let us know what our public IP is. We are going to use one of these, available at https://api.ipify.org. We can see it in action with a simple curl command:

```
$ curl https://api.ipify.org 54.164.95.231
```

We are going to take advantage of that service in our script. One of the reasons for using this particular service is that it has been packaged into a Python library. You can read more on this at https://github.com/rdegges/python-ipify. You can first install that library as follows:

```
$ pip install ipify
```

In case you come across some pip related errors, as shown in the following code block, the fix would be to downgrade the pip version, install ipify, and then upgrade the pip version again to the latest version:

```
Cannot uninstall 'requests'. It is a distutils installed project and thus
we cannot accurately determine which files belong to it which would lead to
only a partial uninstall.
```

The preceding error can be fixed with the following commands:

```
$ pip install --upgrade --force-reinstall pip==9.0.3
$ pip install ipify
$ pip install --upgrade pip
```

Our script requires a CIDR. In order to convert our IP address to CIDR, we will also install another library, called ipaddress. The main advantage of combining these libraries is that we don't have to worry about handling IPv4 versus IPv6:

```
$ pip install ipaddress
```

Once those libraries are installed, reopen helloworld-cf-template.py in your editor. At the top of our script, we are going to import the libraries, then, after the ApplicationPort variable definition, we will define a new variable called PublicCidrIp and, combining the two libraries mentioned previously, we can extract our CIDR as follows:

```
...
from ipaddress import ip_network
from ipify import get_ip
from troposphere import (
```

```
        Base64,
        ec2,
        GetAtt,
        Join,
        Output,
        Parameter,
        Ref,
        Template,
    )

ApplicationPort = "3000"
PublicCidrIp = str(ip_network(get_ip()))
...
```

Lastly, we can change the `CidrIp` declaration for the SSH group rule as follows:

```
SecurityGroupIngress=[
        ec2.SecurityGroupRule(
            IpProtocol="tcp",
            FromPort="22",
            ToPort="22",
            CidrIp=PublicCidrIp,
        ),
    ....
    ]
```

We can now save these changes. The file created should look like the file at https://github.com/yogeshraheja/Effective-DevOps-with-AWS/blob/master/Chapter03/EffectiveDevOpsTemplates/helloworld-cf-template.py.

We can now generate a new `diff` command to visually verify the change:

```
$ python helloworld-cf-template.py > helloworld-cf-v2.template
$ diff helloworld-cf-v2.template helloworld-cf.template
46c46
<             "CidrIp": "54.164.95.231/32",
---
>             "CidrIp": "0.0.0.0/0",
            91a92
>
$
```

As we can see, our CIDR IP is now correctly restricting the connection to our IP. We can now apply that change.

Updating our stack

Having generated the new JSON CloudFormation template, we can get in the
CloudFormation console and update the stack as follows:

1. Open the CloudFormation web console in your browser at `https://console.`
   `aws.amazon.com/cloudformation`.
2. Select the `HelloWorld` stack that we created previously .
3. Click on the **Actions** drop-down menu, and then choose the **Update Stack**
   option.
4. Choose the `helloworld-cf-v2.template` file by clicking the **Browse** button,
   selecting the file, and then clicking on the **Next** button.
5. This brings us to the next screen that lets us update the details of our stack. In our
   case, nothing has changed in the parameters, so we can continue by clicking on
   the **Next** button.
6. In the next screen as well, since we simply want to see the effect of our IP change,
   we can click on the **Next** button:

7. This brings us to the review page, where, after a couple of seconds, we can see CloudFormation giving us a preview of our change:

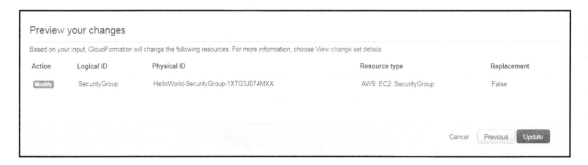

8. As you can see, the only change will be an update on the security group. Now click on the **Update** button. This will bring us back to the CloudFormation template, where we will see the change being applied.

9. In this particular example, AWS is able to simply update the security group to take our change into account. We can verify the change by extracting the physical ID from either the review page, or in the **Resources** tab back in the console:

```
$ aws ec2 describe-security-groups \
--group-names HelloWorld-SecurityGroup-1XTG3J074MXX
```

Change sets

Our template only includes a web server and a security group that makes updating CloudFormation a fairly harmless operation. Furthermore, our change was fairly trivial, as AWS could simply update the existing security group, as opposed to having to replace it. As you can imagine, as the architecture becomes more and more complex, so does the CloudFormation template. Depending on the update you want to perform, you might encounter unexpected changes when you review the change set in the final step of updating a template. AWS offers an alternative and safer way to update templates; this feature is called **change sets** and is accessible from the CloudFormation console. Follow this procedure in order to use change sets to review the updates, followed by execution:

1. Open the CloudFormation web console in your browser at `https://console.aws.amazon.com/cloudformation`
2. Select the `HelloWorld` stack that we previously created
3. Click on the **Actions** drop-down menu and then click the **Create Change Set For Current Stack** option

From there, you can follow the same steps you took to create a simple update in the *Updating our stack* section. The main difference happens on the last screen, shown here:

Unlike the regular stack updates, change sets have a strong emphasis on giving you the ability to review a change before applying it. If you are satisfied with the changes displayed, you have the ability to execute the update. Lastly, when using a change set to update your stack, you can easily audit recent changes using the **Change Sets** tab of your stack in the CloudFormation console. Finally, we will commit the changes to the Troposphere script with the following command:

```
$ git commit -am "Only allow ssh from our local IP"
$ git push
```

Deleting our CloudFormation stack

In the last section, we saw how CloudFormation was able to update resources as we update our template. The same goes when you want to remove a CloudFormation stack and its resources. In a couple of clicks, you can delete your template and the various resources that were created at launch time. From a best practice standpoint, it is highly recommended to always use CloudFormation to make changes to your resources that were previously initialized with CloudFormation, including when you don't need your stack any more.

Deleting a stack is very simple, and you should proceed as follows:

1. Open the CloudFormation web console in your browser at `https://console.aws.amazon.com/cloudformation`
2. Select the `HelloWorld` stack that we created previously
3. Click on the **Actions** drop-down menu, and then click on the **Delete Stack** option

As always, you will be able to track completion in the **Events** tab:

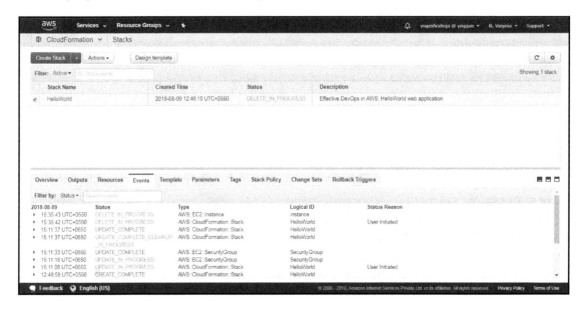

CloudFormation has a unique place in the AWS ecosystem. As complex as they are, most architectures can be described and managed through CloudFormation, allowing you to keep tight control over your AWS resources creation. While CloudFormation does a great job of managing the creation of resources, it doesn't always make things easy. This is especially the case when you want to make simple changes on services such as EC2. Because CloudFormation doesn't keep track of the state of the resources once they are launched, the only reliable way to update an EC2 instance is, for example, to recreate a new instance and swap it with the existing instance when it is ready. This creates somewhat of an immutable design (assuming that you don't run any extra commands when the instance is created). This may be an attractive architecture choice and, in some cases, it may take you a long way, but you may wish to have the ability to have long-running instances where you can, as this allows you to quickly and reliably make changes through a controlled pipeline, like we did with CloudFormation. This is what configuration management systems excel at.

Adding a configuration management system

Configuration management systems are probably the most well known components of classic DevOps-driven organizations. Present in most companies (including in the enterprise market), configuration management systems are quickly replacing home-grown Shell, Python, and Perl scripts. There are many reasons why configuration management systems should be a part of your environment. One reason is that they offer domain-specific languages, which improves the readability of the code, and they are tailored to the specific needs that arise in organizations when trying to configure systems. This results in a lot of useful built-in features. Furthermore, the most common configuration management tools have a big and active user community, which often means that you will be able to find existing code for the system you are trying to automate.

Some of the most popular configuration management tools include **Puppet**, **Chef**, **SaltStack**, and **Ansible**. While all of those options are fairly good, this book will focus on Ansible, the easiest of the four tools mentioned. There are a number of key characteristics that make Ansible a very popular and easy-to-use solution. Unlike other configuration management systems, Ansible is built to work without a server, a daemon, or a database. You can simply keep your code in source control and download it on the host whenever you need to run it or use a push mechanism through SSH. The automation code you write is in YAML static files, which makes the learning curve a lot less steep than some of the other alternatives that use Ruby or specific DSL. In order to store our configuration files, we will instead rely on our version control system (in our case, GitHub.)

AWS OpsWorks and its Chef integration: While Amazon hasn't really released a service dedicated to configuration management, it supports Chef and Puppet within the OpsWorks service. Unlike the services we have explored so far in the book, OpsWorks aims at being a *complete application life cycle, including resource provisioning, configuration management, application deployment, software updates, monitoring, and access control.* If you are willing to sacrifice some flexibility and control, OpsWorks might be able to handle what you need in order to run a simple web application. You can learn more about this at `http://amzn.to/1O8dTsn`.

Getting started with Ansible

Begin by installing Ansible on your computer. After doing this, create an EC2 instance that will let us illustrate the basic usage of Ansible. After that, we will work on recreating the Hello World Node.js application by creating and executing what Ansible calls a playbook. We will then look at how Ansible can run in pull mode, which offers a new approach to deploying changes. Finally, we will look at replacing the `UserData` block in our CloudFormation template with Ansible to combine the benefits of both CloudFormation and our configuration management system.

Ansible is fairly easy to use and well documented throughout the web. This book will cover enough to get you started and up to speed on simple configurations, such as the one we need in our examples. However, you might be interested in spending a bit more time learning about Ansible in order to be really efficient with it.

Installing Ansible on your computer

As mentioned before, Ansible is a really simple application with very few dependencies. You can install Ansible on your computer using your operating system package manager, or through `pip`, as Ansible is written in Python. We will be demonstrating all of the outputs from a CentOS 7.x-based Linux distribution, but the process applies equally to all supported platforms. (For more information, refer to the following link in order to find and install Ansible binaries on your operating system: https://docs.ansible.com/ansible/latest/installation_guide/intro_installation.html#installing-the-control-machine.) The following command will install a number of binaries, libraries, and Ansible modules:

```
$ yum install ansible
```

Note that no daemon or database is installed at this point. This is because, by default, Ansible relies on static files and SSH in order to run. At this point, we are ready to use Ansible:

```
$ ansible --version

ansible 2.6.2
  config file = /etc/ansible/ansible.cfg
  configured module search path = [u'/root/.ansible/plugins/modules',
  u'/usr/share/ansible/plugins/modules']
  ansible python module location = /usr/lib/python2.7/site-
  packages/ansible
  executable location = /bin/ansible
```

```
python version = 2.7.5 (default, Aug 4 2017, 00:39:18) [GCC 4.8.5
20150623 (Red Hat 4.8.5-16)]
```

Creating our Ansible playground

To illustrate the basic functionalities of Ansible, we are going to start by re-launching our Hello World application.

In the previous section, we saw how to create a stack using the web interface. As you would expect, it is also possible to launch a stack using the command-line interface. Go into the EffectiveDevOpsTemplates directory where you previously generated the helloworld-cf-v2.template file and run the following command:

```
$ aws cloudformation create-stack \
    --capabilities CAPABILITY_IAM \
    --stack-name ansible \
    --template-body file://helloworld-cf-v2.template \
    --parameters ParameterKey=KeyPair,ParameterValue=EffectiveDevOpsAWS
{
    "StackId": "arn:aws:cloudformation:us-east-
    1:094507990803:stack/ansible/bb29cb10-9bbe-11e8-9ee4-500c20fefad2"
}
```

Our instance will soon be ready. We can now bootstrap our environment by creating a workspace.

Creating our Ansible repository

With Ansible, our first goal is to be able to run commands on remote hosts. In order to do that efficiently, we need to configure our local environment. Because we don't want to have to redo those steps repeatedly, and because, ultimately, we want to source-control everything, we will create a new Git repository. To do that, we will repeat the same steps that we used when we created our EffectiveDevOpsTemplate repository.

Once logged into GitHub, create a new repository for the CloudFormation template as follows:

1. In your browser, open this link: `https://github.com/new`.
2. Give the new repository the name `ansible`, as shown here:

3. Check the **Initialize this repository with a README** checkbox.
4. Finally, click on the **Create repository** button.
5. Once your repository is created, clone it onto your computer as follows:

    ```
    $ git clone https://github.com/<your_github_username>/ansible
    ```

6. Now that the repository is cloned, we will go into this and copy the template created previously in the new GitHub repository:

    ```
    $ cd ansible
    ```

At its base, Ansible is a tool that can run commands remotely on the hosts in your inventory. The inventory can be managed manually by creating an INI file where you list all your hosts and/or IPs. It can also be managed dynamically if it can query an API. As you can imagine, Ansible is perfectly capable of taking advantage of the AWS API in order to fetch our inventory. To do so, we will download a Python script from the official Ansible Git repository and give the execution permissions as follows:

```
$ curl -Lo ec2.py http://bit.ly/2v4SwE5
$ chmod +x ec2.py
```

Before we can start testing this Python script, we also need to provide a configuration for it. Create a new file in the same directory and call it ec2.ini. In this file, we will put the following configuration:

```
[ec2]
regions = all
regions_exclude = us-gov-west-1,cn-north-1 destination_variable =
public_dns_name vpc_destination_variable = ip_address route53 = False
cache_path = ~/.ansible/tmp cache_max_age = 300
rds = False
```

Once this is done, you can finally validate that the inventory is working by executing the ec2.py script as follows:

```
$ ./ec2.py
```

This command should return a big nested JSON of the different resources found on your AWS account. Among these is the public IP address of the EC2 instance that we created in the previous section. The last step in our bootstrapping is to configure Ansible itself, such that it knows how to get the inventory of our infrastructure; which user to use when it tries to SSH into our instances; how to become a root; and so on. We will create a new file in the same location and call it ansible.cfg. Its content should be as follows:

```
[defaults]
inventory       = ./ec2.py
remote_user   = ec2-user
become = True
become_method   = sudo
become_user     = root
nocows      = 1
```

At that point, we are ready to start running Ansible commands. Ansible has a few commands and some simple concepts. We will first look at the ansible command and the concept of modules.

Executing modules

The `ansible` command is the main command that drives the execution of the different modules on the remote hosts. Modules are libraries that can be executed directly on remote hosts. Ansible comes with a number of modules, as listed at `http://bit.ly/24rU0yk`. In addition to the standard modules, you can also create your own custom modules using Python. These are the modules for most common use cases and technologies. The first module we will see is a simple module called `ping`, which tries to connect to a host and returns `pong` if the host is usable.

 Module documentation can also be accessed using the `ansible-doc` command, shown as follows:
```
$ ansible-doc <Module-Name>
$ ansible-doc ping
```
Here, `ping` is one of the Ansible module names.

When creating our Ansible playground section, we created a new EC2 instance using CloudFormation. So far, we haven't looked up the IP address for this. Using Ansible and the `ping` module, we will discover that information. As mentioned before, we need to be in the `ansible` directory in order to run the `ansible` command. The command is as follows:

```
$ ansible --private-key ~/.ssh/EffectiveDevOpsAWS.pem ec2 -m ping
18.206.223.199 | SUCCESS => {
    "changed": false,
    "ping": "pong"
}
```

As we can see, Ansible was able to find our EC2 instance by querying the AWS EC2 API. The newly created instance is now ready to be used.

 Configuring SSH: As Ansible relies heavily on SSH, it is worth dedicating a bit of time to configuring SSH through the `$HOME/.ssh/config` file. For instance, you can use the following options to avoid having to specify `--private-key` and `-u` in the preceding example:
```
IdentityFile ~/.ssh/EffectiveDevOpsAWS.pem
User ec2-user StrictHostKeyChecking no
PasswordAuthentication no
ForwardAgent yes
```

Once configured, you won't need to provide the `--private-key` option to Ansible.

Running arbitrary commands

The `ansible` command can also be used to run arbitrary commands on remote servers. In the following example, we will only run the `df` command on hosts matching `18.206.223.*` for their public IP address (you will need to adapt this command to match your instance public IP, as returned in the `ping` command in the previous example):

```
$ ansible --private-key ~/.ssh/EffectiveDevOpsAWS.pem '18.206.223.*' \
-a 'df -h'
18.206.223.199 | SUCCESS | rc=0 >>
Filesystem  Size  Used  Avail  Use%  Mounted on
devtmpfs    484M  56K   484M   1%    /dev
tmpfs       494M  0     494M   0%    /dev/shm
/dev/xvda1  7.8G  1.1G  6.6G   15%   /
```

Now that we have a basic understanding of how Ansible works, we can start combining calls to different Ansible modules to put in place for automation. This is called creating a **playbook**.

Ansible playbooks

Playbooks are the files that contain Ansible's configuration, deployment, and orchestration language. By creating those files, you sequentially define the state of your systems, from the OS configuration down to application deployment and monitoring. Ansible uses YAML, which is fairly easy to read. For that reason, an easy way to get started with Ansible, similarly to what we did with CloudFormation, is to look at some examples inside the official Ansible GitHub repository, available at `https://github.com/ansible/ansible-examples`. Alternatively, you can even look in my repository, which makes it fairly simple and easy to understand playbooks, and which can be found at `https://github.com/yogeshraheja/Automation-with-Ansible-By-Yogesh-Raheja` for the book *Automation with Ansible*.

Creating a playbook

Ansible provides a number of best practices on their website, available at `http://bit.ly/1ZqdcLH`. One emphasis in their documentation is on using roles. One crucial way to organize your playbook content is Ansible's *roles* organization feature, which is documented as part of the main playbooks page. Creating roles is a key component in making Ansible code sharable and modular enough so that you can reuse your code across services and playbooks. To demonstrate a proper structure, we are going to create a role that our playbook will then call.

Creating roles to deploy and start our web application

We are going to use roles to recreate the Hello World stack we made previously using the `UserData` block of CloudFormation. If you recall, the `UserData` section looked roughly like this:

```
yum install --enablerepo=epel -y nodejs
wget http://bit.ly/2vESNuc -O /home/ec2-user/helloworld.js
wget http://bit.ly/2vVvT18 -O /etc/init/helloworld.conf start helloworld
```

You will notice three different types of operation in the preceding script. We are first preparing the system to run our application. To do that, in our example, we are simply installing a Node.js package. Next, we copy the different resources needed to run the application. In our case, this is the JavaScript code and the upstart configuration. Finally, we start the service. As always when doing programming, it is important to keep the code DRY. If deploying and starting our application is very unique to our Hello World project, installing Node.js likely isn't. In order to make the installation of Node.js a reusable piece of code, we are going to create two roles—one to install Node.js, and one to deploy and start the Hello World application.

By default, Ansible expects to see roles inside a `roles` directory at the root of the Ansible repository. So, the first thing we need to do is to go inside the `ansible` directory that we created under the *Creating our Ansible repository* section. Create the `roles` directory inside, and `cd` the following into it:

```
$ mkdir roles
$ cd roles
```

We can now create our roles. Ansible has an `ansible-galaxy` command that can be used to initialize the creation of a role. The first role we will look into is the role that will install Node.js:

```
$ ansible-galaxy init nodejs
- nodejs was created successfully
```

 As briefly mentioned, Ansible, like most other configuration management systems, has a strong support community who share roles online through `https://galaxy.ansible.com/`. In addition to using the `ansible-galaxy` command to create the skeleton for new roles, you can also use `ansible-galaxy` to import and install community supported roles.

This creates a `nodejs` directory, and a number of sub-directories that will let us structure the different sections of our role. We will enter this directory with the following command:

```
$ cd nodejs
```

The most important directory inside the `nodejs` directory is the one called `tasks`. When Ansible executes a playbook, it runs the code present in the `tasks/main.yml` file. Open the file with your favorite text editor.

When you first open `tasks/main.yml`, you will see the following:

```
---
# tasks file for nodejs
```

The goal of the `nodejs` role is to install Node.js and `npm`. To do so, we will proceed similarly to how we did with the `UserData` script, and use the `yum` command to perform those tasks.

When writing a task in Ansible, you sequence a number of calls to various Ansible modules. The first module we are going to look at is a wrapper around the `yum` command. The documentation on it is available at `http://bit.ly/28joDLe`. This will let us install our packages. We are also going to introduce the concept of loops. Since we have two packages to install, we will want to call the `yum` module twice. We will use the operator's `with_items`. All Ansible codes are written in YAML, which is very easy to start with and use. After the initial three dashes and comments, which indicate the start of a YAML file, we are going to call the `yum` module in order to install our packages:

```
---
# tasks file for nodejs

name: Installing node and npm yum:
name: "{{ item }}" enablerepo: epel state: installed
with_items:
nodejs
npm
```

Whenever Ansible runs that playbook, it will look at packages installed on the system. If it doesn't find the `nodejs` or `npm` packages, it will install them.

Your file should look like the example available at https://github.com/yogeshraheja/
Effective-DevOps-with-AWS/blob/master/Chapter03/ansible/roles/nodejs/tasks/
main.yml. This first role is complete. For the purpose of this book, we are keeping the role
very simple, but you can imagine how, in a more production-type environment, you might
have a role that will install specific versions of Node.js and npm, fetch the binaries directly
from https://nodejs.org/en/, and maybe even install specific dependencies. Our next
role will be dedicated to deploying and starting the Hello World application that we built
previously. We are going to go one directory up back into the roles directory, and call
ansible-galaxy one more time:

```
$ cd ..
$ ansible-galaxy init helloworld
- helloworld was created successfully
```

Like before, we will now go inside the newly created helloworld directory as follows:

```
$ cd helloworld
```

This time, we will explore some of the other directories present. One of the sub-directories
that was created when we ran the ansible-galaxy command was the directory called
files. Adding files to that directory will give us the ability to copy files on the remote
hosts. To do so, we are first going to download our two files in this directory as follows:

```
$ wget http://bit.ly/2vESNuc -O files/helloworld.js
$ wget http://bit.ly/2vVvT18 -O files/helloworld.conf
```

We can now use task files to perform the copy on the remote system. Open the
tasks/main.yml file and, after the initial three dashes and comments, add the following:

```
---
# tasks file for helloworld
- name: Copying the application file copy:
src: helloworld.js dest: /home/ec2-user/ owner: ec2-user group: ec2-user
mode: 0644
notify: restart helloworld
```

We are taking advantage of the copy module documented at http://bit.ly/1WBv08E to
copy our application file in the home directory of the ec2-user. On the last line of that call,
we add a notify option at the end (note how the notify statement is aligned with the call
to the copy module). Notify actions are triggers that can be added at the end of each block
of tasks in a playbook. In this example, we are telling Ansible to call the restart
helloworld directive if the file helloworld.js changed, and not to perform a restart if
nothing is changed in the code (we will define how to do a restart of the helloworld
application in a different file a bit later).

One of the big differences between CloudFormation and Ansible is that Ansible is expected to run multiple times throughout the lifetime of your systems. A lot of the functionalities built into Ansible are optimized for long-running instances. As such, the notify option makes it easy to trigger events when a system changes state. Similarly, Ansible will know to stop the execution when an error encountered prevents outages as far as possible.

Now that we have copied our application file, we can add our second file, the upstart script. After the previous call to copy the helloword.js file, we are going to add the following call:

```
- name: Copying the upstart file copy:
src: helloworld.conf
dest: /etc/init/helloworld.conf owner: root
group: root mode: 0644
```

The last task we need to perform is to start our service. We will use the service module for that. The module documentation is available at http://bit.ly/22I7QNH:

```
- name: Starting the HelloWorld node service service:
name: helloworld state: started
```

Our task file is now completed. You should end up with something resembling the sample available
at https://github.com/yogeshraheja/Effective-DevOps-with-AWS/blob/master/Chapter03/ansible/roles/helloworld/tasks/main.yml.

Having finished our task file, we are going to move on to the next file, which will give Ansible knowledge of how and when to restart helloworld, as called out in the notify parameter of our task. These types of interaction are defined in the handler section of the role. We are going to edit the handlers/main.yml file. Here too, we are going to use the service module. The following is a comment:

```
---
# handlers file for helloworld
```

Add the following to the main.yml file:

```
- name: restart helloworld service:
name: helloworld state: restarted
```

No surprises here; we are using the same module we previously used to manage the service. We need one more step in our role. In order for the `helloworld` role to work, the system needs to have Node.js installed. Ansible supports the concept of role dependencies. We can explicitly tell that our `helloworld` role depends on the `nodejs` role we previously created, so that, if the `helloworld` role is executed, it will first call the `nodejs` role and install the necessary requirements to run the app.

Open the `meta/main.yml` file. This file has two sections. The first one, under `galaxy_info`, lets you fill in the information on the role you are building. If you wish, you can ultimately publish your role on GitHub and link it back into `ansible-galaxy` to share your creation with the Ansible community. The second section at the bottom of the file is called `dependencies` and this is the one we want to edit to make sure that `nodejs` is present on the system prior to starting our application. Remove the square brackets ([]) and add an entry to call `nodejs` as follows:

```
dependencies:
- nodejs
```

Your file should look like the sample available at `https://github.com/yogeshraheja/Effective-DevOps-with-AWS/blob/master/Chapter03/ansible/roles/helloworld/meta/main.yml`. This concludes the creation of the code for the role. From a documentation standpoint, it is good practice to also edit `README.md`. Once done, we can move on to creating a playbook file that will reference our newly created role.

Creating the playbook file

At the top level of our Ansible repository (two directories up from the `helloworld` role), we are going to create a new file called `helloworld.yml`. In this file, we are going to add the following:

```
---
- hosts: "{{ target | default('localhost') }}" become: yes
roles:
- helloworld
```

This basically tells Ansible to execute the `helloworld` role onto the hosts listed in the `target` variable, or `localhost` if the target isn't defined. The `become` option will tell Ansible to execute the role with elevated privileges (in our case, `sudo`). At this point, your Ansible repository should look like the example at `https://github.com/yogeshraheja/Effective-DevOps-with-AWS/tree/master/Chapter03/ansible`. We are now ready to test our playbook.

Note that in practice, on a bigger scale, the roles sections could include more than a single role. If you deploy multiple applications or services to a target, you will often see playbook looking like this. In later chapters, we will see more examples of this:

```
---
hosts: webservers roles:
foo
bar
baz
```

Executing a playbook

The execution of playbooks is done using the dedicated `ansible-playbook` command. This command relies on the same Ansible configuration file that we used previously, and therefore, we want to run the command from the root of our Ansible repository. The syntax of the command is as follows:

```
ansible-playbook <playbook.yml> [options]
```

We will first run the following command (adapt the value of the `private-key` option):

```
$ ansible-playbook helloworld.yml \
    --private-key ~/.ssh/EffectiveDevOpsAWS.pem \
    -e target=ec2 \
    --list-hosts
```

The option `-e` (or `--extra-vars`) allows us to pass extra options for execution. In our case, we are defining the `target` variable (which we declared in the `hosts` section of our playbook) to be equal to ec2. This first `ansible-playbook` command will tell Ansible to target all EC2 instances. The `--list-hosts` option will make Ansible return a list of hosts that match the hosts criteria, but it won't actually run anything against those hosts. The output of the command will be something like this:

```
playbook: helloworld.yml
  play #1 (ec2): ec2 TAGS: []
    pattern: [u'ec2']
    hosts (1):
      18.206.223.199
```

The `list-hosts` option is a good way to verify your inventory and, on more complex playbooks with more specific host values, to verify which hosts would run actual playbooks, allowing you to verify that they are targeting the hosts you expect.

We now know which hosts will be impacted if we were to use this value for the target. The next thing we want to check is what will happen if we run our playbook. The `ansible-playbook` command has an option `-C` (or `--check`) that will try to predict the change a given playbook will make; this is sometimes also called **dry-run** mode in Ansible:

```
$ ansible-playbook helloworld.yml \
    --private-key ~/.ssh/EffectiveDevOpsAWS.pem \
    -e target=18.206.223.199 \
    --check

PLAY [18.206.223.199]
***********************************************************************
***********************************************************************

TASK [Gathering Facts]
***********************************************************************
***********************************************************************
ok: [18.206.223.199]

TASK [nodejs : Installing node and npm]
***********************************************************************
*******************************************************
changed: [18.206.223.199] => (item=[u'nodejs', u'npm'])

TASK [helloworld : Copying the application file]
***********************************************************************
********************************************
changed: [18.206.223.199]

TASK [helloworld : Copying the upstart file]
***********************************************************************
**********************************************
changed: [18.206.223.199]

TASK [helloworld : Starting the HelloWorld node service]
***********************************************************************
***********************************
changed: [18.206.223.199]

RUNNING HANDLER [helloworld : restart helloworld]
***********************************************************************
********************************************
changed: [18.206.223.199]
```

```
PLAY RECAP
**********************************************************************
**********************************************************************
******
18.206.223.199 : ok=6 changed=5 unreachable=0 failed=0
```

Running that command will execute our playbook in dry-run mode. Through that mode, we can ensure that the proper tasks will be executed. Because we are in dry-run mode, some of the modules don't really find everything they need in order to simulate how they would run. This is the reason why we sometimes see service start errors at the end of the service module. If you see this, then don't worry, it will get executed when the packages are installed in the real-mode. Having verified the hosts and code, we can finally run `ansible-playbook` and execute our changes in a real-mode as follows:

```
$ ansible-playbook helloworld.yml \
    --private-key ~/.ssh/EffectiveDevOpsAWS.pem \
    -e target=18.206.223.199
```

The output is very similar to the `--check` command, except that this time, the execution is performed in real-mode. Our application is now installed and configured, and we can verify that it is running correctly as follows:

```
$ curl 18.206.223.199:3000
Hello World
```

We were able to reproduce what we did previously with CloudFormation using Ansible. Now that we have tested our first playbook, we can commit our changes. We will do that in two commits to break down the initialization of the repository and the creation of the role. From the root of your Ansible repository, run the following commands:

```
$ git add ansible.cfg ec2.ini ec2.py
$ git commit -m "Configuring ansible to work with EC2"
$ git add roles helloworld.yml
$ git commit -m "Adding role for nodejs and helloworld"
$ git push
```

Canary-testing changes

One of the great benefits of using Ansible to manage services is that you can easily make changes to your code and quickly push the change. In some situations where you have a big fleet of services managed by Ansible, you may wish to push out a change only to a single host to make sure things are how you expect them to be. This is often called **canary testing**. With Ansible, doing this is really easy. To illustrate that, we are going to open the `roles/helloworld/files/helloworld.js` file and then simply change the response on line 11 from `Hello World` to `Hello World, Welcome again`:

```
// Send the response body as "Hello World"
response.end('Hello World, Welcome again\n');
}).listen(3000);
```

Save the file, and then run `ansible-playbook` again. Do this with the `--check` option first:

```
$ ansible-playbook helloworld.yml \
    --private-key ~/.ssh/EffectiveDevOpsAWS.pem \
    -e target=18.206.223.199 \
    --check
```

This time, Ansible detects only two changes. The first one overwrites the application file and the second one executes the `notify` statement, which means restarting the application. Seeing that it is what we expect, we can run our playbook without the `--check` options:

```
$ ansible-playbook helloworld.yml \
    --private-key ~/.ssh/EffectiveDevOpsAWS.pem \
    -e target=18.206.223.199
```

This produces the same output as in our previous command, but this time the change is in effect:

```
$ curl 18.206.223.199:3000
Hello World, Welcome again
```

Our change was very simple, but if we had done this by updating our CloudFormation template, CloudFormation would have had to create a new EC2 instance to make it happen. Here, we simply updated the code of the application and pushed it through Ansible on the target host. We will now revert this change locally in Git as follows:

```
$ git checkout roles/helloworld/files/helloworld.js
```

We will demonstrate this by removing the changes from the EC2 instance as we illustrate a new concept. In the next section, we will be running Ansible asynchronously in a reverse mode (in this case, in pull mode).

The sooner, the better: Being able to push changes in seconds instead of minutes may seem like a small win, but it isn't. Speed matters; it is what sets apart successful start-ups and technologies. The ability to deploy new servers in minutes instead of days is a big factor in cloud adoption. Similarly, the recent success of containers, as we will see later in the book, is also likely driven by the fact that it only takes seconds to run a new container, while it still takes minutes to start a virtual server.

Running Ansible in pull mode

Having the ability to instantly make a change like we just did is a very valuable feature. We could easily and synchronously push the new code out and verify that the Ansible execution was successful. On a larger scale, while being able to change anything across a fleet of servers remains as valuable as in our example, it is also sometimes a bit trickier. The risk with making changes that way is that you have to be very disciplined with regards to not pushing changes to only a subset of hosts, and forgetting other hosts that are also sharing the role that just got updated. Otherwise, the increasing number of changes between the Ansible configuration repository and the running servers quickly makes running Ansible a riskier operation. For those situations, it is usually preferable to use a pull mechanism that will automatically pull in the changes. Of course, you don't have to choose one or the other—it is easy to configure both push and pull mechanisms to deploy changes. Ansible provides a command called `ansible-pull`, which, as its name suggests, makes it easy to run Ansible in pull mode. The `ansible-pull` command works very much like `ansible-playbook`, except that it starts by pulling your code from your GitHub repository.

Installing Git and Ansible on our EC2 instance

Since we need to be able to run Ansible and Git remotely, we first need to install those packages on our EC2 instance. For now, we will do that by manually installing those two packages. We will implement a reusable solution later in this chapter. Since Ansible is a perfect tool for running remote commands and this has a module to manage most common requirements such as installing packages, instead of logging in on the host through ssh and running some commands, we are going to use Ansible to push out those changes. We will install Git and Ansible from the EPEL yum repository. This will require running commands as **root**, which you can do with the help of the become option. After adapting the IP address of your EC2 instance, run the following commands:

```
$ ansible '18.206.223.199' \
    --private-key ~/.ssh/EffectiveDevOpsAWS.pem \
    --become \
    -m yum -a 'name=git enablerepo=epel state=installed'

$ ansible '18.206.223.199' \
    --private-key ~/.ssh/EffectiveDevOpsAWS.pem \
    --become \
    -m yum -a 'name=ansible enablerepo=epel state=installed'
```

With ansible-pull, our goal is for Ansible to apply the change locally. We can make a change to our Ansible repository in order to optimize this operation.

Configuring Ansible to run on localhost

Since ansible-pull relies on Git to locally clone the repository and execute it, we don't need the execution to happen over SSH. Go to the root directory of your Ansible repository to create a new file. The file should be called localhost and it should contain the following:

```
[localhost]
localhost ansible_connection=local
```

Essentially, what we are doing is creating a static inventory and asking ansible to run commands in local mode (as opposed to using SSH) when the target host is localhost. We can save the changes and commit the new file to GitHub as follows:

```
$ git add localhost
$ git commit -m "Adding localhost inventory"
$ git push
```

Adding a cron job to our EC2 instance

We are now going to create a cron tab entry to periodically call `ansible-pull`. Here, too, we will rely on Ansible to create our cron job remotely. Run the following command by adapting the IP address:

```
$ ansible '18.206.223.199' \
--private-key ~/.ssh/EffectiveDevOpsAWS.pem \
-m cron -a 'name=ansible-pull minute="*/10" job="/usr/bin/ansible-pull -U
https://github.com/<your_username>/ansible helloworld.yml -i localhost --
sleep 60"'
```

In the preceding command, we are telling Ansible to use the `cron` module targeting our `ec2` instance. Here, we are providing a name that Ansible will use to track the cron job over time, telling `cron` to run the job every `10` minutes, followed by the command to execute and its parameters. The parameters we are giving to `ansible-pull` are the GitHub URL of our branch, the inventory file we just added to our repository, and a `sleep` parameter that will make the command start sometime between `1` and `60` seconds after the call started. This will help spread out the load on the network and prevent all node services from restarting at the same time if we have more than one server. After waiting for a bit, we can verify that our change is effective through the following:

```
$ curl 54.175.86.38:3000
Hello World
```

After manually integrating Ansible to the EC2 instance we created using CloudFormation, we can now formalize the procedure.

Integrating Ansible with CloudFormation

While there are different strategies to integrate Ansible to CloudFormation, in our situation there is an obvious path to take. We are going to take advantage of the `UserData` field, and initialize Ansible through the `ansible-pull` command.

We are now going to start the Troposphere script that we created earlier in this chapter. We will duplicate this and call the new script as follows:

```
ansiblebase-cf-template.py.
```

Go to your template repository and duplicate the previous template as follows:

```
$ cd EffectiveDevOpsTemplates
$ cp helloworld-cf-template.py ansiblebase-cf-template.py
```

Next, open the `ansiblebase-cf-template.py` script with your editor. To keep the script readable, we will first define several variables. Before the declaration of the application port, we will define an application name:

```
ApplicationName = "helloworld"
ApplicationPort = "3000"
```

We will also set a number of constants around the GitHub information. Replace the value of `GithubAccount` with your GitHub username or GitHub organization name as follows:

```
ApplicationPort = "3000"

GithubAccount = "EffectiveDevOpsWithAWS"
GithubAnsibleURL = "https://github.com/{}/ansible".format(GithubAccount)
```

After the definition of `GithubAnsibleURL`, we are going to create one more variable that will contain the command line we want to execute in order to configure the host through Ansible. We will call `ansible-pull` and use the `GithubAnsibleURL` and `ApplicationName` variables that we just defined. This is what this looks like:

```
AnsiblePullCmd = \
"/usr/bin/ansible-pull -U {} {}.yml -i localhost".format( GithubAnsibleURL,
ApplicationName
)
```

We are now going to update the `UserData` block. Instead of installing Node.js, downloading our application files and starting the service, we will change this block to install `git` and `ansible`, execute the command contained in the `AnsiblePullCmd` variable, and finally create a cron job to re-execute that command every 10 minutes. Delete the previous `ud` variable definition and replace it with the following:

```
ud = Base64(Join('\n', [ "#!/bin/bash",
"yum install --enablerepo=epel -y git", "pip install ansible",
AnsiblePullCmd,
"echo '*/10 * * * * {}' > /etc/cron.d/ansible- pull".format(AnsiblePullCmd)
]))
```

We can now save our file, use it to create our JSON template, and test it. Your new script should look like the sample at `https://github.com/yogeshraheja/EffectiveDevOpsTemplates/blob/master/ansiblebase-cf-template.py`:

```
$ python ansiblebase-cf-template.py > ansiblebase.template
$ aws cloudformation update-stack \
    --stack-name ansible \
    --template-body file://ansiblebase.template \
    --parameters ParameterKey=KeyPair,ParameterValue=EffectiveDevOpsAWS
{
"StackId": "arn:aws:cloudformation:us-
east-1:511912822958:stack/HelloWorld/ef2c3250-6428-11e7-a67b-50d501eed2b3"
}
```

You can even create a new stack yourself. For example, let's say `helloworld`, instead of changing the existing `ansible` stack. In this case, you need to run the following command for stack creation:

```
$ aws cloudformation create-stack \
    --stack-name helloworld \
    --template-body file://ansiblebase.template \
    --parameters ParameterKey=KeyPair,ParameterValue=EffectiveDevOpsAWS
{
    "StackId": "arn:aws:cloudformation:us-east-
    1:094507990803:stack/helloworld/5959e7c0-9c6e-11e8-b47f-
    50d5cd26c2d2"
}
```

We can now wait until the execution is complete:

```
$ aws cloudformation wait stack-update-complete \
        --stack-name ansible
```

Now that the stack creation is complete, we can query CloudFormation to get the output of the stack and, more specifically, its public IP address:

```
$ aws cloudformation describe-stacks \
    --stack-name ansible \
    --query 'Stacks[0].Outputs[0]'
  {
    "Description": "Public IP of our instance.",
    "OutputKey": "InstancePublicIp",
    "OutputValue": "35.174.138.51"
  }
```

And finally, we can verify that our server is up and running as follows:

```
$ curl 35.174.138.51:3000
Hello World
```

We can now commit our newly created `troposphere` script to our GitHub repository as follows:

```
EffectiveDevOpsTemplates repository:
$ git add ansiblebase-cf-template.py
$ git commit -m "Adding a Troposphere script to create a stack that relies
on Ansible to manage our application"
$ git push
```

We now have a complete solution for efficiently managing our infrastructure using code. We demonstrated this through a very simple example. However, as you can imagine, everything is applicable to bigger infrastructure with a greater number of services. This section is almost over; we can now delete our stack to free up the resources that we are currently consuming. In the earlier part of the chapter, we did this using the web interface. As you can imagine, this can also be done easily using the following command-line interface:

```
$ aws cloudformation delete-stack --stack-name ansible
```

Note that if you have created a new `helloworld` stack for this example, then remove that too using the following command:

```
aws cloudformation delete-stack --stack-name helloworld
```

Monitoring

As you probably know by now, monitoring and measuring everything is an important aspect of a DevOps-driven organization. On the internet, you will find a number of well written blog posts and examples of how to efficiently monitor CloudFormation and Ansible. When working on monitoring CloudFormation, you will want to subscribe to an SNS topic for your stack creation to receive all events relating to your stack life cycle. It is also important to look out for CloudFormation stack creation failure. Ansible has a system of callbacks that will also give you a way to create some automation around the Ansible execution. Similarly to CloudFormation, receiving notifications when Ansible fails to run is important (it's even more important when Ansible is configured to run in pull mode).

Summary

In this chapter, we learned how to efficiently manage infrastructure by using code. We also explored CloudFormation, an AWS service that allows you to create templates for your different services in order to describe each AWS component used, as well as its configuration. In order to simplify the creation of those templates, we looked at a couple of options, ranging from CloudFormation designer, a tool with a graphic user interface, to Troposphere, a Python library. After that, we looked at configuration management, one of the most well-known aspects of the DevOps philosophy. To illustrate this topic, we looked at Ansible, one of the most popular configuration management solutions. We first looked at the different ways to use Ansible commands and ran simple commands against our infrastructure. We then looked at how to create playbooks, which allowed us to orchestrate the different steps to deploy our web server. Finally, we looked at how Ansible can be used in pull mode, which usually makes more sense when managing sizable infrastructure.

We now have a good production environment that is ready to host any application, and we have seen how to architect it and monitor our servers. In Chapter 5, *Adding Continuous Integration and Continuous Deployment*, we will continue to use CloudFormation and Ansible, but in the context of software delivery: we will learn how to put in place continuous integration testing and continuous deployment.

Questions

1. What does IaC stand for?
2. How can a simple Hello World application be deployed using the AWS CloudFormation Console?
3. List some of the popular SCM offerings. How is a GitHub account useful for source control management?
4. Install Git (Local Version Control) package, clone your GitHub global repository created in the previous example and push your `helloworld-cf.template` to your GitHub repository.
5. What is Ansible? List some of its important characteristics.

Further reading

In order to explore this topic in more detail, please visit the following links:

- *AWS CloudFormation details* at `https://console.aws.amazon.com/cloudformation`
- *Troposphere – Python library to create AWS CloudFormation descriptions* at `https://github.com/cloudtools/troposphere`
- *Ansible configuration management tool* at `https://docs.ansible.com/ansible`

Infrastructure as Code with Terraform

4

In Chapter 3, *Treating Your Infrastructure as Code*, we familiarized ourselves with AWS CloudFormation and Ansible. We created a CloudFormation template to create an EC2 environment and deployed a HelloWorld web application on it. Taking a step further in the world of automation, we then introduced the **Ansible** configuration management tool. We learnt about how Ansible takes care of application deployment and orchestration so that CloudFormation templates remain neat and confined until provisioning. This approach is well accepted by the tech giants as far as the AWS cloud is concerned, but when we talk about heterogeneous environments where we have multiple cloud platforms such as AWS, Azure, Google cloud, OpenStack, and VMware then CloudFormation service, as it is a AWS-native service, is not applicable.

Hence, we need an alternative solution that will not only help us to provision compute services but also other cloud native services without much effort. Obviously, this is possible using complex, unmanageable scripts in imperative way, but we'd end up making the environments even more complex. We need a solution that will keep the heterogeneous environment simple and manageable, with a declarative approach that follows the recommended guidelines regarding using **Infrastructure as Code** (**IaC**). This solution is **Terraform**, a tool for building, changing, and versioning infrastructure safely and efficiently.

In this chapter, we will cover the following topics:

- What is Terraform?
- Creating a Terraform repository
- Integrating AWS, Terraform, and Ansible

Technical requirements

The technical requirements are as follows:

- AWS Console
- Git
- GitHub
- Terraform
- Ansible

The following websites provide further information about Terraform:

- Terraform official website for product information: `https://terraform.io`
- Terraform supported provide details: `https://www.terraform.io/docs/providers/`
- HashiCorp configuration language details: `https://github.com/hashicorp/hcl`
- GitHub link for Terraform template for the first project: `https://raw.githubusercontent.com/yogeshraheja/EffectiveDevOpsTerraform/master/firstproject/ec2.tf`
- GitHub link for Terraform template for the second project: `https://raw.githubusercontent.com/yogeshraheja/EffectiveDevOpsTerraform/master/secondproject/helloworldec2.tf`
- Github link for Terraform template for the third project: `https://raw.githubusercontent.com/yogeshraheja/EffectiveDevOpsTerraform/master/thirdproject/helloworldansible.tf`
- Github link for Terraform template for the fourth project: `https://raw.githubusercontent.com/yogeshraheja/EffectiveDevOpsTerraform/master/fourthproject/helloworldansiblepull.tf`

What is Terraform?

Terraform is an open-source, IaC software that was released in July 2014 by a company named **HashiCorp**. This is the same company that produced tools including Vagrant, Packer, and Vault. Terraform was released under the **Mozilla Public License (MPL)** version 2.0. The source code for Terraform is available on GitHub at `https://github.com/hashicorp/terraform`. Anyone can use this source code and contribute to Terraform's development.

Terraform allow users to define a datacenter infrastructure in a high-level configuration language called **HashiCorp Configuration Language** (**HCL**). HashiCorp also provide the Enterprise version of Terraform, which comes with added support. There are lot of features available with Terraform, which makes it a perfect high-level infrastructure orchestration tool. It has the following features:

- It has very easy and minimal installation steps.
- It has a declarative approach to write Terraform templates.
- It is available as both open-source and Enterprise offerings.
- It has idempotency, which means the Terraform templates provide the same result every time you apply them in your environment.
- It is a perfect match for almost all majorly available cloud platforms such as AWS, Azure, GCP, OpenStack, DigitalOcean, and so on. Refer to `https://www.terraform.io/docs/providers/` for more details.

However, Terraform is not:

- A configuration management tool like Puppet, Chef, Ansible, or SaltStack. You can install some lightweight programs or software to ship some important configuration files inside your instances, but when it comes to the deployment and orchestration of more complex applications, you need to use configuration tools like those listed in the preceding section.
- A low-level tool like Boto for AWS.

Getting started with Terraform

In this book, we will focus on open-source Terraform. We will be demonstrating the complete Terraform setup on the CentOS 7.x machine that we used in the previous chapters. HashiCorp does not provide native packages for operating systems, so Terraform is distributed as a single binary, packaged inside a ZIP archive.

Let's set up Terraform on our CentOS server. Follow these steps:

1. We have to download the Terraform binaries from the official website: `https://www.terraform.io/downloads.html`. In our case, we will be using Linux 64-bit:

```
[root@yogeshraheja ~]# curl -O https://releases.hashicorp.com/terraform/0.11.8/terraform_0.11.8_linux_amd64.zip
  % Total    % Received % Xferd  Average Speed   Time    Time     Time  Current
                                 Dload  Upload   Total   Spent    Left  Speed
100 17.0M  100 17.0M    0     0  34.5M      0 --:--:-- --:--:-- --:--:-- 34.6M
[root@yogeshraheja ~]#
[root@yogeshraheja ~]# ls -lrt terraform_0.11.8_linux_amd64.zip
-rw-r--r--. 1 root root 17871447 Sep 12 06:40 terraform_0.11.8_linux_amd64.zip
[root@yogeshraheja ~]#
```

2. Unzip the extracted Terraform `.zip` file. You need to install the unzip package if it is not already present:

```
$ yum -y install unzip
$ echo $PATH
$ unzip terraform_0.11.8_linux_amd64.zip -d /usr/bin/
```

This will extract the Terraform binary to the `/usr/bin`, which is available in the **PATH** environment variable for your Linux systems.

3. Finally, check the installed version of Terraform. The latest version of Terraform software available at the time of writing is the following:

```
$ terraform -v
Terraform v0.11.8
```

As you can observe, setting up Terraform takes just a matter of minutes and it has very lightweight binaries. We are now all set to use the Terraform environment for AWS service provisioning.

Terraform and AWS for automated provisioning

As mentioned previously, Terraform supports multiple providers such as AWS, Azure, and GCP for high level infrastructure orchestration. In this book, we will use only the AWS platform. As we saw at in `Chapter 2`, *Deploying Your First Web Application*, we can deploy compute services or any AWS service using two modes:

- AWS Management Console
- AWS **Command Line Interface** (**CLI**)

Deployment using AWS Management Console

Here, we will focus on deploying the AWS compute service as we did previously. Deploying AWS instances using the AWS Management Console is fairly simple. Follow the steps below:

1. Log in into your AWS Management Console at `https://console.aws.amazon.com` or use your IAM user account to log in . We created an IAM user account in `Chapter 2`, *Deploying Your First Web Application* at `https://AWS-account-ID-or-alias.signin.aws.amazon.com/console`.
2. Select the **Services** tab, followed by **EC2** from the **Compute** section, and click on the **Launch Instance** button.
3. On the next screen, search for and select **Amazon Machine Image** (**AMI**). In this book, we are using `ami-cfe4b2b0`, which is Amazon Linux AMI.
4. Select the `t2.micro` type from the **Choose an Instance Type** step and click on the **Next: Configure Instance Details** button.
5. Accept the default settings and click the **Next: Add Storage** button.
6. Again, accept the default setting for storage and click on the **Next: Add tags** button followed by the **Next: Configure Security Group** button.

7. Here, select the security group you created in `Chapter 2`, *Deploying Your First Web Application*, which in my case is `sg-01864b4c`, as shown in the following screenshot:

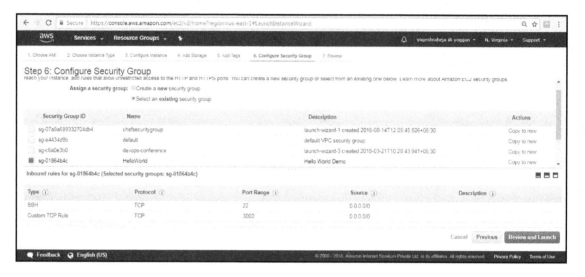

8. Now, click on the **Review and Launch** button. Ignore any warnings that appear and press the **Launch** button.
9. Select the key-pair, which in my case is `EffectiveDevOpsAWS`. Click the **Launch Instances** button.

Within a few minutes, your AWS instance will be up and running. Once the server is up, log in to the server from your local instance, which is CentOS in my case. Proceed with the following process to deploy the Hello World application manually and verify it locally or from the browser:

```
$ ssh -i ~/.ssh/EffectiveDevOpsAWS.pem ec2-user@34.201.116.2 (replace this
IP with your AWS public IP)
$ sudo yum install --enablerepo=epel -y nodejs
$ sudo wget
https://raw.githubusercontent.com/yogeshraheja/Effective-DevOps-with-AWS/ma
ster/Chapter02/helloworld.js -O /home/ec2-user/helloworld.js
$ sudo wget
https://raw.githubusercontent.com/yogeshraheja/Effective-DevOps-with-AWS/ma
ster/Chapter02/helloworld.conf -O /etc/init/helloworld.conf
$ sudo start helloworld

$ curl http://34.201.116.2:3000/
Hello World
```

Remember to terminate the instance from the AWS Management Console once you are done with the test.

The termination process is also very straightforward. Select the created instance, click the **Actions** drop-down, followed by the **Instance State** option and then click **Terminate,** as shown in the following screenshot:

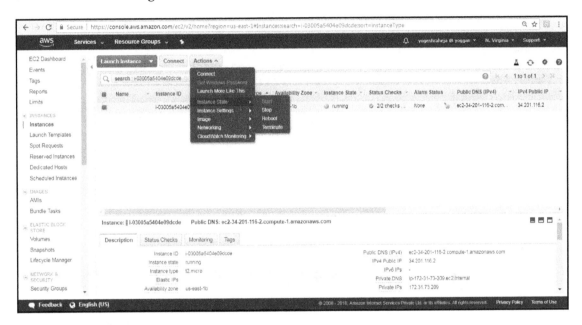

Deployment using AWS CLI

The steps for creating an instance and deploying the Hello World web application using AWS CLI have already been demonstrated in Chapter 2, *Deploying Your First Web Application.* You need to make sure to install the awscli utility before proceeding further. Here is a quick overview for deploying the Hello World web application using AWS CLI:

```
$ aws ec2 run-instances \
    --instance-type t2.micro \
    --key-name EffectiveDevOpsAWS \
    --security-group-ids sg-01864b4c \
    --image-id ami-cfe4b2b0

$ aws ec2 describe-instances \
```

```
--instance-ids i-0eb05adae2bb760c6 \
--query "Reservations[*].Instances[*].PublicDnsName"
```

Make sure to replace `i-0eb05adae2bb760c6` with the AWS instance ID that you created in the previous command.

```
$ ssh -i ~/.ssh/EffectiveDevOpsAWS.pem ec2-
user@ec2-18-234-227-160.compute-1.amazonaws.com
$ sudo yum install --enablerepo=epel -y nodejs
$ sudo wget
https://raw.githubusercontent.com/yogeshraheja/Effective-DevOps-with-AWS/ma
ster/Chapter02/helloworld.js -O /home/ec2-user/helloworld.js
$ sudo wget
https://raw.githubusercontent.com/yogeshraheja/Effective-DevOps-with-AWS/ma
ster/Chapter02/helloworld.conf -O /etc/init/helloworld.conf
$ sudo start helloworld

$ curl http://ec2-18-234-227-160.compute-1.amazonaws.com:3000/
 Hello World
```

Remember to terminate the instance using `aws ec2 terminate-instances --instance-ids <AWS INSTANCE ID>` once you are done with the testing.

Creating our Terraform repository

We have now looked at two modes for creating AWS EC2 instances: using AWS Management Console and using AWS CLI. These can be automated using the AWS cloud native service called **CloudFormation template**, as we saw in Chapter 3, *Treating Your Infrastructure as Code.* This is only applicable for use with the AWS cloud. In this chapter, we will achieve the same results of provisioning AWS instances using Terraform. Refer to https://www.terraform.io/intro/vs/cloudformation.html to understand the differences between Terraform and CloudFormation.

Let's create a dedicated repository in our GitHub account and start our journey with Terraform. Once you've logged in to GitHub, create a new repository for the Terraform templates by following the steps below:

1. In your browser, open `https://github.com/new`.
2. Call the new repository `EffectiveDevOpsTerraform` as shown in the following screenshot:

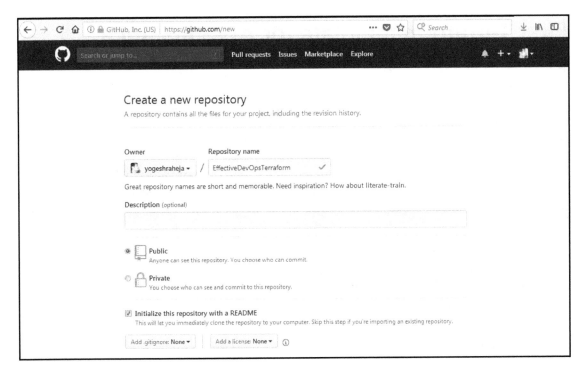

3. Check the **Initialize this repository with a README** checkbox.
4. Finally, click the **Create repository** button.
5. Once your repository is created, you will want to clone it to your system. To do this, you need to have Git installed. If you don't have Git yet, search on Google for instructions on how to install it for your operating system. For CentOS, you just need to run `yum -y install git` as the Git package is part of the Linux distribution now:

```
$ git clone
https://github.com/<your_github_username>/EffectiveDevOpsTerraf
orm
```

Now that the repository is cloned, it's time to start developing Terraform templates. Go into the `EffectiveDevOpsTerraform` repository and create a directory called `firstproject`:

```
$ cd EffectiveDevOpsTerraform
$ mkdir firstproject
$ cd firstproject
```

First Terraform template for AWS instance provisioning

Terraform is used to create, manage, and update infrastructure resources such as virtual machines, cloud instances, physical machines, containers, and much more. Almost any infrastructure type can be represented as a resource in Terraform. We are going to create a resource in the next step. Before that, we need to understand *Terraform providers*, which are responsible for understanding API interactions and exposing resources. A provider could be IaaS (such as AWS, GCP, and so on), PaaS (such as Heroku) or SaaS (such as DNSimple). The provider is the first section with which we have to start our Terraform templates. Before using Terraform to create an instance, we need to configure the AWS provider. This is the first piece of code that we are going to write in our template.

Templates are written in a special language called HCL. More details about HCL can be found at `https://github.com/hashicorp/hcl`. You can also write your templates in JSON, but we will be using HCL here. Terraform template files must have the extension `.tf`, which stands for **Terraform file**. Let's create our first template, `ec2.tf`:

```
provider "aws" {
access_key = "<YOUR AWS ACCESS KEY>"
secret_key = "<YOUR AWS SECRET KEY>"
region = "us-east-1"
}
```

Visit `https://www.terraform.io/docs/providers/aws/index.html` to explore more options about the AWS provider.

This type of declaration for providers in Terraform is called *configuring providers using static credentials*. It is not a secure way of declaring providers; there are other options in Terraform, such as environment variables, Terraform variable files, AWS native credential files (`~/.aws/credentials`), and so on, for storing providers with sensitive information.

Do not push your AWS access key or your secret key on GitHub or any other public website. Doing so will allow hackers to hack your AWS account.

Before moving on, we need to install the plugin or reinitialize the plugins that are related to AWS for Terraform. We don't need to do much here; the configured file with the `provider` plugins will perform this task for us.

Run the following command:

```
$ terraform init
```

The output of the preceding command is as follows:

```
[root@yogeshraheja firstproject]# terraform init

Initializing provider plugins...
- Checking for available provider plugins on https://releases.hashicorp.com...
- Downloading plugin for provider "aws" (1.36.0)...

The following providers do not have any version constraints in configuration,
so the latest version was installed.

To prevent automatic upgrades to new major versions that may contain breaking
changes, it is recommended to add version = "..." constraints to the
corresponding provider blocks in configuration, with the constraint strings
suggested below.

* provider.aws: version = "~> 1.36"

Terraform has been successfully initialized!

You may now begin working with Terraform. Try running "terraform plan" to see
any changes that are required for your infrastructure. All Terraform commands
should now work.

If you ever set or change modules or backend configuration for Terraform,
rerun this command to reinitialize your working directory. If you forget, other
commands will detect it and remind you to do so if necessary.
[root@yogeshraheja firstproject]# []
```

The next step is to configure our infrastructure. This is where we start developing the ec2.ft file with Terraform resources. Resources are components of your infrastructure. They can be as complex as a complete virtual server that has multiple other services, or as simple as a DNS record. Each resource belongs to a provider and the type of the resource is suffixed with the provider name. The configuration of a resource, which is called a resource block, takes the following form:

```
resource "provider-name_resource-type" "resource-name" {
parameter_name = "parameter_value"
parameter_name = "parameter_value"
.
.
.
}
```

In our case, we have to create an EC2 instance. The aws_instance resource in Terraform is responsible for this job. To create an instance, we need to set at least two parameters: ami and instance_type. These two parameters are required, whereas the others are optional. In order to get a list and a description of all the aws_instance resource parameters, check out the following website: https://www.terraform.io/docs/providers/aws/r/instance.html.

In our case we will create an instance with the same details with which we created and tested the instance using the AWS Management Console and the AWS CLI utility. We have ami-cfe4b2b0 as AMI and t2.micro as our instance type. EffectiveDevOpsAWS is the key name that we created in the past and sg-01864b4c is our security group. We are also tagging the instance with the name helloworld for easy recognition. It's worth mentioning that like any other scripting or automation language, you can put *comments* in the Terraform template with the # sign. Our complete file should now look as follows:

```
# Provider Configuration for AWS
provider "aws" {
access_key = "<YOUR AWS ACCESS KEY>"
secret_key = "<YOUR AWS SECRET KEY>"
region = "us-east-1"
}

# Resource Configuration for AWS
resource "aws_instance" "myserver" {
ami = "ami-cfe4b2b0"
instance_type = "t2.micro"
key_name = "EffectiveDevOpsAWS"
vpc_security_group_ids = ["sg-01864b4c"]
tags {
```

```
Name = "helloworld"
  }
}
```

The created file should look like the file at the following website: `https://raw.` `githubusercontent.com/yogeshraheja/EffectiveDevOpsTerraform/master/` `firstproject/ec2.tf`.

Let's validate the Terraform template first to ensure that the template doesn't have any syntax errors. Terraform has a dedicated `terraform validate` utility, which checks the syntax of the Terraform template and provides us with the outputs if there are any syntax errors that need our attention:

```
$ terraform validate
```

As there are no outputs, this signifies that our Terraform template is free from syntax errors. It's time to perform a dry run to see what this template will execute. This is just a smoke test to find out which changes or implementations will be performed by the template we have created. This step in Terraform is known as **plan**:

```
[root@yogeshraheja firstproject]# terraform plan
Refreshing Terraform state in-memory prior to plan...
The refreshed state will be used to calculate this plan, but will not be
persisted to local or remote state storage.


------------------------------------------------------------------------

An execution plan has been generated and is shown below.
Resource actions are indicated with the following symbols:
  + create

Terraform will perform the following actions:

  + aws_instance.myserver
      id: <computed>
      ami: "ami-cfe4b2b0"
      arn: <computed>
      associate_public_ip_address: <computed>
      availability_zone: <computed>
      cpu_core_count: <computed>
      cpu_threads_per_core: <computed>
      ebs_block_device.#: <computed>
      ephemeral_block_device.#: <computed>
      get_password_data: "false"
      instance_state: <computed>
      instance_type: "t2.micro"
```

```
          ipv6_address_count: <computed>
          ipv6_addresses.#: <computed>
          key_name: "EffectiveDevOpsAWS"
          network_interface.#: <computed>
          network_interface_id: <computed>
          password_data: <computed>
          placement_group: <computed>
          primary_network_interface_id: <computed>
          private_dns: <computed>
          private_ip: <computed>
          public_dns: <computed>
          public_ip: <computed>
          root_block_device.#: <computed>
          security_groups.#: <computed>
          source_dest_check: "true"
          subnet_id: <computed>
          tags.%: "1"
          tags.Name: "helloworld"
          tenancy: <computed>
          volume_tags.%: <computed>
          vpc_security_group_ids.#: "1"
          vpc_security_group_ids.1524136243: "sg-01864b4c"


Plan: 1 to add, 0 to change, 0 to destroy.

-------------------------------------------------------------------------
```

Here, we didn't specify an -out parameter to save this plan, so Terraform can't guarantee that these actions exactly will be performed if terraform apply is subsequently run:

```
[root@yogeshraheja firstproject]#
```

Our plan stage indicates the same parameters that we want in the real execution while creating our instance. Again, don't get confused with the <computed> parameters, this just signifies that their value will be assigned when the resources are created

Let's now execute our plan for real and look at how a Terraform template can be used to create an AWS instance with the defined resource parameters. Terraform does this using the terraform apply utility and you can think of this stage as **apply**. Once you execute terraform apply, it will ask for your approval by default for confirmation. Type yes to start the resource creation.

In case you want to skip this interactive approval of the plan before applying it, use the --auto-approve option with the terraform apply command:

```
[root@yogeshraheja firstproject]# terraform apply

An execution plan has been generated and is shown below.
Resource actions are indicated with the following symbols:
  + create

Terraform will perform the following actions:

  + aws_instance.myserver
      id: <computed>
      ami: "ami-cfe4b2b0"
      arn: <computed>
      associate_public_ip_address: <computed>
      availability_zone: <computed>
      cpu_core_count: <computed>
      cpu_threads_per_core: <computed>
      ebs_block_device.#: <computed>
      ephemeral_block_device.#: <computed>
      get_password_data: "false"
      instance_state: <computed>
      instance_type: "t2.micro"
      ipv6_address_count: <computed>
      ipv6_addresses.#: <computed>
      key_name: "EffectiveDevOpsAWS"
      network_interface.#: <computed>
      network_interface_id: <computed>
      password_data: <computed>
      placement_group: <computed>
      primary_network_interface_id: <computed>
      private_dns: <computed>
      private_ip: <computed>
      public_dns: <computed>
      public_ip: <computed>
      root_block_device.#: <computed>
      security_groups.#: <computed>
      source_dest_check: "true"
      subnet_id: <computed>
      tags.%: "1"
      tags.Name: "helloworld"
      tenancy: <computed>
      volume_tags.%: <computed>
      vpc_security_group_ids.#: "1"
      vpc_security_group_ids.1524136243: "sg-01864b4c"
```

```
Plan: 1 to add, 0 to change, 0 to destroy.

Do you want to perform these actions?
  Terraform will perform the actions described above.
  Only 'yes' will be accepted to approve.

  Enter a value: yes

aws_instance.myserver: Creating...
  ami: "" => "ami-cfe4b2b0"
  arn: "" => "<computed>"
  associate_public_ip_address: "" => "<computed>"
  availability_zone: "" => "<computed>"
  cpu_core_count: "" => "<computed>"
  cpu_threads_per_core: "" => "<computed>"
  ebs_block_device.#: "" => "<computed>"
  ephemeral_block_device.#: "" => "<computed>"
  get_password_data: "" => "false"
  instance_state: "" => "<computed>"
  instance_type: "" => "t2.micro"
  ipv6_address_count: "" => "<computed>"
  ipv6_addresses.#: "" => "<computed>"
  key_name: "" => "EffectiveDevOpsAWS"
  network_interface.#: "" => "<computed>"
  network_interface_id: "" => "<computed>"
  password_data: "" => "<computed>"
  placement_group: "" => "<computed>"
  primary_network_interface_id: "" => "<computed>"
  private_dns: "" => "<computed>"
  private_ip: "" => "<computed>"
  public_dns: "" => "<computed>"
  public_ip: "" => "<computed>"
  root_block_device.#: "" => "<computed>"
  security_groups.#: "" => "<computed>"
  source_dest_check: "" => "true"
  subnet_id: "" => "<computed>"
  tags.%: "" => "1"
  tags.Name: "" => "helloworld"
  tenancy: "" => "<computed>"
  volume_tags.%: "" => "<computed>"
  vpc_security_group_ids.#: "" => "1"
  vpc_security_group_ids.1524136243: "" => "sg-01864b4c"
aws_instance.myserver: Still creating... (10s elapsed)
aws_instance.myserver: Still creating... (20s elapsed)
aws_instance.myserver: Creation complete after 22s (ID: i-dd8834ca)

Apply complete! Resources: 1 added, 0 changed, 0 destroyed.
[root@yogeshraheja firstproject]#
```

Let's confirm the newly created instance from our AWS console to ensure the `helloworld` instance has been created by the Terraform template:

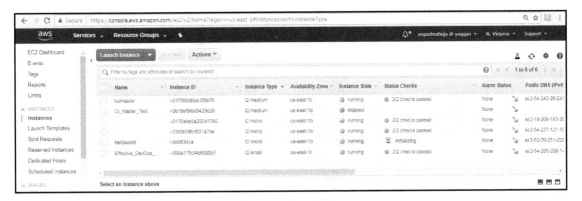

Terraform didn't simply create an instance and forget about it. In fact, Terraform actually saves everything it knows about the resources (in our case, the instance) to a special file, which is known as the **state file** in Terraform. In this file, Terraform stores the state of all the resources it has created. It is saved to the same directory where the Terraform template is present and with the `.tfstate` extension. The format of the state file is a simple JSON format:

```
[root@yogeshraheja firstproject]# cat terraform.tfstate
{
    "version": 3,
    "terraform_version": "0.11.8",
    "serial": 1,
    "lineage": "9158b0ed-754a-e01e-094e-6b0827347950",
    "modules": [
        {
            "path": [
                "root"
            ],
            "outputs": {},
            "resources": {
                "aws_instance.myserver": {
                    "type": "aws_instance",
                    "depends_on": [],
                    "primary": {
                        "id": "i-dd8834ca",
                        "attributes": {
                            "ami": "ami-cfe4b2b0",
                            "arn": "arn:aws:ec2:us-
east-1:094507990803:instance/i-dd8834ca",
                            "associate_public_ip_address": "true",
```

```
                                "availability_zone": "us-east-1b",
                                "cpu_core_count": "1",
                                "cpu_threads_per_core": "1",
                                "credit_specification.#": "1",
                                "credit_specification.0.cpu_credits":
"standard",

                                "disable_api_termination": "false",
                                "ebs_block_device.#": "0",
                                "ebs_optimized": "false",
                                "ephemeral_block_device.#": "0",
                                "get_password_data": "false",
                                "iam_instance_profile": "",
                                "id": "i-dd8834ca",
                                "instance_state": "running",
                                "instance_type": "t2.micro",
                                "ipv6_addresses.#": "0",
                                "key_name": "EffectiveDevOpsAWS",
                                "monitoring": "false",
                                "network_interface.#": "0",
                                "network_interface_id": "eni-b0683ee7",
                                "password_data": "",
                                "placement_group": "",
                                "primary_network_interface_id": "eni-b0683ee7",
                                "private_dns": "ip-172-31-74-203.ec2.internal",
                                "private_ip": "172.31.74.203",
                                "public_dns":
"ec2-52-70-251-228.compute-1.amazonaws.com",
                                "public_ip": "52.70.251.228",
                                "root_block_device.#": "1",
                                "root_block_device.0.delete_on_termination":
"true",

                                "root_block_device.0.iops": "100",
                                "root_block_device.0.volume_id":
"vol-024f64aa1bb805237",

                                "root_block_device.0.volume_size": "8",
                                "root_block_device.0.volume_type": "gp2",
                                "security_groups.#": "1",
                                "security_groups.2004290681": "HelloWorld",
                                "source_dest_check": "true",
                                "subnet_id": "subnet-658b6149",
                                "tags.%": "1",
                                "tags.Name": "helloworld",
                                "tenancy": "default",
                                "volume_tags.%": "0",
                                "vpc_security_group_ids.#": "1",
                                "vpc_security_group_ids.1524136243":
"sg-01864b4c"
                        },
```

```
                    "meta": {
                        "e2bfb730-ecaa-11e6-8f88-34363bc7c4c0": {
                            "create": 600000000000,
                            "delete": 1200000000000,
                            "update": 600000000000
                        },
                        "schema_version": "1"
                    },
                    "tainted": false
                },
                "deposed": [],
                "provider": "provider.aws"
            }
        },
        "depends_on": []
    }
  ]
}
[root@yogeshraheja firstproject]#
```

The special part about Terraform is that you can read this JSON output in a human-readable format using the `terraform show` command:

```
[root@yogeshraheja firstproject]# terraform show
aws_instance.myserver:
  id = i-dd8834ca
  ami = ami-cfe4b2b0
  arn = arn:aws:ec2:us-east-1:094507990803:instance/i-dd8834ca
  associate_public_ip_address = true
  availability_zone = us-east-1b
  cpu_core_count = 1
  cpu_threads_per_core = 1
  credit_specification.# = 1
  credit_specification.0.cpu_credits = standard
  disable_api_termination = false
  ebs_block_device.# = 0
  ebs_optimized = false
  ephemeral_block_device.# = 0
  get_password_data = false
  iam_instance_profile =
  instance_state = running
  instance_type = t2.micro
  ipv6_addresses.# = 0
  key_name = EffectiveDevOpsAWS
  monitoring = false
  network_interface.# = 0
  network_interface_id = eni-b0683ee7
  password_data =
```

```
          placement_group =
          primary_network_interface_id = eni-b0683ee7
          private_dns = ip-172-31-74-203.ec2.internal
          private_ip = 172.31.74.203
          public_dns = ec2-52-70-251-228.compute-1.amazonaws.com
          public_ip = 52.70.251.228
          root_block_device.# = 1
          root_block_device.0.delete_on_termination = true
          root_block_device.0.iops = 100
          root_block_device.0.volume_id = vol-024f64aa1bb805237
          root_block_device.0.volume_size = 8
          root_block_device.0.volume_type = gp2
          security_groups.# = 1
          security_groups.2004290681 = HelloWorld
          source_dest_check = true
          subnet_id = subnet-658b6149
          tags.% = 1
          tags.Name = helloworld
          tenancy = default
          volume_tags.% = 0
          vpc_security_group_ids.# = 1
          vpc_security_group_ids.1524136243 = sg-01864b4c

[root@yogeshraheja firstproject]#
```

Up to here, we have created a Terraform template, validated it to ensure there are no syntax errors, performed a smoke test in the form of `terraform plan`, and then finally applied our Terraform template using `terraform apply` to create resources.

The question remaining is *how can we delete or destroy all of the resources that are created by the Terraform template?* Do we need to find and delete resources one after another? The answer is No, this will also be taken care of by Terraform. By referring to the state file Terraform created during the **apply** phase, any resources that have been created by Terraform can be destroyed using the simple `terraform destroy` command from the `template` directory:

```
[root@yogeshraheja firstproject]# terraform destroy
aws_instance.myserver: Refreshing state... (ID: i-dd8834ca)

An execution plan has been generated and is shown below.
Resource actions are indicated with the following symbols:
  - destroy

Terraform will perform the following actions:

  - aws_instance.myserver
```

```
Plan: 0 to add, 0 to change, 1 to destroy.

Do you really want to destroy all resources?
   Terraform will destroy all your managed infrastructure, as shown above.
   There is no undo. Only 'yes' will be accepted to confirm.

   Enter a value: yes

aws_instance.myserver: Destroying... (ID: i-dd8834ca)
aws_instance.myserver: Still destroying... (ID: i-dd8834ca, 10s elapsed)
aws_instance.myserver: Still destroying... (ID: i-dd8834ca, 20s elapsed)
aws_instance.myserver: Still destroying... (ID: i-dd8834ca, 30s elapsed)
aws_instance.myserver: Still destroying... (ID: i-dd8834ca, 40s elapsed)
aws_instance.myserver: Still destroying... (ID: i-dd8834ca, 50s elapsed)
aws_instance.myserver: Destruction complete after 1m0s

Destroy complete! Resources: 1 destroyed.
[root@yogeshraheja firstproject]#
```

Check your AWS console to ensure that the instance is in a terminated state.

> Check the `terraform show` command now. It should be empty as none of your resources will be available.

A second Terraform template for deploying a Hello World application

Go into the **EffectiveDevOpsTerraform** repository and create a directory called second project:

```
$ mkdir secondproject
$ cd secondproject
```

Now that we have created our EC2 instance with the Terraform template in the previous section, we are ready to extend the provisioning of our Hello World web application. We are going to use **Terraform Provisioner** to recreate the Hello World stack that we previously made using the UserDatablock field of CloudFormation in Chapter 2, *Deploying Your First Web Application* and using Ansible roles in Chapter 3, *Treating Your Infrastructure as Code*. If you recall, the UserData field looked roughly like this:

```
yum install --enablerepo=epel -y nodejs
wget
https://raw.githubusercontent.com/yogeshraheja/Effective-DevOps-with-AWS/ma
ster/Chapter02/helloworld.js -O /home/ec2-user/helloworld.js
wget
https://raw.githubusercontent.com/yogeshraheja/Effective-DevOps-with-AWS/ma
ster/Chapter02/helloworld.conf -O /etc/init/helloworld.conf
start helloworld
```

You will observe that there are three different types of operations for the deployment of our Hello World web application. First, we prepare the system to run our application. To do this, in our example, we are simply installing the Node.js package. Next, we copy the different resources that are needed to run the application. In our case, these resources include the JavaScript code and the upstart configuration. Finally, we start the service.

In order to deploy our Hello World web application, we need to introduce **Terraform Provisioner**. Provisioners in Terraform are configuration blocks available for several resources that allow you to perform actions after the resource has been created. It is mostly used for EC2 instances. Provisioners are primarily used as **post build steps** to install lightweight applications or configuration management agents such as **Puppet agents** or **chef-clients**. They can even be used to run configuration management tools such as **playbooks**, **Puppet modules**, **Chef cookbooks,** or **Salt formulas**. In the next section, we'll look at a few examples of how to use Terraform with Ansible.

Let's create the helloworldec2.tf Terraform template to create the instance and then introduce the provisioner block with remote-exec to establish a connection with the newly created instance and download and deploy Hello World application on top of it. Our completed Terraform template should look like this:

```
# Provider Configuration for AWS
provider "aws" {
  access_key = "<YOUR AWS ACCESS KEY>"
  secret_key = "<YOUR AWS SECRET KEY>"
  region = "us-east-1"
}

# Resource Configuration for AWS
resource "aws_instance" "myserver" {
```

```
  ami = "ami-cfe4b2b0"
  instance_type = "t2.micro"
  key_name = "EffectiveDevOpsAWS"
  vpc_security_group_ids = ["sg-01864b4c"]

  tags {
    Name = "helloworld"
  }

# Helloworld Appication code
  provisioner "remote-exec" {
    connection {
      user = "ec2-user"
      private_key = "${file("/root/.ssh/EffectiveDevOpsAWS.pem")}"
    }
    inline = [
      "sudo yum install --enablerepo=epel -y nodejs",
      "sudo wget
https://raw.githubusercontent.com/yogeshraheja/Effective-DevOps-with-AWS/ma
ster/Chapter02/helloworld.js -O /home/ec2-user/helloworld.js",
      "sudo wget
https://raw.githubusercontent.com/yogeshraheja/Effective-DevOps-with-AWS/ma
ster/Chapter02/helloworld.conf -O /etc/init/helloworld.conf",
      "sudo start helloworld",
    ]
  }
}
```

The created file should look like the file at: https://raw.githubusercontent.com/
yogeshraheja/EffectiveDevOpsTerraform/master/secondproject/helloworldec2.tf.

As we are creating the Terraform template inside a new directory, secondproject, we
need to install the plugin or reinitialize the plugins that are related to AWS for Terraform.
The configured file with the provider section will perform this task for us:

```
$ terraform init
```

Now, it's time to validate the Terraform template file to ensure that it doesn't have any
syntax errors. Upon successful verification, run the plan command followed by the
complete execution of the template using the terraform apply command:

```
$ terraform validate
$ terraform plan
$ terraform apply
```

We will get the following output:

Our Terraform template has been executed successfully. We have provisioned our EC2 instance and deployed our Hello World web application. Let's find the public IP of the instance by executing the `terraform show` command followed by the `curl` command to ensure the application has deployed correctly:

```
$ terraform show | grep -i public_ip
$ curl <PUBLIC_IP>:3000
```

The output of running the preceding commands is as follows:

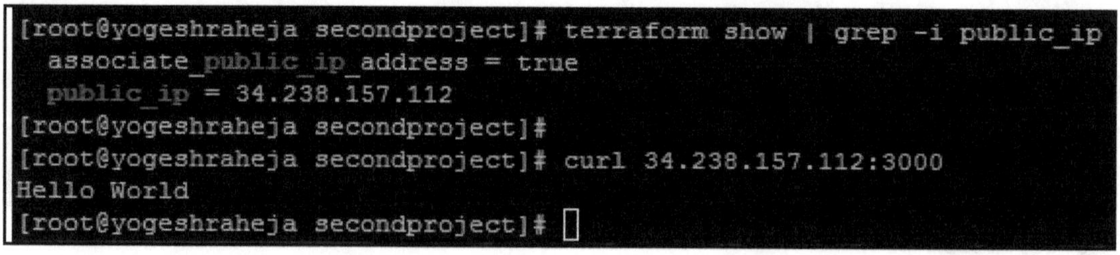

Let's verify the application outputs from our browser as well, as shown in the following screenshot:

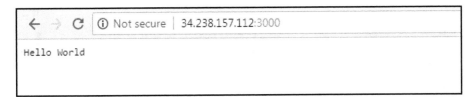

We have now successfully deployed our Hello World web application using the power of Terraform. Once you've tested it, make sure to remove all of the created resources before you proceed to the next section. Execute the `terraform destroy` command, which will take care of removing all of the created resources by referring to the Terraform state file.

Run the following command:

```
$ terraform destroy
```

Integrating AWS, Terraform, and Ansible

In the previous sections, we looked at how to provision a vanilla instance using Terraform. We then learnt how to provision a vanilla EC2 instance and execute **post builds** using the Terraform `remote-exec` provisioner. Now, we'll look at how Terraform can be integrated with Ansible to perform configuration management tasks. We will consider two different scenarios. In scenario one, we will provision an EC2 instance and run Ansible using **push** mode, which is the primary way that we can use Ansible to perform automation. In scenario two, we will provision an EC2 instance and run Ansible in **pull** mode using the `ansible pull` approach.

Terraform with Ansible using a push-based approach

Go into the `EffectiveDevOpsTerraform` repository and create a directory called `thirdproject`:

```
$ mkdir thirdproject
$ cd thirdproject
```

In this example, we will use the recommended practices to create Terraform templates. We will remove our AWS `access_key` and our AWS `secret_key` from our Terraform template first. We have AWS CLI installed on our system, which means that we have already configured this system to talk to our AWS account. If we don't already have AWS CLI installed, we will use the `aws configure` to install it. This will create a `credentials` file inside the `/root/.aws` directory, which will contain our AWS access and secret keys. We will take the advantage of this file for our Terraform template and use the same credentials to build resources on our AWS account:

```
[root@yogeshraheja thirdproject]# cat /root/.aws/credentials
[default]
aws_access_key_id = <YOUR AWS SECRET KEY>
aws_secret_access_key = <YOUR AWS SECRET KEY>
[root@yogeshraheja thirdproject]#
```

It's now time to start writing our `helloworldansible.tf` Terraform template. In this case, we will provision an EC2 instance and wait for the SSH services to appear by verifying the connection using the `remote-exec` provisioner. We will then use the `local-exec` provisioner to create the inventory with the new IP and run the Ansible playbooks on it using the primary push model by executing `ansible-playbook` locally from the system.

 Inside provisioners (and only inside provisioners), we can use a special keyword, **self**, to access the attributes of a resource being provisioned.

We are also using another block in our code, which is called the `output` block. Outputs allow you to return data from the Terraform template after it was applied, using the Terraform `output` command:

```
# Provider Configuration for AWS
provider "aws" {
  region = "us-east-1"
}

# Resource Configuration for AWS
resource "aws_instance" "myserver" {
  ami = "ami-cfe4b2b0"
  instance_type = "t2.micro"
  key_name = "EffectiveDevOpsAWS"
  vpc_security_group_ids = ["sg-01864b4c"]

  tags {
    Name = "helloworld"
  }
```

```
# Provisioner for applying Ansible playbook
  provisioner "remote-exec" {
    connection {
      user = "ec2-user"
      private_key = "${file("/root/.ssh/EffectiveDevOpsAWS.pem")}"
    }
  }
  provisioner "local-exec" {
    command = "sudo echo '${self.public_ip}' > ./myinventory",
  }

  provisioner "local-exec" {
    command = "sudo ansible-playbook -i myinventory --private-
key=/root/.ssh/EffectiveDevOpsAWS.pem helloworld.yml",
  }
}

# IP address of newly created EC2 instance
output "myserver" {
 value = "${aws_instance.myserver.public_ip}"
}
```

The created file should look like the file at: https://raw.githubusercontent.com/ yogeshraheja/EffectiveDevOpsTerraform/master/thirdproject/helloworldansible.tf.

We will call the helloworld role in our helloworld.yml Ansible playbook to deploy the Hello World web application:

```
---
- hosts: all
  become: yes
  roles:
    - helloworld
```

The Ansible configuration file ansible.cfg should look like as follows. It should be pointing to the myinventory file that is present in our thirdproject directory structure:

```
[defaults]
inventory = $PWD/myinventory
roles_path = ./roles
remote_user = ec2-user
become = True
become_method = sudo
become_user = root
nocows = 1
host_key_checking = False
```

The complete project should look like the file at: `https://github.com/yogeshraheja/` `EffectiveDevOpsTerraform/tree/master/thirdproject`.

As we have created a new directory, `thirdproject`, we again need to install the plugin or reinitialize the plugins that are related to AWS for Terraform. The configured file with the `provider` section will perform this task for us:

```
$ terraform init
```

It's now time to validate the Terraform template file to ensure that it doesn't have any syntax errors. Upon successful verification, execute the plan followed by the real run using `terraform apply`:

```
$ terraform validate
$ terraform plan
$ terraform apply
```

The outputs are clearly showing the logs for Ansible playbook and returning the `output` block with the public IP. Let's use this public IP to verify the application deployment:

```
$ curl 54.85.107.87:3000
```

The output of running the preceding command is as follows:

```
[root@yogeshraheja thirdproject]# curl 54.85.107.87:3000
Hello World
[root@yogeshraheja thirdproject]#
```

Let's verify the application outputs from the browser, as shown in the following screenshot:

Upon successful deployment, execute `terraform destroy` to clean up the created resources:

```
$ terraform destroy
```

Terraform with Ansible using the pull-based approach

Go into the `EffectiveDevOpsTerraform` repository and create a directory called `fourthproject`:

```
$ mkdir fourthproject
$ cd fourthproject
```

Again, we will follow the best practices for Terraform templates here and use the `credentials` file located in the `/root/.aws` directory, which contains our AWS access and secret keys. In this case, we will use Ansible in the inverted form: the *Ansible pull-based approach*. To use Ansible in this inverted approach, we have to make sure to install Ansible on the provisioned EC2 instance and run `ansible-pull` by referring to the Ansible code that is present at the source code repository.

In our case we will be using the same Ansible code that we created in Chapter 3, *Treating Your Infrastructure as Code*, which is present at https://github.com/yogeshraheja/ ansible. In our helloworldansiblepull.tf Terraform template, we will be using a remote-exec Terraform provisioner to establish a connection with the newly created instance. We will use the inline attribute to execute multiple commands remotely on the newly created EC2 installation. Our Terraform template should look as follows:

```
# Provider Configuration for AWS
provider "aws" {
  region = "us-east-1"
}

# Resource Configuration for AWS
resource "aws_instance" "myserver" {
  ami = "ami-cfe4b2b0"
  instance_type = "t2.micro"
  key_name = "EffectiveDevOpsAWS"
  vpc_security_group_ids = ["sg-01864b4c"]

  tags {
    Name = "helloworld"
  }

# Provisioner for applying Ansible playbook in Pull mode
  provisioner "remote-exec" {
    connection {
      user = "ec2-user"
      private_key = "${file("/root/.ssh/EffectiveDevOpsAWS.pem")}"
    }
    inline = [
      "sudo yum install --enablerepo=epel -y ansible git",
      "sudo ansible-pull -U https://github.com/yogeshraheja/ansible
helloworld.yml -i localhost",
    ]
  }
}

# IP address of newly created EC2 instance
output "myserver" {
 value = "${aws_instance.myserver.public_ip}"
}
```

The created file should look like the file at: https://raw.githubusercontent.com/
yogeshraheja/EffectiveDevOpsTerraform/master/fourthproject/
helloworldansiblepull.tf.

As we have again created a new directory, `fourthproject`, we need to install the plugin
or reinitialize the plugins related to AWS for Terraform. The configured file with
the `provider` section will perform this task for us.

```
$ terraform init
```

It's now time to validate the Terraform template file to ensure that it doesn't have any
syntax errors. Upon successful verification, execute the plan followed by the real run using
`terraform apply`:

```
$ terraform validate
$ terraform plan
$ terraform apply
```

```
aws_instance.myserver (remote-exec): PLAY [localhost] ************************************************************

aws_instance.myserver (remote-exec): TASK [Gathering Facts] *****************************************************
aws_instance.myserver (remote-exec): ok: [localhost]

aws_instance.myserver (remote-exec): TASK [nodejs : Installing node and npm] ************************************
aws_instance.myserver: Still creating... (1m10s elapsed)
aws_instance.myserver: Still creating... (1m20s elapsed)
aws_instance.myserver (remote-exec): changed: [localhost] => (item=[u'nodejs', u'npm'])

aws_instance.myserver (remote-exec): TASK [helloworld : Copying the application file] **************************
aws_instance.myserver (remote-exec): changed: [localhost]

aws_instance.myserver (remote-exec): TASK [helloworld : Copying the upstart file] ******************************
aws_instance.myserver (remote-exec): changed: [localhost]

aws_instance.myserver (remote-exec): TASK [helloworld : Starting the HelloWorld node service] ******************
aws_instance.myserver (remote-exec): changed: [localhost]

aws_instance.myserver (remote-exec): RUNNING HANDLER [helloworld : restart helloworld] *************************
aws_instance.myserver (remote-exec): changed: [localhost]

aws_instance.myserver (remote-exec): PLAY RECAP *****************************************************************
aws_instance.myserver (remote-exec): localhost                  : ok=6    changed=5    unreachable=0    failed=0

aws_instance.myserver: Creation complete after 1m28s (ID: i-5d84384a)

Apply complete! Resources: 1 added, 0 changed, 0 destroyed.

Outputs:

myserver = 18.212.64.84
[root@yogeshraheja fourthproject]#
```

As expected, the Ansible code is running locally on the newly created EC2 instance. The `output` block configured in the Terraform template has also returned the expected value of the public IP. Let's verify the outputs using the `curl` command:

```
$ curl 18.212.64.84:3000/
```

The output of running the preceding command is as follows:

```
[root@yogeshraheja fourthproject]# curl 18.212.64.84:3000
Hello World
[root@yogeshraheja fourthproject]#
```

Finally, verify the outputs from the browser, as shown in the following screenshot:

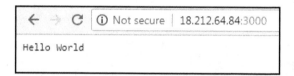

Great—the application is deployed and verified. Once you are done, don't forget to destroy the resource using the following command, to avoid unwanted AWS bills:

```
$ terraform destroy
```

Summary

In this chapter, we learned how to efficiently manage infrastructure using Terraform templates. First, we learned about how Terraform can be used to provision an EC2 instance in just a few lines. We then looked at how to create Terraform templates using Terraform provisioners to deploy lightweight applications. We then extended the Terraform templates with Ansible, which allowed us to orchestrate the different steps to deploy our web application. Finally, we looked at how Terraform can be integrated with Ansible in a pull-based approach, which usually makes more sense when managing sizable infrastructures, as we observed in Chapter 3, *Treating Your Infrastructure as Code*.

We now have a good production environment ready to host any application. We have seen how to architect it using CloudFormation, Ansible, and Terraform. In Chapter 5, *Adding Continuous Integration and Continuous Deployment*, we will continue to use CloudFormation and Ansible, but in the context of software delivery, as we will learn how to put in place continuous integration testing and continuous deployment.

Questions

1. What is Terraform and how it is different from other configuration management tools?
2. How do you install Terraform on a Linux-based operating system?
3. How do you provision your first AWS instance using a Terraform template?
4. How do you write a Terraform template to integrate Ansible with a pull-based approach?

Further reading

Read the following articles for more information:

- **Terraform reference** at `https://terraform.io`
- **Terraform GitHub reference** at `https://github.com/hashicorp/terraform`

5
Adding Continuous Integration and Continuous Deployment

In the previous chapters, we focused on improving the creation and management of infrastructure. The DevOps culture doesn't stop there, however. As you might recall from Chapter 1, *The Cloud and the DevOps Revolution*, DevOps culture also includes having a very efficient process to test and deploy code. At the 2009 Velocity conference, John Allspaw and Paul Hammond made a very inspirational speech about how Flickr was carrying out over 10 deployments a day (http://bit.ly/292AS1W). This presentation is often mentioned as a pivotal moment that contributed to the creation of the DevOps movement. In their presentation, John and Paul talk about the conflicts between development and operations teams but also outline a number of best practices that allow Flickr to deploy new code to production multiple times a day.

With innovations such as virtualization, the public and private cloud, and automation, creating new start ups has never been so easy. Because of that, the biggest problem many companies are now facing is being able to stand apart from their competitors. Having the ability to iterate faster than most competitors can be a detrimental to a company's success. An effective DevOps organization uses a number of tools and strategies to increase the velocity at which engineering organizations release new code to production. This is what we will focus on in this chapter.

We will first look at creating a **Continuous Integration** (**CI**) pipeline. A CI pipeline will allow us to test proposed code changes automatically and continuously. This will free up the time of developers and QAs who no longer have to carry out as much manual testing. It also makes the integration of code changes much easier. To implement our pipeline, we will use GitHub and one of the most widely used integration tools—**Jenkins**.

We will then look at creating a **Continuous Deployment** (**CD**) pipeline. Once the code has gone through the CI pipeline, we will use this continuous deployment pipeline to automatically deploy the new code. We will rely on two AWS services to implement this pipeline—**AWS CodeDeploy** and **AWS CodePipeline**. CodeDeploy lets us define how the new code needs to be deployed on our EC2 instances while CodePipeline lets us orchestrate the full life cycle of our application.

In order to deploy our code to production, we will add an extra step that will allow the operator to deploy the latest build that is present in the staging to the production process at the press of a button. This ability to deploy code to production on-demand is called CD. Its main advantage is that it provides the ability for the deployment operator to validate a build in a staging environment before it gets deployed to production. At the end of the chapter, we will see a couple of techniques and strategies that effective engineering organizations use to convert their continuous delivery pipelines into continuous deployment pipelines so that the entire process of deploying code up to production can happen without any human intervention. We will cover the following topics:

- Building a continuous integration pipeline
- Building a continuous deployment pipeline

Technical requirements

The technical requirements for this chapter as follows:

- GitHub
- Jenkins
- Ansible
- AWS CodeDeploy
- AWS CodePipeline

The links are as follows:

- **Jenkins package repository**: https://pkg.jenkins.io/
- **Jenkins setup playbook**: https://raw.githubusercontent.com/yogeshraheja/ansible/master/roles/jenkins/tasks/main.yml
- **Jenkinsfile**: https://raw.githubusercontent.com/yogeshraheja/helloworld/master/Jenkinsfile
- **Code deploy library**: https://raw.githubusercontent.com/yogeshraheja/Effective-DevOps-with-AWS/master/Chapter05/ansible/library/aws_codedeploy

Building a CI pipeline

Initially, working in a CI environment meant that developers had to commit their code in a common branch as frequently as possible, as opposed to working off a separate branch or not committing changes for weeks. This allowed for improved visibility of the ongoing work and encouraged communication to avoid integration problems, a situation that is commonly known as **Integration Hell**. As the toolset related to source control and build and release management matured, so did the vision of how code integration should look in an ideal world.

Nowadays, most effective engineering organizations will continue down the path of integrating early and often. They often use, however, a more modern development process, where developers are required to edit the code and, at the same time, add or edit the different relevant tests to validate the change. This drastically increases overall productivity; it is now easier to find new bugs as the amount of code that changes between merges is fairly small.

To adopt such a workflow, using a source control tool such as Git for example, you can proceed as follows:

1. When as a developer, you want to make changes, start by creating a new Git branch that branches off the HEAD of the master branch.
2. Edit the code and, at the same time, add or edit the different relevant tests to validate the change.
3. Test the code locally.
4. When the code is ready, rebase the branch to integrate new eventual changes from other developers. If needed, resolve conflicts and test the code again.
5. If everything went well, the next step consists of creating a `pull request`. In this process, you tell other developers that your code is ready to be reviewed.
6. Once the pull request is created, an automated testing system such as the one we will build in this chapter will pick up the change and run the entire test suite to make sure nothing fails.
7. In addition, other interested parties will review the code and the different tests that were added to the branch. If they are satisfied with the proposed change, they will approve it, giving the developers the green light to merge their changes.
8. In the last step, the developers merge their pull requests, which will translate into merging their new code and testing the master branch. Other developers will now integrate this change when they rebase or create new branches.

In the following section, we will create a CI server using Jenkins running on top of an EC2 instance and GitHub.

As projects get bigger, the number of tests, the time it takes to run them. While certain advanced build systems such as Bazel (`https://bazel.build/`) have the ability to run only those tests relevant to a particular change, it is usually easier to start simply and create a CI system that runs all the tests available every time a new pull request is proposed. Having an external test infrastructure with the elasticity of AWS becomes a huge time saver for the developers who don't want to wait minutes or even hours for all the tests to be executed. In this book, we will focus on web application development. You may face a more challenging environment in which you need to build software for specific hardware and operating system. Having a dedicated CI system will allow you to run your tests on the hardware and software you are ultimately targeting.

Creating a Jenkins server using Ansible and CloudFormation

As mentioned before, we are going to use Jenkins as our central system to run our CI pipeline. With over 10 years of development, Jenkins has been the leading open-source solution to practice continuous integration for a long time. Famous for its rich plugin ecosystem, Jenkins has gone through a major new release (Jenkins 2.x), which has put the spotlight on a number of very DevOps-centric features, including the ability to create native delivery pipelines that can be checked in and version-controlled. It also provides better integration with source control systems such as GitHub, which we are using in this book.

We are going to continue using **Ansible** and **CloudFormation** in the same way as we did in Chapter 3, *Treating Your Infrastructure as Code*, to manage our Jenkins server.

Creating the Ansible playbook for Jenkins

Start by navigating to our `ansible` roles directory:

```
$ cd ansible/roles
```

This directory should contain the `helloworld` and `nodejs` directories, with the configurations that we created previously in `Chapter 3`, *Treating Your Infrastructure as Code*. We are now going to create our Jenkins role with the `ansible-galaxy` command:

```
$ ansible-galaxy init jenkins
```

We are now going to edit the task definition for this new role by editing the file: `jenkins/tasks/main.yml`. Open up the file with your favorite text editor.

The goal of our task is to install and start Jenkins. In order to do this, since we are on a Linux-based operating system (AWS Amazon Linux, in our case), we are going to install an RPM package through `yum`. Jenkins maintains a `yum` repository, so the first step will consist of importing this to our `yum` repository configuration, basically as an entry in `/etc/yum.repos.d`:

The following is the initial comment of the tasks file, add the following:

```
- name: Add Jenkins repository
  shell: wget -O /etc/yum.repos.d/jenkins.repo
https://pkg.jenkins.io/redhat/jenkins.repo
```

The next step will consist of importing the GPG key of that repository. Ansible has a module to manage these kinds of keys:

```
- name: Import Jenkins GPG key
  rpm_key:
    state: present
    key: https://pkg.jenkins.io/redhat/jenkins.io.key
```

We have now reached the point where we can use `yum` to install Jenkins. We will do that with the following call:

```
- name: Install Jenkins
  yum:
    name: jenkins-2.99
    enablerepo: jenkins
    state: present
```

Since the `jenkins` repository is disabled by default, we are enabling it through the `enablerepo` flag for the execution of this `yum` command.

At this point, Jenkins will be installed. To conform with best practice guidelines, we will specify which version of Jenkins we want to install (in our case the version is 2.99). We also want to start the service and have it enabled at the `chkconfig` level so that if the EC2 instance where Jenkins is installed restarts, Jenkins will start automatically. We can do that using the service module. Add the following after the previous call:

```
- name: Start Jenkins
  service:
    name: jenkins
    enabled: yes
    state: started
```

For a simple Jenkins role, that's all we need.

We should now have a `main.yml` file that looks as follows: `https://raw.githubusercontent.com/yogeshraheja/ansible/master/roles/jenkins/tasks/main.yml`.

AWS Amazon Linux comes with Java 7 but Jenkins has pre-requisites to install Java 8 for Jenkins version 2.54 and above. So you will see two extra tasks in the preceding link, which will uninstall Java 7 and install Java 8:

```
- name: Removing old version of JAVA from Amazon Linux
  yum:
    name: java-1.7.0-openjdk
    state: absent

- name: Install specific supported version of JAVA
  yum:
    name: java-1.8.0-openjdk
    state: present
```

> As you gain more experience with Jenkins and Ansible, explore the web or the Ansible galaxy, you will find more advanced roles allowing you to configure Jenkins in more detail, generate jobs, and select the plugins to install. It is an important step to go through that this book won't cover, but ideally, you want your entire system to be described by code. In addition, in this chapter, we are using Jenkins over HTTP. It is strongly encouraged to use it over an encrypted protocol such as HTTPS or, as we will see in Chapter 8, *Hardening the Security of Your AWS Environment*, in a private subnet with a VPN connection.

We have now built a role that will allow us to install Jenkins. We want to create a new EC2 instance and install Jenkins on it with the end goal of testing our Node.js code on the instance. In order to be able to do that, the Jenkins host will need to also have the node and `npm` installed.

We have two options. We can either add our `nodejs` role as a dependency of the Jenkins role, as we did for the `helloworld` role, or we can list the `nodejs` role in the list of roles for our playbook. Since ultimately Jenkins doesn't really require a node to run, we will opt for the second approach. In the root directory of our `ansible` repository, create the `playbook` file. The filename is `jenkins.yml` and it should look as follows:

```
---
- hosts: "{{ target | default('localhost') }}"
  become: yes
  roles:
    - jenkins
    - nodejs
```

Our role is now complete, so we can commit our new role and push it to GitHub. Following the best practices described previously, we will start by creating a new branch:

```
$ git checkout -b jenkins
```

Add our files with the following command:

```
$ git add jenkins.yml roles/jenkins
```

Commit and finally push the changes:

```
$ git commit -m "Adding a Jenkins playbook and role"
$ git push origin jenkins
```

From there, submit a pull request inside GitHub and merge the branch back to the master:

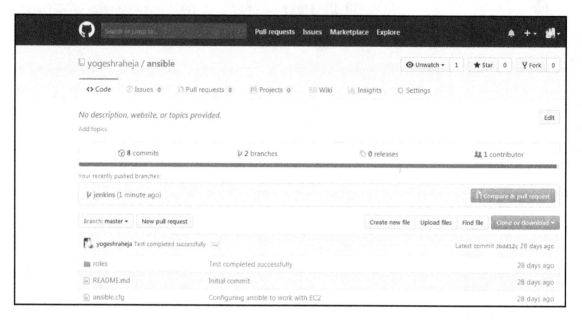

Once done, get back to the master branch with the following command:

```
$ git checkout master
$ git branch
    jenkins
  * master
$ git pull
```

In a real-life situation, you likely also want to periodically run the following:

```
$ git pull
```

This will retrieve the changes made by other developers.

We can now create our CloudFormation template in order to call the role.

Creating the CloudFormation template

In order to keep our code fairly similar to the code we looked at in Chapter 3, *Treating Your Infrastructure as Code,* we are going to start off with the helloworld Trosphere code that we created in that chapter. First, we are going to duplicate the Python script. Go to your EffectiveDevOpsTemplates directory, where you have your Troposphere templates, and then clone the ansiblebase-cf-template.py file as follows:

```
$ cp ansiblebase-cf-template.py jenkins-cf-template.py
```

The Jenkins host will need to interact with AWS. To allow this, we will create an instance profile, which we will describe in more detail later, taking advantage of another library that is developed by the same authors as Troposphere. We will install it as follows:

```
$ pip install awacs
```

We are now going to edit the jenkins-cf-template.py file. The first two changes we will make are to the name and port of the application. Jenkins runs by default on TCP/8080:

```
ApplicationName = "jenkins"
ApplicationPort = "8080"
```

We will also set a number of constants around the GitHub information. Replace the value of your GithubAccount with your GitHub username or organization name:

```
GithubAccount = "yogeshraheja"
```

We also want to add an instance IAM profile to better control how our EC2 instance can interact with AWS services such as EC2. We previously used the IAM service in Chapter 2, *Deploying Your First Web Application,* when we created our user. You may recall that in addition to creating the user, we also assigned it the administrator policy, which gives the user full access to all AWS services. On top of that, we generated an access key and a secret access key, which we are currently using to authenticate ourselves as that administrator user and interact with services such as CloudFormation and EC2.

When you are using EC2 instances, the **instance profile** feature provided lets you specify an IAM role to your instance. In other words, we can assign IAM permissions directly to EC2 instances without having to use access keys and secret access keys.

Having an instance profile will be very useful later on in this chapter, when we work on the CI pipeline and integrate our Jenkins instance with the AWS managed services. To do this, we will first import some extra libraries. The following is from Troposphere `import()` section, add the following:

```
from troposphere.iam import (
    InstanceProfile,
    PolicyType as IAMPolicy,
    Role,
)

from awacs.aws import (
    Action,
    Allow,
    Policy,
    Principal,
    Statement,
)

from awacs.sts import AssumeRole
```

Then, in between the instantiation of the variables `ud` and the creation of the instance, we are going to create and add our role resource to the template as follows:

```
t.add_resource(Role(
    "Role",
    AssumeRolePolicyDocument=Policy(
        Statement=[
            Statement(
                Effect=Allow,
                Action=[AssumeRole],
                Principal=Principal("Service", ["ec2.amazonaws.com"])
            )
        ]
    )
))
```

As we did previously for the role, we can now create our instance profile and reference the role. The following code is the creation of the role:

```
t.add_resource(InstanceProfile(
    "InstanceProfile",
    Path="/",
    Roles=[Ref("Role")]
))
```

Finally, we can reference our new instance profile by updating the declaration of our instance. We will add a period after `UserData=ud` and on the line after initializing the `IamInstanceProfile` as follows:

```
t.add_resource(ec2.Instance(
    "instance",
    ImageId="ami-cfe4b2b0",
    InstanceType="t2.micro",
    SecurityGroups=[Ref("SecurityGroup")],
    KeyName=Ref("KeyPair"),
    UserData=ud,
    IamInstanceProfile=Ref("InstanceProfile"),
)
```

The file should now look like this https://github.com/yogeshraheja/ EffectiveDevOpsTemplates/blob/master/jenkins-cf-template.py. You can save the changes, commit the new script to GitHub, and generate the CloudFormation template:

```
$ git add jenkins-cf-template.py
$ git commit -m "Adding troposphere script to generate a Jenkins instance"
$ git push
$ python jenkins-cf-template.py > jenkins-cf.template
```

Launching the stack and configuring Jenkins

In order to create our EC2 instance with Jenkins running on it, we will proceed as we did in Chapter 3, *Treating Your Infrastructure as Code*, using either the web interface or the command-line interface as follows:

```
$ aws cloudformation create-stack \
        --capabilities CAPABILITY_IAM \
        --stack-name jenkins \
        --template-body file://jenkins-cf.template \
        --parameters
        ParameterKey=KeyPair,ParameterValue=EffectiveDevOpsAWS
```

As we did before, we can then wait until the execution is complete:

```
$ aws cloudformation wait stack-create-complete \
        --stack-name jenkins
```

After that, we can extract the host's public IP:

```
$ aws cloudformation describe-stacks \
    --stack-name jenkins \
    --query 'Stacks[0].Outputs[0]'
  {
      "Description": "Public IP of our instance.",
      "OutputKey": "InstancePublicIp",
      "OutputValue": "18.208.183.35"
  }
```

Because we kept the **Ansible Jenkins** role fairly simple, we need to complete its configuration in order to complete the installation of Jenkins. Follow these steps:

1. Open port `8080` of the instance public IP in your browser (that is, in my case, `http://18.208.183.35:8080`). Wait for a while to get Jenkins configurations to get configured before you get the screen):

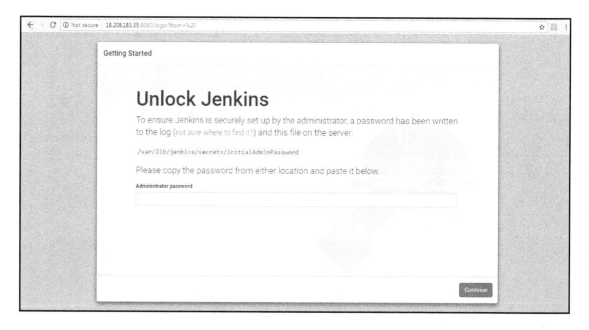

2. Using the following `ssh` command (adapt the IP address) and its ability to run commands remotely, we can extract the admin password, and provide it to that first configuration screen with the following command:

```
$ ssh -i ~/.ssh/EffectiveDevOpsAWS.pem ec2-user@18.208.183.35 \
sudo cat /var/lib/jenkins/secrets/initialAdminPassword
```

3. On the next screen, choose to install the suggested plugins.
4. Create your first admin user on the next screen and click on the **Save and Finish** button.
5. Finally, click on the **Start using Jenkins** button.

Our Jenkins instance is now ready to be used.

Preparing our CI environment

We are going to use our Jenkins instance in conjunction with GitHub to recreate our `helloworld` application using a proper CI pipeline. To do this, we are going to go through a number of preliminary steps, starting with the creation of a new GitHub organization that has a new repository named `helloworld`.

Creating a new GitHub organization and repository

We are now going to create a new organization having a new repository dedicated to hosting our `helloworld` node application. We will create the organization by going through the following steps and then will create a new repository inside the organization using the same steps as in Chapter 3, *Treating Your Infrastructure as Code*:

1. Open `https://github.com/organizations/new` in your browser.
2. Set the organization name, which will be a separate GitHub account inside your main GitHub account. I am creating mine with the name `yogeshrahejahelloworld`.
3. Provide your email ID and select the free plan.

4. Click on the **Create organization** button and select the default settings for the next two steps:

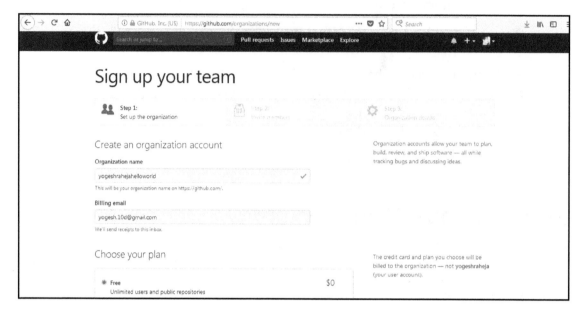

5. Create a new repository for the newly created organization:

6. Call your repository `helloworld`.
7. Check the **Initialize this repository with a README** checkbox.
8. Click on the **Create Repository** button:

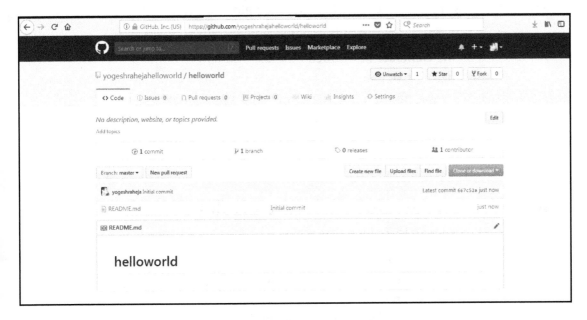

This will create the repository, a master branch, and a `README.md` file.

A proper CI pipeline works silently in the background. In order to achieve this, when the code is hosted on GitHub, Jenkins needs to get notifications from GitHub to indicate that the code has changed so that it can trigger a build automatically. This is something we can easily implement thanks to a plugin called `github-organization-plugin`. This plugin is one of those that were installed when we chose to install the suggested plugins in Jenkins. In order to use it, we first need to create a personal access token in GitHub.

Creating a GitHub personal access token

Creating a personal access token will give the plugins the ability to access the code pushed to GitHub and create the necessary hooks to get notifications when new commits and pull requests occur. In order to create the token, use the following steps:

1. Open `https://github.com/settings/tokens` in your browser.
2. Click on the **Generate new token** button.
3. Give it a descriptive name, such as `Effective DevOps with AWS Jenkins`.
4. Select the **repo, admin:repo_hook,** and **admin:org_hook** scopes.
5. Click on the **Generate token** button.
6. This brings you back to the main token page. Save the token that is generated. We will need it later.

Adding the access token to the credentials in Jenkins

We can now add the token to Jenkins as follows:

1. Open Jenkins, in my case `http://18.208.183.35:8080`.
2. Click on **Credentials** in the menu on the left, then click on **System** just after it it, and then **Global credentials**.
3. On the next screen, click on **Add credentials**.
4. The credentials we are going to create are of the type **Username with password**.
5. The scope should be global.
6. Use your GitHub organization as a username.
7. Use the token generated in the previous section as your password.
8. The ID can be something like `GitHub` as shown in the following screenshot:

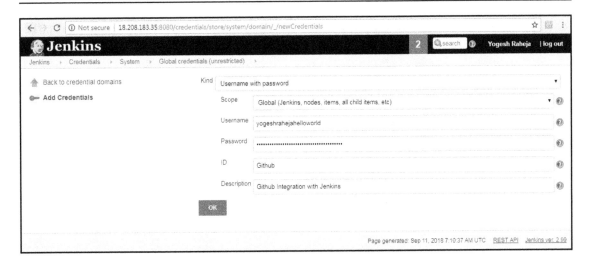

9. You can also choose to give it a description. After that, click **OK**.

The last step of our initialization process consists of creating the Jenkins job.

Creating the Jenkins job to automatically run the builds

As mentioned previously, Jenkins has a plugin to help with the GitHub integration. We can easily take advantage of this by creating a GitHub organization job. To do this, go through the following steps:

1. Open your Jenkins home page in your browser, enter `http://18.208.183.35:8080/` and click on **Create new jobs**.
2. Enter an item name, provide your GitHub username or organization name, click on **GitHub Organization**, and then click on **OK**.
3. This will bring us to a new page, where we will be able to configure the project:
    1. In the **Credentials** drop-down menu, select your newly created credential.
    2. Validate that the owner is your username or organization name or the name you provided while creating the job. This will be used by Jenkins to scan all your repositories.
    3. Since we already know that we are only interested in the `helloworld` repository, click on the **Add** button at the bottom of the **Behaviors** section and select the first option, which should be **Filter by Name (with regular expression)**.

4. In the newly populated field, **Regular expression**, replace `.*` with `helloworld`. Select strategy as **All branches** from the **Discover branches** section and scroll down to select one minute from the **Scan Organization Triggers** section on the same page:

5. Click on **Save**.

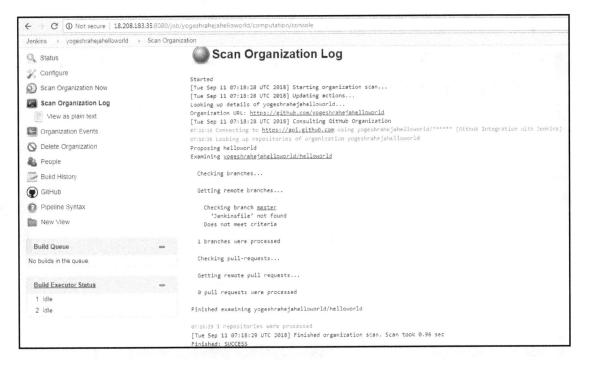

The job will be created and will scan the project to find a branch. It will find the master branch with the README file in it, but because we don't have any code yet we will not do anything. In the following section, we are going to remediate that lack of code and implement our `helloworld` application:

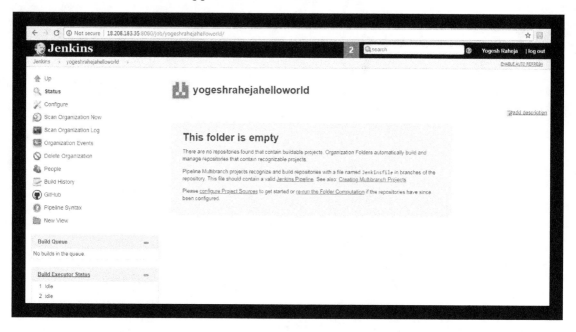

Implementing the helloworld application using our CI environment

Here, we will once again use the simple `helloworld` web application that we created in Chapter 2, *Deploying Your First Web Application*. The goal here is more to illustrate the use of our CI pipeline than to build a complex web application:

Initializing the project

We are going to use the same AWS instance that we deployed and configured in the previous section for Jenkins, as a development environment. Therefore, we need to have `nodejs` and `npm` installed on our instance. If you haven't installed these yet, refer to the instructions in Chapter 2, *Deploying Your First Web Application*:

```
$ ssh -i ~/.ssh/EffectiveDevOpsAWS.pem ec2-user@18.208.183.35
```

```
$ node -v
$ npm -v
```

The output of running the preceding command is as follows:

```
[root@yogeshraheja EffectiveDevOpsTemplates]# ssh -i ~/.ssh/EffectiveDevOpsAWS.pem ec2-user@18.208.183.35

      __|  __|_  )
      _|  (     /   Amazon Linux AMI
     ___|\___|___|

https://aws.amazon.com/amazon-linux-ami/2018.03-release-notes/
6 package(s) needed for security, out of 13 available
Run "sudo yum update" to apply all updates.
[ec2-user@ip-172-31-68-115 ~]$ sudo -i
[root@ip-172-31-68-115 ~]# node -v
v0.10.48
[root@ip-172-31-68-115 ~]# npm -v
1.3.6
```

Our first step will be to clone the `helloworld` GitHub repository that we created in the preceding section:

```
$ git clone https://github.com/<your_github_organization>/helloworld.git
$ cd helloworld
```

We can now create a new branch:

```
$ git checkout -b initial-branch
```

Create an empty file called `helloworld.js`:

```
$ touch helloworld.js
```

One of the best ways to write tests for these types of projects is to use a **Test Driven Development** (**TDD**) approach. In a TDD process, developers create the tests first, then run them to make sure they are failing, write the code, and then test again. At that point, the tests should pass. We can create a pull request and merge it once it has been reviewed and approved.

Creating a functional test using Mocha

In order to illustrate the process of writing tests for our TDD approach, we will use a tool called **Mocha** (`https://mochajs.org/`). Mocha is a very common and easy-to-use JavaScript test framework to create a test.

We will install it locally on our system using the following `npm`, the Node.js package manager command.

First, we will initialize npm with the following command:

```
$ npm config set registry http://registry.npmjs.org/
$ npm init -yes
```

The output of running the preceding command is as follows:

```
[root@ip-172-31-68-115 helloworld]# npm init -yes
This utility will walk you through creating a package.json file.
It only covers the most common items, and tries to guess sane defaults.

See `npm help json` for definitive documentation on these fields
and exactly what they do.

Use `npm install <pkg> --save` afterwards to install a package and
save it as a dependency in the package.json file.

Press ^C at any time to quit.
name: (helloworld)
version: (0.0.0) 1.0.0
description:
entry point: (helloworld.js)
test command:
git repository: (https://github.com/yogeshrahejahelloworld/helloworld.git)
keywords:
author:
license: (BSD)
About to write to /root/helloworld/package.json:

{
  "name": "helloworld",
  "version": "1.0.0",
  "description": "",
  "main": "helloworld.js",
  "scripts": {
    "test": "echo \"Error: no test specified\" && exit 1"
  },
  "repository": {
    "type": "git",
    "url": "https://github.com/yogeshrahejahelloworld/helloworld.git"
  },
  "author": "",
  "license": "BSD",
  "bugs": {
    "url": "https://github.com/yogeshrahejahelloworld/helloworld/issues"
  }
}


Is this ok? (yes)
[root@ip-172-31-68-115 helloworld]# 
```

This will create a new file called `package.json`. Next, we will install Mocha and add it to our list of development dependencies as follows:

```
$ npm install mocha@2.5.3 --save-dev
```

This will create a directory called `node_modules`. Mocha will be installed in that directory.

In addition to Mocha, we will use a headless browser testing module to render our `helloworld` application, called **Zombie**. We can install it with the same command as follows:

```
$ npm install zombie@3.0.15 --save-dev
```

In order to separate the tests from the rest of the project, we are now going to create a directory called `test` in the root location of our `helloworld` project. By default, Mocha will look for tests in that directory:

```
$ mkdir test
```

The last piece of boilerplate code we will use will configure npm to use Mocha to run our tests. With your editor, open the `package.json` file and replace the test scripts with the following command:

```
"scripts": {
  "test": "node_modules/mocha/bin/mocha"
},
```

Inside the `test` directory, create and edit the file `helloworld_test.js`.

The first step consists of loading two modules that we are going to use and need in our test. The first one is `zombie`, our headline browser, and the second one is the `assert` module, which is the standard module used to create unit testing in Node.js applications:

```
var Browser = require('zombie')
var assert = require('assert')
```

Next, we need to load our application. This is done by calling the same `require()` function, but this time we will ask it to load the `helloworld.js` file that we will soon implement. For now, it's an empty file:

```
var app = require('../helloworld')
```

We can now start creating the test. The basic syntax of Mocha tries to mimic what it thinks specification document could require. The following are the three required statements, add the following:

```
describe('main page', function() {
  it('should say hello world')
})
```

We now need to add hooks into that test to interact with our web application.

The first step will be to point the test to our application endpoint. As you might remember from the previous chapters, the application is running on http://localhost:3000. We will use the hook called before() to set up a precondition. Above the call to it(), add the following to point our headless browser to the proper server:

```
describe('main page', function() {
before(function() {
   this.browser = new Browser({ site: 'http://localhost:3000' })
})

it('should say hello world')
})
...
```

At this point, our headless browser will connect to our application, but it won't request any page. Let's add that in another before() hook, as follows:

```
describe('main page', function() {
  before(function() {
    this.browser = new Browser({ site: 'http://localhost:3000' })
  })

  before(function(done) {
    this.browser.visit('/', done)
  })

  it('should say hello world')
})
...
```

Now that the home page has loaded, we need to implement the code in the it() function to validate our assertion. We will edit the line with the it() call to add a callback function, as follows:

```
describe('main page', function() {
  before(function() {
    this.browser = new Browser({ site: 'http://localhost:3000' })
```

```
  })
  before(function(done) {
    this.browser.visit('/', done)
  })
  it('should say hello world', function() {
    assert.ok(this.browser.success)
    assert.equal(this.browser.text(), "Hello World")
  })
})
```

Our test is now ready. If everything went well, your code should look like the one shown at the following link: https://raw.githubusercontent.com/yogeshraheja/helloworld/master/test/helloworld_test.js.

We can test it in Terminal by simply calling the Mocha command, as follows:

```
$ npm test

./node_modules/mocha/bin/mocha
  main page
    1) "before all" hook
  0 passing (48ms)
  1 failing
  1) main page "before all" hook:
      TypeError: connect ECONNREFUSED 127.0.0.1:3000
```

As you can see, our test is failing. It can't connect to the web application. This is, of course, expected, since we haven't implemented the application code yet.

Developing the remainder of the application

We are now ready to develop our application. Since we already went through creating the exact code in Chapter 2, *Deploying Your First Web Application*, we are simply going to copy it or download it directly as follows:

```
$ curl -L
https://raw.githubusercontent.com/yogeshraheja/Effective-DevOps-with-AWS/master/Chapter02/helloworld.js > helloworld.js
```

We can now test the code again using the npm command:

```
$ npm test
Server running
  main page
      should say hello world
  1 passing (78ms)
```

The output of running the preceding command is as follows:

```
[root@ip-172-31-68-115 helloworld]# npm test

> helloworld@1.0.0 test /root/helloworld
> node_modules/mocha/bin/mocha

Server running


  main page
    ✓ should say hello world


  1 passing (62ms)

[root@ip-172-31-68-115 helloworld]# []
```

Our test is now passing.

We are almost there. We have satisfied one of our first goals, which was to have test coverage for our code. Of course, a real application with more complexity would have many more tests, but what we want to focus on now is automation. Now that we've learned how to test our code manually, we want to see how Jenkins can do this for us.

Creating the CI pipeline in Jenkins

As we saw earlier, Jenkins works by creating and executing jobs. Historically, one way to create the pipeline would be to open Jenkins in the browser, navigate to the job we previously created, and edit it to outline the different steps involved in testing our code. The problem with that solution is that there isn't a good review process involved and it's hard to track every change made over time. In addition, it's very hard for developers to make changes in a project that involves adding new build steps as the code of the project and the job building the project aren't synced together. Jenkins 2 made the concept of describing the build process into a local file a standard feature, which we're going to use in the following section.

We are going to create and edit a new file in the project called Jenkinsfile (capital J, no file extension). The file will be written in **Groovy** (http://www.groovy-lang.org).

On the first line of the file, we are going to put the following:

```
#!groovy
```

This is useful for the different IDEs and GitHub as it indicates the nature of the file. The first step of our script will consist of asking Jenkins to assign the job to a node as follows:

```
node { }
```

Our Jenkins installation is fairly simple. We only have one server and therefore only one node. If we had more nodes, we could add parameters to the call to target a node with a specific architecture, or even drive the parallel execution.

Our CI testing can be logically broken up into a few steps:

1. Get the code from GitHub.
2. Install the different dependencies by calling the npm install command.
3. Run our run with the command mocha.
4. Clean up.

These steps have an equivalent concept in Jenkins called **stages**. We are going to add them inside the node routing. Here is what the first stage will look like:

```
node {
    stage 'Checkout'
        checkout scm
}
```

This tells Jenkins to get the code from the source control. When we created the job, we stated that it was a GitHub organization job, so Jenkins will know how to interpret that correctly.

Next, we need to call the npm install command. Groovy doesn't understand native language specific features such as calling npm. To do this, therefore, we will use the sh command, which will allow us to spawn a shell and run a command. Here is what our second stage looks like:

```
stage 'Checkout'
    checkout scm

stage 'Setup'
    sh 'npm config set registry http://registry.npmjs.org/'
    sh 'npm install'
```

In our next stage, we are going to run Mocha. The following is the `Setup` stage; add the following:

```
stage 'Mocha test'
      sh './node_modules/mocha/bin/mocha'
```

Finally, we can proceed to clean up the repository with the following stage:

```
stage 'Cleanup'
      echo 'prune and cleanup'
      sh 'npm prune'
      sh 'rm node_modules -rf'
```

The Jenkins file is now ready, it should look like this: `https://raw.githubusercontent.com/yogeshraheja/helloworld/master/Jenkinsfile`.

We can now commit our code and test it:

```
$ git add Jenkinsfile helloworld.js package.json test
$ git commit -m "Helloworld application"
$ git push origin initial-branch
```

This will create a remote branch called `initial-branch`. As the branch gets created, Jenkins will get a notification from GitHub about the change and will run the CI pipeline. In a matter of seconds, our test will run on Jenkins, which in turn will send the result back to GitHub. We can observe this as follows:

1. Open GitHub in your browser and navigate to the `helloworld` project you created.
2. Click on **Branch** and select **initial-branch**.
3. From that screen, click on **New pull request**, provide a title and a good description of the change you are making. If possible, mention other developers so that they can thoroughly review the change you are proposing.
4. Click on **Create pull request** and follow the steps to create a pull request. Once the pull request is created, you will be able to see how GitHub shows that the pull request has passed all checks:

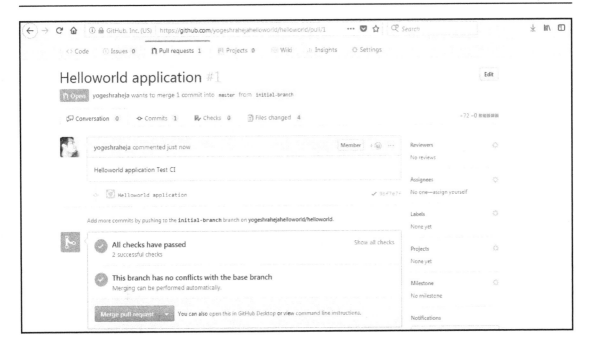

5. You can also go to your Jenkins browser and check the build history. You can even check the details from Jenkins by clicking the organization, followed by repository and branch. This will bring us back to the Jenkins job, where you can observe the execution of the job and its pipeline in more detail:

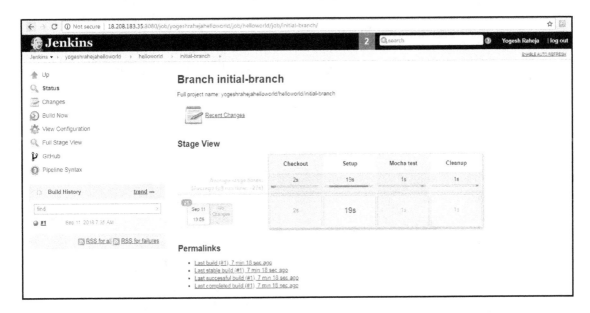

6. At that point, if you mentioned other developers, they should get a notification so that they can look at the content of the pull request. Once it is reviewed and approved, the pull request can be merged. From that point on, when developers pull the master branch or rebase their branch, they will see your code.

 Depending on the size of the team working on a repository, it is common to have to rebase a branch. The two most important times to do that are before creating the pull request (step 2) and before merging it (step 6).

Productionizing the CI pipeline

We have now put in place a basic, yet functional, CI pipeline. While this is a good starting point, you are likely to want to perfect certain details of this system. As mentioned previously, our Ansible recipe for Jenkins can be improved to include the configuration of the jobs such as the `helloworld` job we manually created.

We only created a single functional test to illustrate how to use a TDD approach and how to integrate a testing step in our pipeline. The success of a continuous integration pipeline depends strongly on the quality and quantity of the tests produced. Tests will typically be broken up into functional and non-functional tests. In order to best take advantage of your pipeline, you will want to catch possible errors as early as possible. This means focusing on the functional tests and in particular the **unit tests,** which are used to validate small units of code such as a method in a class.

After this, you can focus on **integration testing,** which covers a bit more ground and usually interacts with data stores and other functions in the code. Finally, you will want to add **acceptance testing** to verify that all the requirements for your stories are complete:

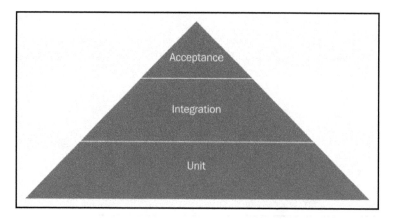

In terms of non-functional testing, you will usually want to look at **performance, security, usability,** and **compatibility** testing.

Finally, you can complement your own tests with code analyzer tools to get a sense of the code coverage (how many lines of code are executed by your automated tests).

As always with DevOps, it is important to collect metrics. In a CI pipeline, you will typically want to monitor the number of builds that go through the CI pipeline and the quality of the pull requests.

Like any other system, you will need to spend a bit of time setting up backups and monitoring. You may decide to back up the Jenkins home directory if you haven't moved to a model where your jobs and the Jenkins configuration are managed by your configuration management system (Ansible). In terms of metrics, keeping an eye on the system performance, its availability, and health are paramount. A breakage in the build pipeline should be considered a critical issue as it impacts the productivity of all the developers and operators.

Finally, you should expect to have to scale up your CI infrastructure over time. As code and tests get added, it will take longer and longer to run the tests. You may decide to add more Jenkins slaves, which will allow you to run tests in parallel and/or use bigger instances. In the current format, Jenkins will run the `helloworld` pipeline every time a change is pushed to a branch. You may also decide to only run the pipeline once the pull requests are created.

In the initial section of this chapter, we adopted a new workflow where developers commit code and tests to individual branches and send frequent pull requests to share the proposed changes with the rest of the engineering organization. In addition, we made sure that the new code is fully tested by creating a continuous integration pipeline. To do this, we created a Jenkins server and hooked it to GitHub. Thanks to that system, all the tests committed with the project get automatically executed and the results are sent back to GitHub. We are now in an ideal situation to take our workflow to the next level and automate deployment.

Are the QA teams no longer needed with DevOps?
Yes and no. In an effective DevOps organization, non-technical QA jobs are not usually needed. If everything is fully automated and the developers write sufficient tests to cover all aspects of the code, the organization doesn't need to task anyone to write and execute test plans. Instead of that, DevOps-focused organizations will have engineers, sometimes called QA engineers, who focus on quality but with an emphasis on automation. This involves working on tooling and processes to improve the ability to automatically test code.

Building a continuous deployment pipeline

By creating a CI pipeline, we have taken the first step toward being an effective **engineering** organization. Because our workflow now involves working in individual branches and merging them back to the master branch after going through automated testing and human reviews, we can assume that the code present in the master branch is of high quality and is safe to deploy. We can now focus on the next challenge, which is to release code automatically as new code gets merged into the master branch.

By continuously releasing new code, you drastically accelerate the feedback loop process that DevOps provides. Releasing new code to production at high speed lets you collect real customer metrics, which often leads to exposing new and often unexpected issues. For many companies, deploying new code to production is a challenge. It can be quite worrying, especially if it involves thousands of new commits all going out to production at the same time in a process that occurs only a few times a year. Companies that do this often schedule their maintenance late at night and during weekends. Adopting a more modern approach, such as the one we will go through in the remainder of the chapters, will have a significant positive impact on the work-life balance of the engineering team.

 Most well-known tech companies such as Google or Facebook don't deploy code on Fridays. The goal is to avoid pushing bugs out just before the weekend, which could otherwise lead to unexpected pages on Saturdays or Sundays. Because they aren't scared of deploying code, a lot of those changes will go out to production at peak hours so that they can quickly catch any issues related to load.

In order to implement our continuous deployment pipeline, we are going to look at two new AWS services—**CodePipeline** and **CodeDeploy**:

- CodePipeline let us create our deployment pipeline. We will tell it to take our code from GitHub, like we did before, and send it to Jenkins to run CI testing on it. Instead of simply returning the result to GitHub, however, we will then take the code and deploy it to our EC2 instance with the help of AWS CodeDeploy.
- CodeDeploy is a service that lets us properly deploy code to our EC2 instances. By adding a certain number of configuration files and scripts, we can use CodeDeploy to deploy and test our code reliably. Thanks to CodeDeploy, we don't have to worry about any kind of complicated logic when it comes to sequencing our deployment. It is tightly integrated with EC2 and knows how to perform rolling updates across multiple instances and, if needed, perform a rollback.

In Chapter 3, *Treating Your Infrastructure as Code*, we looked at how to configure servers and deploy the helloworld application using Ansible. While this solution allowed us to illustrate how to use configuration management, this solution is not good enough for a more critical service. There isn't any notion of sequencing, there are no good feedback mechanisms to tell us how the deploy went, and we didn't implement any validation steps.

Having a dedicated service geared towards carrying out deployments in AWS will make deploying applications a lot better, as we will see in the following section. In order to demonstrate these services, we will first build a new generic Node.js web server using Ansible.

Creating new web servers for continuous deployment

In order to use CodeDeploy, the EC2 instances need to be running the CodeDeploy agent. This is normally done by downloading an executable from an S3 bucket, which varies depending on the region your instances are running in. Conveniently, AWS has also released a custom Ansible library, which can automate these steps. Because that library isn't a part of the standard Ansible library, we first need to add it to our Ansible repository.

Importing a custom library to Ansible for AWS CodeDeploy

By default, Ansible expects to find the custom libraries in the /usr/share/my_modules/ directory. Previously, when we looked at the inventory script in Chapter 3, *Treating Your Infrastructure as Code*, we changed this default behavior by editing the ansible.cfg file. We will make the necessary changes so that the library is being downloaded onto the host with the rest of the Ansible files. The simplest way to accomplish this is to create a new directory at the root of our ansible repository and put the library in it.

On your computer, open a Terminal and go to your ansible directory:

In the root directory of our ansible repository, where the ansible.cfg file is located, we are going to add the new directory library to store the AWS CodeDeploy ansible library:

```
$ mkdir library
```

Once the folder is created, we can download the `ansible` library in it:

```
$ curl -L
https://raw.githubusercontent.com/yogeshraheja/Effective-DevOps-with-AWS/ma
ster/Chapter05/ansible/library/aws_codedeploy > library/aws_codedeploy
```

Lastly, we are going to edit the `ansible.cfg` file that is present in the root directory of the `ansible` repository to specify the location of the library folder as follows:

```
# update ansible.cfg
[defaults]
inventory = ./ec2.py
remote_user = ec2-user
become = True
become_method = sudo
become_user = root
nocows = 1
library = library
```

We are now ready to start using the library. CodeDeploy is a service that we are likely to reuse over time as new services get added to our system. In order to ensure that our Ansible repository code conforms to the **Don't Repeat Yourself** (**DRY**) principle, we are going to create an Ansible role that is dedicated to CodeDeploy.

Creating a CodeDeploy Ansible role

We are first going to go into the role directory that is present at the root location of our `ansible` repository:

```
$ cd roles
```

As before, we will rely on `ansible-galaxy` to put in place the scaffolding that is needed to create our role:

```
$ ansible-galaxy init codedeploy
```

Our role will be very simple. We are going to edit the `codedeploy/tasks/main.yml` file and make a call to the new module that the `aws_codedeploy` library provides, as follows:

```
---
# tasks file for codedeploy
- name: Installs and starts the AWS CodeDeploy Agent
  aws_codedeploy:
    enabled: yes
```

At this point, we can create our new playbook for generic `nodejs` web servers. First, go back in the root directory of the `ansible` repository:

```
$ cd ..
```

Create a new file called `nodeserver.yml`:

```
$ touch nodeserver.yml
```

We will take the same approach we did previously with our other playbooks. The goal of our servers will be to run Node.js applications and run the CodeDeploy daemon. Edit the `nodeserver.yml` file and add the following to it:

```
---
- hosts: "{{ target | default('localhost') }}"
  become: yes
  roles:
    - nodejs
    - codedeploy
```

 When using CodeDeploy in a config management system such as Ansible or CloudFormation, it is important to always install all the dependencies for your application prior to starting it. This allows you to avoid a race condition.

We can now commit our changes to `git`. First, create a new branch and then add new files and directories that we created:

```
$ git checkout -b code-deploy
$ git add library roles/codedeploy nodeserver.yml ansible.cfg
```

Finally, `commit` and `push` the changes:

```
$ git commit -m "adding aws_codedeploy library, role and a nodeserver
playbook"
$ git push origin code-deploy
```

As before, you can now create a pull request. Once the pull request has been reviewed and approved, merge it back to the master. After you have followed these steps, your Ansible repository should look as follows: `https://github.com/yogeshraheja/Effective-DevOps-with-AWS/tree/master/Chapter05/ansible`.

Creating the web server CloudFormation template

As we now have our Ansible playbook ready, we can create our CloudFormation template using Troposphere. Start by duplicating the Troposphere script that we created for Jenkins earlier in the chapter:

```
$ cd EffectiveDevOpsTemplates
$ cp jenkins-cf-template.py nodeserver-cf-template.py
```

Edit the `nodeserver-cf-template.py` file to make the following changes. First, change the application name and port by updating the variables as follows:

```
ApplicationName = "nodeserver"
ApplicationPort = "3000"
```

In addition, our instances will need to download files from S3. To allow this to happen, replace the policy that allowed CodePipeline on our Jenkins instance with a policy to allow S3. Edit the policy called `AllowCodePipeline` and update its name and action. Above the instantiation of our instance, add a new IAM policy resource as follows:

```
t.add_resource(IAMPolicy(
    "Policy",
    PolicyName="AllowS3",
    PolicyDocument=Policy(
        Statement=[
            Statement(
                Effect=Allow,
                Action=[Action("s3", "*")],
                Resource=["*"])
        ]
    ),
    Roles=[Ref("Role")]
))
```

The new script should look as follows: https://raw.githubusercontent.com/yogeshraheja/EffectiveDevOpsTemplates/master/nodeserver-cf-template.py.

As the new script is now ready, we can save it and generate the CloudFormation template as follows:

```
$ git add nodeserver-cf-template.py
$ git commit -m "Adding node server troposhere script"
$ git push
$ python nodeserver-cf-template.py > nodeserver-cf.template
```

Launching our web server

As before, we are going to launch our instance using CloudFormation. Note that we are calling this first stack `helloworld-staging`. We will first look at CodeDeploy as a way to deploy our code to a staging environment. We will use this name in CodeDeploy so that we can target the deployments to that specific stack:

```
$ aws cloudformation create-stack \
    --capabilities CAPABILITY_IAM \
    --stack-name helloworld-staging \
    --template-body file://nodeserver-cf.template \
    --parameters ParameterKey=KeyPair,ParameterValue=EffectiveDevOpsAWS
```

In a few minutes, our instance will be ready.

We are now at an important point in our DevOps transformation. We have now created generic `nodejs` web servers that allow you to deploy code on them easily. We are really close to a realistic environment that effective companies traditionally use to deploy and run their services. The fact that we are able to create these environments simply and on demand is our key to success.

 When architecting services, always make sure that the infrastructure can easily be recreated. Being able to troubleshoot an issue is great, but being able to quickly rebuild a service host and stop the impact on the user is often even more desirable.

Integrating our helloworld application with CodeDeploy

Now that our servers are initiated and the CodeDeploy agent is running, we can start using them. First, we need to create an IAM service role for CodeDeploy. We then need to add an entry in the CodeDeploy service to define our application. Finally, we need to add our application specification file and a few scripts to help with deploying and running our service to the `helloworld` application.

Creating the IAM service role for CodeDeploy

CodeDeploy permissions work with IAM at the level of the individual application. In order to provide sufficient permissions, we will create a new IAM service role with the following policy:

```
{
    "Version": "2012-10-17",
    "Statement": [
        {
            "Sid": "",
            "Effect": "Allow",
            "Principal": {
                "Service": [
                    "codedeploy.amazonaws.com"
                ]
            },
            "Action": "sts:AssumeRole"
        }
    ]
}
```

We will create a new role that will be called CodeDeployServiceRole using the following command in the command-line interface:

```
$ aws iam create-role \
    --role-name CodeDeployServiceRole \
    --assume-role-policy-document \
    https://raw.githubusercontent.com/yogeshraheja/Effective-DevOps-
    with-AWS/master/Chapter05/misc/CodeDeploy-Trust.json
```

We now need to attach the role policy to provide the proper permissions to the service role:

```
$ aws iam attach-role-policy \
    --role-name CodeDeployServiceRole \
    --policy-arn \
    arn:aws:iam::aws:policy/service-role/AWSCodeDeployRole
```

Our IAM service role is now ready. We can finally start interacting with the CodeDeploy web interface.

Creating the CodeDeploy application

Now that we have launched EC2 instances with the CodeDeploy service running on them and defined our IAM service role, we have all the requirements to create a CodeDeploy application. As always, there are many ways to use AWS services, but we will demonstrate the basic uses with the web interface in this section:

1. Open `https://console.aws.amazon.com/codedeploy` in your browser.

2. If prompted, click on **Get Started Now**.

3. This leads us to a welcome screen with two options, **Sample Deployment** and **Custom Deployment**. Choose **Custom Deployment** and click on **Skip Walkthrough**. This brings us to a form called **Create Application**.

4. In that form, under **Application Name**, give our application the name `helloworld`.

5. The deployment groups can be viewed as the environment in which the application will live. We will first create a staging environment. Under **Deployment Group Name**, provide the name `staging`.

6. We now need to add instances to our application. Our goal is to target the EC2 instance that we previously created with CloudFormation. As you might recall, we called our stack `helloworld-staging`. In the section **Environment configuration**, select **Amazon EC2 instances**, and select `aws:cloudformation:stack-name` in the Key field and `helloworld-staging` in the **Value** field. This will make sure that CodeDeploy only selects the instance that we intend to use for our application. AWS CodeDeploy should confirm that it matched one instance:

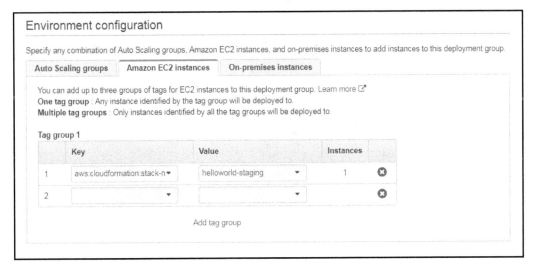

7. The next section is called **Deployment configuration**. One of the strengths of CodeDeploy is its ability to understand how to deploy code to a cluster of servers. This features makes it easy to avoid outages during deployment. By default, the service comes with three deployment options—one at a time, all at once, and half at a time. It is possible to create custom deployment configurations, but in our case, since we have only one instance, we can leave the default option `CodeDeployDefault.OneAtATime`.

8. The next two sections are called triggers and alarms. We aren't going to cover these in detail in this book, but basically triggers are useful when it comes to collecting metrics around deployment and monitoring. By creating triggers to push notifications in SNS and creating CloudWatch metrics, you can easily collect metrics around deployments. This helps you answer questions such as how many deployments are happening, how many fail, how many deploys lead to rollback, and so on.

9. Our application is somewhat stateless, therefore enabling rollback upon failure is a good idea. Select the **Roll back when a deployment fails** option.

10. Lastly, we need to select the service role that we created in the previous steps. Under **Service Role ARN**, select the role that ends with **CodeDeployServiceRole**.

11. Finally, click on **Create Application**.

This brings us back to the CodeDeploy application page for our newly created `helloworld` application.

Creating the application in CodeDeploy allows us to define where our newly created application will be deployed. We will now look at how to deploy our code.

Adding the CodeDeploy configuration and scripts to our repository

When we worked on creating a Jenkins pipeline earlier in this chapter, we created a Jenkinsfile file inside the `helloworld` GitHub repository. The reason for this was that we could change the code and the way the code is tested in the same change set. For the same reason, it is a good idea to put the logic about how to deploy our code with the code itself.

Our `helloworld` repository currently contains the application that we created inside a new GitHub organization (`yogeshrahejahelloworld` in my case). It also contains the applications tests and a repository with name `helloworld` . We are now going to add the information that CodeDeploy needs in order to execute the deployment of our service.

CodeDeploy relies on an application specification file called `appspec.yml` to manage deployment. We first need to create this file. Go to the directory where the `helloworld` GitHub project is cloned and create a new branch off the master:

```
$ git clone https://github.com/<YOUR GITHUB ORGANIZATION>/helloworld.git
$ cd helloworld
$ git checkout -b helloworld-codedeploy
```

We are now going to create and edit the file `appspec.yml`:

```
$ touch appspec.yml
```

On the first line of the file, we are going to define which version of the AppSpec file we want to use. Currently, the only version that is supported is `0.0`:

```
version: 0.0
```

On the next line, we are going to specify the operating system on which we wish to deploy our service. In our case, this is Linux:

```
os: linux
```

We are now going to describe which file goes where. To do this, we are going to create a section called `files` and put each file that we want to deploy using a format source destination. Note that the file is written in YAML and therefore the spacing and alignment are important:

```
version: 0.0
os: linux
files:
  - source: helloworld.js
  destination: /usr/local/helloworld/
```

Thanks to this section, CodeDeploy now knows to copy the `helloworld.js` in the target destination, `/usr/local/helloworld`. Our `helloworld` directory will be automatically created by CodeDeploy. In order to start the application, we will also need our upstart script, which isn't currently in the repository.

Back in the Terminal of the root directory of the `helloworld` project, we are going to create a subdirectory called `scripts` and add the upstart script to it:

```
$ mkdir scripts
$ wget
https://raw.githubusercontent.com/yogeshraheja/Effective-DevOps-with-AWS/master/Chapter02/helloworld.conf -O scripts/helloworld.conf
```

We can now add the `helloworld.conf` file that new file to our `appspsec.yml` by adding another block with the source and destination of the upstart script as follows:

```
files:
  - source: helloworld.js
    destination: /usr/local/helloworld/
  - source: scripts/helloworld.conf
    destination: /etc/init/
```

The two files that we need in order to run our application as a service will now be present in the appropriate locations. In order to deploy our application, we need more files. We need CodeDeploy to start and stop the service. Previously, we started the application using Ansible, but this time around we aren't using Ansible to manage our service. CodeDeploy has a much more elegant solution: when a deployment starts, the CodeDeploy agent running on the EC2 instance will go through the following sequence of events:

The archive containing our application will be downloaded on the system during the **DownloadBundle** event. The install section will be used to copy the files defined in our template to their destinations.

CodeDeploy uses the concept of hooks. In the `appspec.yml` file we can create a number of hooks to execute custom scripts during each of the stages described previously. We are going to create three scripts: a script to start our application, a script to stop it, and finally a script to check if the deployment was successful.

We will put these three scripts in the `scripts` directory that we created previously. Let's create the first file `start.sh` and start editing it:

$ touch scripts/start.sh

The script is very straightforward. We are simply going to call upstart to start the service:

#!/bin/sh
start helloworld

This is all we need. We are now going to create our stop script file:

$ touch scripts/stop.sh

As we did before, edit it as follows:

```
#!/bin/sh
[[ -e /etc/init/helloworld.conf ]] \
    && status helloworld | \
        grep -q '^helloworld start/running, process' \
    && [[ $? -eq 0 ]] \
    && stop helloworld || echo "Application not started"
```

The stop script is slightly more complicated than the start script because it will be executed during the `BeforeInstall` step. The basic logic is the same: we are making a call to stop the `helloworld` application. We have some extra calls before this because we need to handle the case of the first deployment where the application hasn't been installed and started before.

The last script we will create is called `validate.sh`:

$ touch scripts/validate.sh

Once again the code is very simple:

#!/bin/sh
curl -I localhost:3000

For the purposes of this book, we are carrying out the most basic validation possible. This consists of a HEAD request on the only route that our application has. In a more realistic application, we would test more routes and anything that could potentially go wrong when new code is pushed out.

Our scripts need to be executable to avoid any unnecessary warnings in CodeDeploy:

$ chmod a+x scripts/{start,stop,validate}.sh

We can now add our hooks in our `appspec.yml` file. Open the file again and create a `hooks` section below the `files` section:

```
version: 0.0
os: linux
files:
[...]
hooks:
```

We will first declare the stop script that we want to run at the BeforeInstall stage. In the hooks section, add the following:

```
hooks:
  BeforeInstall:
    - location: scripts/stop.sh
      timeout: 30
```

We are allowing 30 seconds for the execution of the stop command to complete. We are going to repeat a similar operation to add our start and validate scripts as follows:

```
hooks:
  BeforeInstall:
    - location: scripts/stop.sh
      timeout: 30
  ApplicationStart:
    - location: scripts/start.sh
      timeout: 30
  ValidateService:
    - location: scripts/validate.sh
```

When our deploy pipeline runs, it will try to do the following:

1. Download our application package and decompress it in a temporary directory
2. Run the stop script
3. Copy the application and upstart script
4. Run the start script
5. Run the validate script to make sure everything is working as expected

We can add all our new files to git, commit and push the changes, and send a pull request as follows:

```
$ git add scripts appspec.yml
$ git commit -m "Adding CodeDeploy support to the application"
$ git push
```

The branch will go through Jenkins and be tested. A peer can then review the code change; once it is approved, you can merge your pull request.

In order to perform deployment, we essentially need to answer three questions—*what are we trying to deploy? Where are we trying to deploy it? How can we deploy it?* We answered the second question when we created the job in CodeDeploy and the third question with our appspec file and its helper scripts. We now need to look into the first question—*what are we trying to deploy?* This is where we are going to use AWS CodePipeline.

Building our deployment pipeline with AWS CodePipeline

AWS CodePipeline is a service dedicated to creating delivery pipelines. You can think of it as similar to the Jenkins pipelines feature with an AWS twist. The service is very well integrated with the rest of the AWS ecosystem, which means that it has a number of great features and useful advantages over Jenkins. Because it's a fully managed service, you don't have to worry about its uptime the way we do with a single Jenkins instance. It integrates out of the box with CodeDeploy, which is very handy for our case. While we won't go into too much detail here, the service is fully integrated with the IAM service, which means that you have a very granular level of control over who can do what. The service can, for example, prevent unauthorized users from performing deployments. Thanks to its API, a number of services can be integrated into your pipelines, including Jenkins and GitHub.

We will first look into creating a basic pipeline in two stages. In the first stage, we will get the code from GitHub, package it, and store the package on S3. In the second stage, we will take that package and deploy it to our staging instance using CodeDeploy.

After that, we will go through a more advanced scenario. We will see how we can use our Jenkins instance to run our tests before deploying our code to staging. We will also create a production environment and add an on-demand production deployment process, called a continuous delivery pipeline. Finally, we will look at a couple of strategies that will allow us to build confidence in the code that we push through our pipeline so that we will be able to remove the on-demand production deployment step and turn it into a fully automated pipeline.

Creating a continuous deployment pipeline for staging

To create our first deployment pipeline with `CodePipeline`, we are going to use the AWS console, which offers a very intuitive web interface:

1. Open the following link in your browser: `https://console.aws.amazon.com/cod epipeline`.
2. If prompted, click on **Get started**.
3. On the next screen, give your pipeline the name `helloworld` and click on **Next Step**.

4. For the source location, select GitHub as a **Source provider** and click on **Connect to Github**. If requested, sign into your GitHub account.

5. This will bring you back to the AWS CodePipeline screen. We can now select a **Repository** and **branch**. We will select the `helloworld` project and the master branch. Click on **Next step.**

> If you don't see the organization name/repository name (that is, `yogeshrahejahelloworld/helloworld`) then, as a workaround, clone/copy the organization name/repository name to your global Github repository (that is, `yogeshrahejahelloworld/helloworld` to `yogeshraheja/hellworld` in my case).

6. This brings us to stage three of our pipeline where we can select our **Build provider**. Our application is being written in Node.js so we don't need to build anything. Select **No build** and click on **Next step**.

7. The next step is called **Beta**. This is essentially our staging deployment step. Under **Deployment provider**, select **AWS CodeDeploy**. Under Application name, select `helloworld`. Finally, select **staging** for the **Deployment group**. Click on **Next step**.

8. This brings us to a step in which we have to choose our **Role Name**. Conveniently, AWS have also added a **Create Role** button. Click on this.

9. On the next screen, select **Create a new IAM Role** and give it the name `AWS-CodePipeline-Service`. Use the policy proposed and click on **Allow**.

10. Go back to the CodePipeline step and make sure that role name says `AWS-CodePipeline-Service`. Click on **Next step**.

11. On the review screen, make sure everything is correct. Finally, click on **Create Pipeline.**

> Because we are using the web interface, Amazon automatically creates an S3 bucket on your behalf to store the artifacts that are produced when the pipeline runs.

Review your pipeline

We will create your pipeline with the following resources.

Source Stage

Source provider	GitHub
Repository	yogeshraheja/helloworld
Branch	master

Build Stage

Build provider	No Build

Staging Stage

Deployment provider	AWS CodeDeploy
Application name	helloworld
Deployment group	staging

Pipeline settings

Pipeline name	helloworld
Artifact location	s3://codepipeline-us-east-1-251505940733/
	AWS CodePipeline will create this Amazon S3 bucket to store artifacts for this pipeline. Depending on the size of your artifacts, you might be charged for storage costs. For more information, see Amazon S3 storage pricing
Role name	AWS-CodePipeline-Service

To save this configuration with these resources, choose Create pipeline.

The pipeline will be created in a matter of seconds and run for the first time.

To illustrate the basic functions of CodeDeploy and CodePipeline, we have used the web and command line interface. This process is very manual and doesn't go through any kind of review process. CloudFormation supports these two services. For a real production system, instead of making changes by hand, it is best to use something like Troposphere to generate the templates programmatically to manage the services.

Once both steps have run, you can verify that the code has been deployed by opening in your browser http://<instanceip>:3000. The instance IP can be found in the CloudFormation template or the EC2 console. You can even verify the success with the following one-liner:

```
$ aws cloudformation describe-stacks \
    --stack-name helloworld-staging \
    --query 'Stacks[0].Outputs[0].OutputValue' \
    | xargs -I {} curl {}:3000
Hello World
```

We have finished our basic pipeline. By taking advantage of CodePipeline, CodeDeploy, GitHub, and S3, we have built a very elegant solution to handle the deployment our web application. Every time a pull request is merged to the master, our pipeline will pick up the change, automatically create a new package with the new code, store it on S3, and then deploy it to staging. Thanks to CodeDeploy we can have a basic test in place to verify that the version is working. If needed, we can also roll back to any revisions that were built previously.

Our pipeline doesn't have to be limited to staging; we can actually do a lot more. As we mentioned previously, CodePipeline can integrate with Jenkins. We can use CodePipeline to build artifacts, but also to run some extra series of tests. Let's add it to our pipeline before deploying to staging.

Integrating Jenkins to our CodePipeline pipeline

One of the features that makes Jenkins so popular is its plugin capability. AWS released a number of plugins to integrate different services with Jenkins. We are going to use the one that has been created for CodePipeline. First, this will require us to change the IAM profile role of the instance so that it can interact with CodePipeline. We will then install the CodePipeline plugin in Jenkins and create a job to run our test. Finally, we will edit our pipeline to integrate the new stage.

Updating the IAM profile through CloudFormation

In order to add the new privileges to the instance profile, we are going to edit the `jenkins-cf-template.py` template that we created earlier in the chapter. We are going to add a policy to grant permissions to allow the Jenkins instance to communicate with CodePipeline. This step is very similar to the change we made to grant S3 access to our web server previously.

Above the instance variable instantiation, add the following:

```
t.add_resource(IAMPolicy(
    "Policy",
    PolicyName="AllowS3",
    PolicyDocument=Policy(
        Statement=[
            Statement(
                Effect=Allow,
                Action=[Action("s3", "*")],
                Resource=["*"])
        ]
    ),
))
```

Then, save the changes and regenerate the template. The new template should look as follows: https://raw.githubusercontent.com/yogeshraheja/Effective-DevOps-with-AWS/master/Chapter05/EffectiveDevOpsTemplates/jenkins-cf-template.py:

```
$ git add jenkins-cf-template.py
$ git commit -m "Allowing Jenkins to interact with CodePipeline"
$ git push
$ python jenkins-cf-template.py > jenkins-cf.template
```

Using the web interface, update the stack:

1. Open https://console.aws.amazon.com/cloudformation.
2. Check the checkbox next to the Jenkins stack and in the **Actions** menu, select **Update Stack**.

3. Browse to the newly generated `jenkins-cf.template` and click on **Next** until you get to the review screen:

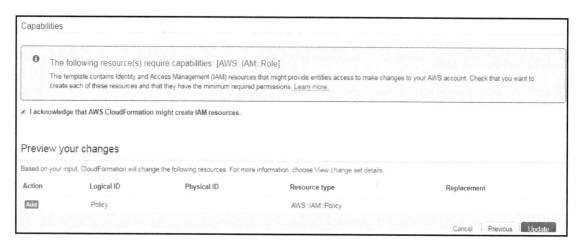

4. As shown in the preceding screenshot, only the IAM policy is being added because we created our instance with an instance profile. Our EC2 instance will stay untouched, making this change safe. Click on **Update** to confirm the change.

The instance policy will get updated, giving Jenkins enough permissions to interact with CodePipeline. We can now install the Jenkins plugin for CodePipeline.

Installing and using the CodePipeline Jenkins plugin

Installing a plugin in Jenkins is very simple:

1. Open your Jenkins instance in your browser (in my case `http://1 8.208.183.35:8080`).
2. If necessary, log in and click on **Manage Jenkins**.
3. on the **Manage Jenkins** page, select **Manage Plugins**.
4. Search for the plugin called **AWS CodePipeline Plugin**, select it, and install it. We can now start using the plugin.
5. Go back to the homepage of your Jenkins server.
6. Click on **New Item** in the menu on the left.
7. Give the new item the name `HelloworldTest`, select **Freestyle project,** and click on the **OK** button at the bottom of the page.

8. On the next screen, under **Source Code Management**, select **AWS CodePipeline**. Because we configured the permissions at the instance profile level, the only options we need to configure are the **AWS Region** and **Category**, which are in our case `US_EAST_1` and `Test` respectively.

9. Under **Build Triggers**, select **Poll SCM** and then type * * * * * to tell Jenkins to check with CodePipeline every minute for possible code test requests.

10. Under the **Build** section, click on **Add build step** and then **Execute shell**.

11. Once again, we are going to run the tests that we created at the beginning of the chapter. In the Command section, type the following:

```
npm config set registry http://registry.npmjs.org/
npm install
./node_modules/mocha/bin/mocha
```

12. Add a **post-build action** and select the action called **AWS CodePipline Publisher**.

13. In the newly generated **AWS CodePipeline Publisher**, click on **Add**, and leave the **Location** blank.

14. You can configure the rest of the job according to your preferences and then click on **Save** to create the new job.

Our test job in Jenkins is ready to be used and we can now update our pipeline.

Adding a test stage to our pipeline

We are going to use the web interface to make this change:

1. Open `https://console.aws.amazon.com/codepipeline` in your browser.
2. Select the `helloworld` pipeline we previously created.
3. On the `helloworld` pipeline page, click on the **Edit** button at the top of the pipeline.
4. Add a stage by clicking on the **+ Stage** button located between the **Source** and **Beta** stages.
5. Call that stage `Test` and click on **Action**.
6. In the menu on the right, under **Action category**, choose the action called `Test`.
7. Call your action Jenkins and, for the **Test provider**, select **Add Jenkins**.
8. In the **Add Jenkins** menu, leave the **Provider Name** set to `Jenkins`. Provide your Jenkins URL, which in my case is `http://18.203.183.35:8080`. The project name needs to match the name of the job on Jenkins. This should be `HelloworldTest`. Once set, click on **Add action**.

9. Apply your change by clicking on **Save pipeline changes** at the top of the pipeline.

10. Run the pipeline again by clicking on **Release change**. After a few minutes, you should be able to see the Jenkins step being executed. If everything goes well it should turn green.

Our pipeline is now starting to look very interesting. Here, we have demonstrated the Jenkins integration in its most rudimentary form, but you can easily imagine more realistic scenarios where you would add a step after deploying your code to staging to carry out better validation with better integration, load, and even penetration testing.

The goal of AWS CodePipeline is to help you take your services from source control all the way up to production. As you first start working on a service, you might not have the test coverage needed to continuously deploy it to production so you might opt for one-click production deployment instead. We are going to take advantage of the automation we have built so far in this chapter and build a continuous delivery pipeline for production.

Building a continuous delivery pipeline for production

In order to build our continuous delivery pipeline, we are first going to create a CloudFormation stack for a production environment. We will then add a new deployment group in CodeDeploy, which will provide us with the ability to deploy code to the new CloudFormation stack. Finally, we will upgrade the pipeline to include an approval process to deploy our code to production and the production deployment stage itself.

Creating the new CloudFormation stack for production

Here, we are going to reuse the exact same template as we used for staging. In your Terminal, go to the location you used to generate the node server template and then run the same command as before, but this time with the stack name helloworld-production:

```
$ aws cloudformation create-stack \
    --capabilities CAPABILITY_IAM \
    --stack-name helloworld-production \
    --template-body file://nodeserver.template \
    --parameters ParameterKey=KeyPair,ParameterValue=EffectiveDevOpsAWS
```

We can then run the following command to wait for the stack to be ready:

```
$ aws cloudformation wait stack-create-complete \
    --stack-name helloworld-production
```

You might realize the weakness of our production stack with only one EC2 instance in it. We will address that concern in `Chapter 6`, *Scaling Your Infrastructure,* when we talk about scaling strategies.

Creating a CodeDeploy group to deploy to production

Previously, we created a CodeDeploy application and a first deployment group that allowed us to deploy our code to staging. Using the command-line interface, we are now going to add a new deployment group to deploy our code to our newly created production environment.

One of the parameters needed to add new deployment groups is the `arn` of the policy we created initially. We can easily extract this from the staging deployment group that we created previously. We will store the result in a variable called `arn`:

```
$ arn=$(aws deploy get-deployment-group \
    --application-name helloworld \
    --deployment-group-name staging \
    --query 'deploymentGroupInfo.serviceRoleArn')
```

We can now run the following command to create the new deployment group:

```
$ aws deploy create-deployment-group \
    --application-name helloworld \
    --ec2-tag-filters Key=aws:cloudformation:stack-
    name,Type=KEY_AND_VALUE,Value=helloworld-production \
    --deployment-group-name production \
    --service-role-arn $arn
```

If everything went well, the new deployment group should be created. We can verify this by browsing to the application in the AWS CodeDeploy web page or using the command-line with the following command:

```
$ aws deploy list-deployment-groups \
    --application-name helloworld
{
"applicationName": "helloworld",
"deploymentGroups": [
    "staging",
        "production"
]
}
```

Adding a continuous delivery step to our pipeline

As we saw earlier in this chapter, pipelines are composed of stages. In CodePipeline, stages are characterized by their categories. We have explored three categories so far: source, deploy, and test. In order to add a confirmation step to deploy our service to production, we will use a new category called **approval**.

Approval actions offer a number of configuration options to send notifications when a job is pending approval. To demonstrate this feature, we are going to create a new SNS topic and subscribe to it. As you might remember from Chapter 3, *Treating Your Infrastructure as Code*, SNS is the simple notification service that we used to monitor our infrastructure.

We are going to use the command-line to create a new topic and subscribe to it:

```
$ aws sns create-topic --name production-deploy-approval
{
"TopicArn": "arn:aws:sns:us-east-1:511912822958:production-deploy-
approval"
}
```

Here, we will use an email subscription. SNS also supports a number of other protocols such as SMS, HTTP, and SQS. In order to subscribe, you need to know the Topic ARN, which is in the output of the previous command:

```
$ aws sns subscribe --topic-arn \
    arn:aws:sns:us-east-1:511912822958:production-deploy-approval \
    --protocol email \
    --notification-endpoint yogeshraheja07@gmail.com
{
"SubscriptionArn": "pending confirmation"
}
```

Go to your inbox to confirm the subscription.

We can now add our new stages, starting with the approval stage:

1. Open https://console.aws.amazon.com/codepipeline in your browser.
2. Select the helloworld application.
3. Click on Edit at the top of the pipeline.
4. Click on the + Stage button at the bottom of the pipeline below the Beta stage.
5. Give it the name Approval.
6. Click on **+ Action.**
7. Select **Approval** in the **Action Category** menu.
8. Call the action **Approval.**

9. Select the approval type **Manual approval.**
10. Pick the **SNS topic** we just created. Typing `production deploy` should allow you to find the topic easily thanks to the autocomplete feature of the form.
11. Finally, click on **Add action**. We are now going to add the deployment to production steps below this approval.
12. Click on the **+ Stage** button below the newly created stage Approval.
13. Call this new stage **Production.**
14. Click on **+ Action**.
15. Select the **Deploy** category.
16. Call the action **Production.**
17. Select the **CodeDeploy** provider.
18. Pick `helloworld` as our application name.
19. Select the deployment group **production**.
20. Select the artifact `MyApp`.
21. Click on **Add action**.
22. Complete the creation of our new stages by clicking on **Save pipeline changes** at the top of the pipeline.

We can once again click on **Release change** to test our updated pipeline.

The pipeline will go through the first three stages and then block at the approval stage. If you check your email inbox, you will find a link where you can review the change. Alternatively, you can simply use the web interface and click on the review button in the approval stage:

After carefully reviewing the changes, you can either approve or reject the change. If it is approved, the deployment will continue to the last step of the pipeline and deploy the code to production.

We have now automated our entire release process. Our `helloworld` application may not reflect what a real application might look like, but the pipeline we built around it does. What we built can be used as a blueprint for deploying more complex applications from environment to environment safely.

There is no question that the ability to move fast and release your new features and services to customers allows you to prevent disruptions. The last step of building a continuous deployment pipeline is to remove the manual approval process to release code to production, thereby taking out the last step involving humans in the release process. Over the years, different companies have come up with a couple of strategies to make production deployments a safe process. In the next section, we will look at some solutions that you can implement.

Strategies to practice continuous deployments in production

As always, your first line of defense is to have enough test coverage and sophisticated validation scripts that cover most of the sensitive routes and features in your product. There are some well-known strategies and techniques to make a continuous deployment pipeline safe for production. We will explore three common ones in this section.

Fail fast

The pipeline that we built is fairly fast and robust. Depending on the nature of your service, you may choose to trust the quality of the code produced by your team and always deploy the code straight to production. With sufficient monitoring around your logs and application metrics, you will be able to catch issues minutes after the code is deployed. You can then rely on CodeDeploy and its ability to deploy older releases fast to recover from that situation.

If you take this approach and a problem is detected, simply roll back to a previous version. You may know exactly what's wrong and know that it's easy to fix, but the pressure caused by knowing that there is an ongoing issue impacting users can cause you to make more mistakes, making the situation worse.

Canary deployment

Similarly, you could try to deploy your code straight to production, but only expose part of the traffic to the new code for some time. You can build a system where only a small percentage of the traffic hits the new servers that are running the new code and compare the error rate and performance originating from each release for a short period of time. Usually, 10% of the traffic for 10 minutes is sufficient to collect enough information about the quality of the new build. If, after that time, everything looks good, you can then move 100% of the traffic to the new version of the service.

Bugs such as memory leaks are usually slower to manifest themselves; once the deployment is complete, continue closely monitoring your different systems and key metrics to make sure that no mistakes have been made:

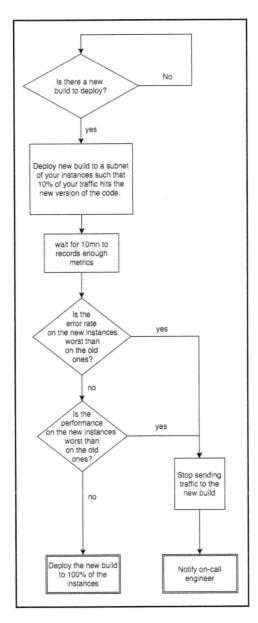

Feature flags

Also known as a dark launch, this last strategy is the hardest one to implement but also the most valuable. It is used by most well-known tech companies. The idea is to have multiple smart switches on each of your features. When you first deploy the code for a new feature, you do so with those switches turned off. You then progressively turn them on for different subsets of users. You might start by only allowing employees of the company to experience the feature. You might then decide to increase the number of people exposed to that feature by adding a set of trusted users. You might then turn the feature on for 20% of your users, then 50%, and so on. As well as allowing you to do a soft launch, this type of features can be used at the product level to carry out A/B testing, maintenance, where you want to turn off a specific feature, or even load testing.

One of the best uses of a dark launch was summarized in a blog post by Facebook. In 2008, Facebook launched their chat functionality. It was a very challenging feature as it was the first service Facebook developed in Erlang. In order to make sure the service would be able to handle the scale at which Facebook operates, they relied on a dark launch strategy. During the months leading up to the official launch, they simulated what the real traffic could look like by releasing the service without the UI. Real users browsers would establish connections to the chat servers and invisibly send and receive messages to simulate the load. When it was time to launch, Facebook didn't push out new code, but simply turned the switch on to make the chat window visible in the UI. More information about this launch can be found at: `https://www.facebook.com/notes/facebook-engineering/facebook-cha t/14218138919/`.

Summary

In this chapter, we have been through one of the most important aspects of the DevOps philosophy—how to change the way in which code is released.

Our first objective was to improve developers' productivity. To that effect, we built a continuous integration pipeline. Taking advantage of Jenkins and GitHub, we created a new workflow where developers commit their code in individual branches and submit pull requests. The branches are automatically tested with Jenkins and a final peer review ensures that the code committed is of high quality.

Thanks to this change, we can guarantee that the code present in the master branch of our project is always good and worth being pushed to staging. To do this, we built a continuous deployment pipeline. Thanks to AWS CodeDeploy and CodePipeline, we were able to easily build a fully functional pipeline. The pipeline has all the desired features an operator could wish for. It automatically picks up changes from developers merging their pull requests, creates a package of the new version of the application, stores the package on S3, and then deploys it to staging. As the new code gets deployed, validation steps ensure that the application isn't misbehaving and, if needed, the application can easily be rolled back.

Once we finished building our continuous deployment pipeline, we extended it to build a continuous delivery capability so that we could carry out production deployment on demand. We also added an extra stage to integrate testing through Jenkins within the pipeline itself. Finally, we discussed different techniques and strategies to have a continuous deployment pipeline for production that will allow us to perform dozens of production deployments a day for any given service.

Since we started to take a more DevOps approach towards managing our architecture and services, we haven't looked at the notions of high availability or load balancing. Even in this chapter, we only created one EC2 instance for our production environment. We will address this in `Chapter 6`, *Scaling Your Infrastructure*. We will look at tools and services to scale our infrastructure and handle massive amounts of traffic.

Questions

1. What is Continuous Integration, Continuous Deployment and Continuous Delivery?
2. What is Jenkins, and how does it help in the SDLC cycle?
3. Describe how to build your first continuous deployment pipeline.

Further reading

Please read the following articles for more information:

- **Jenkins Reference**: `https://jenkins.io/`
- **Mocha Reference**: `https://mochajs.org/`
- **AWS CodeDeploy Reference**: `https://docs.aws.amazon.com/codedeploy/latest/userguide/welcome.html`

- **AWS CodePipeline Reference**: `https://docs.aws.amazon.com/codepipeline/latest/userguide/welcome.html`
- **Jenkins Reference**: `https://jenkins.io/`
- **Mocha Reference**: `https://mochajs.org/`
- **AWS CodeDeploy Reference**: `https://docs.aws.amazon.com/codedeploy/latest/userguide/welcome.html`
- **AWS CodePipeline Reference**: `https://docs.aws.amazon.com/codepipeline/latest/userguide/welcome.html`

6
Scaling Your Infrastructure

In this chapter, we are going to analyze all the technologies used to deploy a complete web application in **Amazon Web Services** (**AWS**). In particular, we will look at how to create a monolithic application in one single machine and decompose the application into multiple pieces in order to achieve scalability and reliability.

Every section of this chapter first has a theoretical part that focuses on the overarching idea as well as the AWS technologies necessary to implement it. It also has a practical example, which makes it possible to put what is explained *into action*.

Starting with the monolith approach to all the software on a single machine, we are going to see when and why it is convenient to break it into multiple pieces to achieve better scalability and reliability. To do this, moving the data (also called the state of the application) outside of the EC2 machine is the first step that can be performed using RDS, the database service in the Amazon cloud universe. Adding a load balancer can add many advantages, from using the **AWS Certification Manager** (**ACM**), to preparing the infrastructure and scaling in and out. Configuring Auto Scaling group / launch configuration is the last step to enabling scalability in and out for our application.

Technical requirements

In this chapter, basic knowledge of the AWS console is assumed. This was covered in the previous chapters as well as in the Terraform configuration already completed in Chapter 4, *Infrastructure as Code with Terraform*.

A public domain is available in the AWS account. This can be useful for testing all aspects of a web application, but this is only an optional step.

Basic knowledge of Linux command-line tool is also required because the example is built with an Amazon Linux 2 operating system. The code files included within the chapter can be found on GitHub at link: `https://github.com/giuseppeborgese/effective_devops_ with_aws__second_edition`.

A monolithic application

The purpose of this chapter is to introduce and lead the reader to transform what is commonly called *monolithic application* into a dynamic and scalable application.

What is a monolithic application?

When people talk about scaling, they often use the term **monolithic application**. But what is this, exactly? Usually, this refers to a software or an infrastructure where everything (including the presentation part, backend, and data part) is combined in a single block, called a monolith. In our case, we are focusing on the infrastructure. To explain the concept of a monolithic application, we are going to build an example application with the following components as shown in the figure below:

- A MySQL database where there is only one table with a single numeric field
- A backend frontend Java/Tomcat listening on the default 8080 port component that reads the database, shows the value, and increments the numeric value
- An Apache 2.2 web server listening on default port 80 that communicates with the Tomcat and shows the web page
- Everything contained in a single EC2 virtual machine with a public IP assigned to it to communicate on the internet

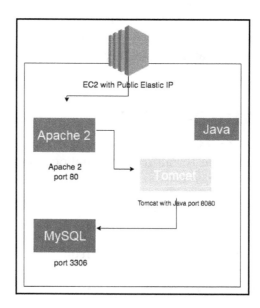

Let's create an example application that allows us to break and scale it:

We learned how to use Terraform in the previous chapters. To build the EC2 machine and the security group showed in the following screenshot, we can use this module called **monolith application**. To use it in your account you need to change the initialization parameters and provide your personal: * vpc-id * subnet * pem key. For the AMI instead you can find the right one following the indication in the following screenshot. This example was tested with North Virginia Amazon region and operative system **Amazon Linux 2**. Find the AMI ID for your region as it is shown in the following screenshot:

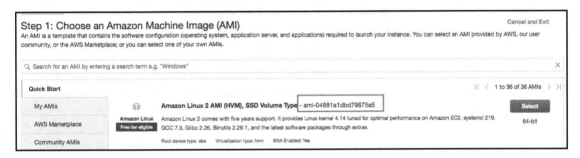

```
module "monolith_application" {
  source =
"github.com/giuseppeborgese/effective_devops_with_aws__second_edition//terr
aform-modules//monolith-playground"
  my_vpc_id = "${var.my_default_vpcid}"
  my_subnet = "subnet-54840730"
  my_ami_id = "ami-04681a1dbd79675a5"
  my_pem_keyname = "effectivedevops"
}
```

The commands that create the modules are always as follows:

```
terraform init -upgrade
terraform plan -out /tmp/tf11.out -target module.monolith_application
terraform apply apply /tmp/tf11.out
```

You should have in the output the following result:

```
Apply complete! Resources: 3 added, 0 changed, 0 destroyed.
Outputs:
monolith_url = http://54.209.174.12/visits
```

If you wait a few minutes to let the application run and install all the software and configurations, you can put the URL in your browser and see the one shown in the following screenshot:

If you receive this result, you should wait a few minutes. If this doesn't resolve the error, something probably went wrong in the installation. The error message is as follows:

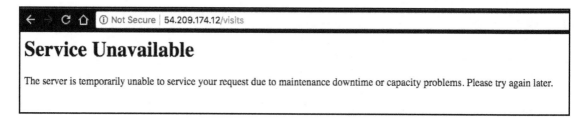

Of course, your public IP will be different from this one. Every time you refresh the page or the URL is opened from any source, the Java application reads the value from the MySQL database, increments the value of 1 unit, and writes in the same database field.

It is worth spending some lines of code to see how everything was installed. This code is found inside the `monolith_application` module shown above:

These lines are the installation script for the `monolith_application`:

```
yum -y install httpd mariadb.x86_64 mariadb-server java

systemctl start mariadb
chkconfig httpd on
chkconfig mariadb on
systemctl restart httpd
```

Now install MySQL (MariaDB)—this is the MySQL type that is available in the Amazon Linux 2 **Long Term Support** (**LTS**) default repository as well as Apache 2 and Java software.

The following is the installation script we started to explain before::

```
echo "<VirtualHost *>" > /etc/httpd/conf.d/tomcat-proxy.conf
echo " ProxyPass /visits http://localhost:8080/visits" >>
/etc/httpd/conf.d/tomcat-proxy.conf
echo " ProxyPassReverse /visits http://localhost:8080/visits" >>
/etc/httpd/conf.d/tomcat-proxy.conf
echo "</VirtualHost>" >> /etc/httpd/conf.d/tomcat-proxy.conf
```

Apache is configured to pass the traffic to the Tomcat on port 8080.

To set up the MySQL in a non-interactive way, I used these lines to create a database, table, and user for the Java application as follows:

```
mysql -u root -e "create database demodb;"
mysql -u root -e "CREATE TABLE visits (id bigint(20) NOT NULL
AUTO_INCREMENT, count bigint(20) NOT NULL, version bigint(20) NOT NULL,
PRIMARY KEY (id)) ENGINE=InnoDB DEFAULT CHARSET=latin1;" demodb
mysql -u root -e "INSERT INTO demodb.visits (count) values (0) ;"
mysql -u root -e "CREATE USER 'monty'@'localhost' IDENTIFIED BY
'some_pass';"
mysql -u root -e "GRANT ALL PRIVILEGES ON *.* TO 'monty'@'localhost' WITH
GRANT OPTION;"
```

The `user_data` script is inside the `module_application` and it is provided as a parameter to the `user_data` field. It downloads an example Java application that saves the result in the database. To simplify the installation, the `.jar` file also contains the Tomcat. This is acceptable for a playground but not for a real usage:

```
runuser -l ec2-user -c 'cd /home/ec2-user ; curl -O
https://raw.githubusercontent.com/giuseppeborgese/effective_devops_with_aws
__second_edition/master/terraform-modules/monolith-playground/demo-0.0.1-
SNAPSHOT.jar'
runuser -l ec2-user -c 'cd /home/ec2-user ; curl -O
https://raw.githubusercontent.com/giuseppeborgese/effective_devops_with_aws
__second_edition/master/terraform-modules/monolith-playground/tomcat.sh'
cd /etc/systemd/system/ ; curl -O
https://raw.githubusercontent.com/giuseppeborgese/effective_devops_with_aws
__second_edition/master/terraform-modules/monolith-
playground/tomcat.service
chmod +x /home/ec2-user/tomcat.sh
systemctl enable tomcat.service
systemctl start tomcat.service
```

To run this Tomcat at startup as a service, the `.jar` and the configuration file are downloaded and the configuration is made automatically.

Anyway, the purpose of the `playground` application is to have something that saves the result of its computation (called the **state**) inside a database. Every time the url is referred to, the state is read from the database, incremented, and saved again.

Associating a DNS name

It is not indispensable for the exercise, but if you have a public domain register, you can create an **A DNS record**.

You need to have a Route 53 public domain registered like mine: `devopstools.link`. If you don't know how to register, go to `https://docs.aws.amazon.com/Route53/latest/DeveloperGuide/domain-register-update.html` and follow the instructions there. Based on my experience, you will need to wait from 30 minutes to two hours and the new domain will then be available. To create a record follow these steps:

1. Go to **Route53 | Hosted zones** and select your zone
2. Click on the **Create Record Set** button
3. Insert a name and choose the `bookapp` name
4. Insert the public IP of your EC2 machine
5. Click on the **Create** button as shown in the following screenshot:

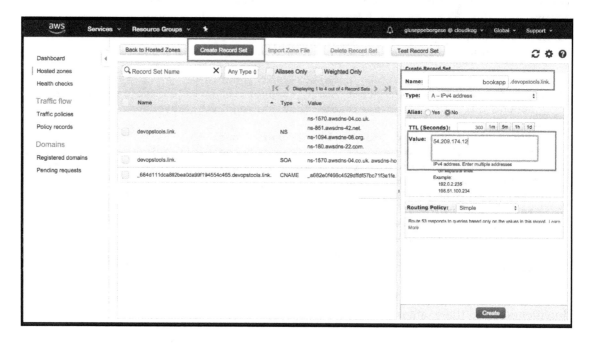

6. Now you can use this record to query the application:

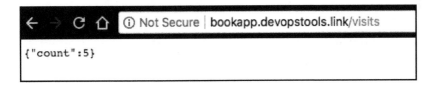

Scaling a monolithic application

We have now created the infrastructure and deployed our application, which is working well. If the application is useful for a large number of people, there is a chance that the number of users, requests, and data will grow quickly. This is exactly what every application owner wants.

It is possible that the EC2 that we chose is not adequate to manage a large amount of data anymore. The following are also possible:

- CPU or RAM are not enough for our three programs: Apache, Tomcat, and MySQL
- The bandwidth of the EC2 virtual machine is not enough for the number of simultaneous requests
- Tomcat or MySQL need to store data for each user and the disk space is not enough anymore
- MySQL and Tomcat need to read a lot of data from a single disk at the same time. Furthermore, there is a context switch for the single disk.

There are two ways to scale an application. These are as follows:

- Scaling it vertically, which means using bigger EC2 instances so that you get an instance with more CPU, more memory, and better network performance
- Scaling it horizontally, which means adding more and more EC2 instances while running the same code and load balancing the traffic across them

Right now we have monolith so we can only scale vertically. In the next section, we are going to break the monolith into different pieces, removing the *state* from the EC2 virtual disk. In this way we can add more machines and also split the load between the balancer and the database using the CDN.

To vertically scale our monolith, you need to follow these steps:

1. Choose a new instance type from the list at `https://aws.amazon.com/ec2/instance-types/`
2. Switch off the instance
3. Change the instance type:

4. Switch on the instance

For the disk space instead, this is a little bit more complex. Here, you must expand the size. This procedure is as follows:

1. Switch off the machine to avoid date incoherency.
2. Detach each volume attached to the instance. However, before doing this, make a note of the device used: `/dev/sda1` or `/dev/xdc` ecc.
3. Make a snapshot for each volume attached to the instance.
4. For each snapshot created in the previous step, create a new volume. You need to specify the desired size of the volume.
5. Attach each new volume to the instance using the same device name as in step 2.
6. Switch the machine on.
7. Log in to the machine and resize the filesystem using the guide for Linux and for Windows. For more details please refer to the *Further reading* section toward the end of the chapter.

Advantages of a monolith

Before breaking and scaling our monolith, it is important to know whether or not it is worth making the effort for our application. Let's examine all the advantages of a single block architecture:

- The first advantage for sure is the infrastructure cost. Here, we are going to break into multiple and scalable pieces but this means that we need to pay for each piece of this architecture. The final cost of the infrastructure will be higher than the single monolith.
- The cost to build a multi-tier scalable architecture will definitely be much more complex than a monolithic one. This means more time to build and more competencies required to do that. The purpose of this book is also to reduce this competency gap.
- An articulated architecture requires many settings. For example, correctly configuring the security group, choosing the right balancer, choosing the right RDS, and configuring S3 or EFS to move out the state from the virtual disk. An exception to this is the SSL configuration. Configuring SSL using the AWS Certificate Manager is much easier than buying and configuring an SSL certificate for Apache.

So, if you do not expect much traffic, your budget is limited. You can consider building a *monolith* infrastructure to host your web application. Of course, keep in mind the scalable limitation and the downtime that you need to accept when you want to scale up or down vertically.

The database

Now that we are aware of the benefits and disadvantages of a monolith application and we have decided to break our app into multiple pieces, it is time to move the first resource outside of the monolith.

As we anticipated in the first section of this chapter, it is necessary to move the data (also called *state*) outside of the EC2 machine. In some web applications, the database is the only data source. However, in others, there are also files uploaded from the users saved directly on the disk or index files if you use an index engine such as **Apache Solr**. For more information on this, refer to `http://lucene.apache.org/solr/` .

When possible, it is always convenient to use a cloud service instead to install a program in a virtual machine. For a database, the RDS service (`https://aws.amazon.com/rds/`) provides a large set of open or closed source (Amazon Aurora, PostgreSQL, MySQL, MariaDB, Oracle, and Microsoft SQL Server), so if you need an **IBM Db2** `https://www.ibm.com/products/db2-database` you can use the RDS service for your database.

To create our MySQL RDS instance, refer to the module is available in the official registry at `https://registry.terraform.io/modules/terraform-aws-modules/rds/aws/1.21.0`:

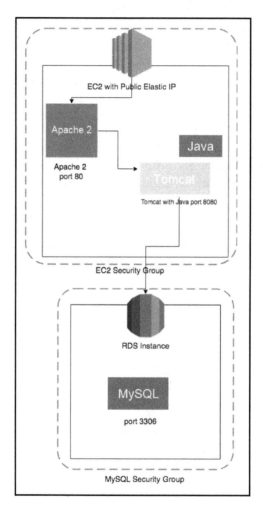

It is important to consider that, when splitting the pieces, it is necessary to correctly configure security groups in order to allow access from the EC2 instance to the RDS instance on port 3306. This also avoids unnecessary access to the database.

For the subnet, it is mandatory to keep a public subnet for the EC2 instance. Instead, it is convenient to choose a private one for the RDS instance. We will explore this topic further in Chapter 8, *Hardening the Security of Your AWS Environment.*

Moving the database to the RDS

To create the MySQL database, we can use a public module that is available in the official repository found here: https://registry.terraform.io/modules/terraform-aws-modules/rds/aws/1.21.0.

In the following code, I will simplify the original example slightly and add a security group as follows. Refer to the main.tf file:

```
resource "aws_security_group" "rds" {
  name = "allow_from_my_vpc"
  description = "Allow from my vpc"
  vpc_id = "${var.my_default_vpcid}"

  ingress {
    from_port = 3306
    to_port = 3306
    protocol = "tcp"
    cidr_blocks = ["172.31.0.0/16"]
  }
}

module "db" {
  source = "terraform-aws-modules/rds/aws"
  identifier = "demodb"
  engine = "mysql"
  engine_version = "5.7.19"
  instance_class = "db.t2.micro"
  allocated_storage = 5
  name = "demodb"
  username = "monty"
  password = "some_pass"
  port = "3306"

  vpc_security_group_ids = ["${aws_security_group.rds.id}"]
  # DB subnet group
  subnet_ids = ["subnet-d056b4ff", "subnet-b541edfe"]
```

```
      maintenance_window = "Mon:00:00-Mon:03:00"
      backup_window = "03:00-06:00"
      # DB parameter group
      family = "mysql5.7"
      # DB option group
      major_engine_version = "5.7"
  }
```

the plan shows 5 these 5 resources to add

```
  + aws_security_group.rds

  + module.db.module.db_instance.aws_db_instance.this

  + module.db.module.db_option_group.aws_db_option_group.this

  + module.db.module.db_parameter_group.aws_db_parameter_group.this

  + module.db.module.db_subnet_group.aws_db_subnet_group.this
```

Plan: 5 to add, 0 to change, 0 to destroy.

Because an RDS needs to work on an option group, a parameter group and a subnet group.

You can see the new instance in the RDS console and click on it to open the properties as follows:

Once the property of the selected instance is opened, note the value of the **Endpoint** field as shown in the following screenshot:

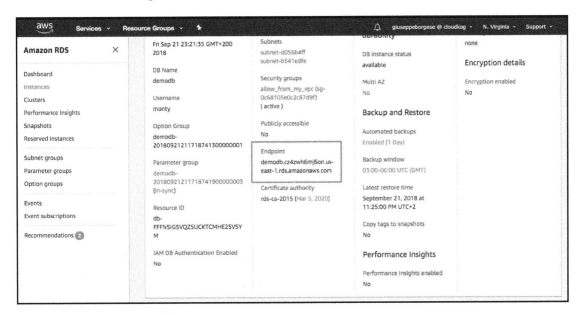

In my case, this is `demodb.cz4zwh6mj6on.us-east-1.rds.amazonaws.com`.

Connect in SSH to the EC2 machine and try the connection to the RDS:

```
[ec2-user@ip-172-31-7-140 ~]$ mysql -u monty -psome_pass -h
demodb.cz4zwh6mj6on.us-east-1.rds.amazonaws.com
Welcome to the MariaDB monitor. Commands end with ; or \g.
Your MySQL connection id is 7
Server version: 5.7.19-log MySQL Community Server (GPL)

Copyright (c) 2000, 2018, Oracle, MariaDB Corporation Ab and others.

Type 'help;' or '\h' for help. Type '\c' to clear the current input
statement.
```

Run the `show databases` command to see if there is the `demodb` schema:

```
MySQL [(none)]> show databases;
+--------------------+
| Database |
+--------------------+
| information_schema |
| demodb |
| innodb |
| mysql |
| performance_schema |
| sys |
+--------------------+
6 rows in set (0.00 sec)
MySQL [(none)]> exit
Bye
[ec2-user@ip-172-31-7-140 ~]$
```

To transfer the database, follow these steps:

1. Close the Java process with the `pkill` java command

2. Dump the local database with the following command:

   ```
   mysqldump -u monty -psome_pass -h localhost demodb >
   demodbdump.sql
   ```

3. We don't need the local database anymore, so stop it with the following command:

   ```
   sudo service mariadb stop
   ```

4. Now restore the dump in the RDS with the following command:

   ```
   mysql -u monty -psome_pass -h demodb.cz4zwh6mj6on.us-
   east-1.rds.amazonaws.com demodb < demodbdump.sql
   ```

5. Check if the content was correctly copied as follows:

```
mysql -u monty -psome_pass -h demodb.cz4zwh6mj6on.us-
east-1.rds.amazonaws.com
Welcome to the MariaDB monitor. Commands end with ; or \g.
Your MySQL connection id is 12
Server version: 5.7.19-log MySQL Community Server (GPL)

Copyright (c) 2000, 2018, Oracle, MariaDB Corporation Ab and
others.

Type 'help;' or '\h' for help. Type '\c' to clear the current input
statement.

MySQL [(none)]> use demodb;
Reading table information for completion of table and column names
You can turn off this feature to get a quicker startup with -A

Database changed
MySQL [demodb]> select * from visits;
+----+-------+---------+
| id | count | version |
+----+-------+---------+
| 1  | 5     | 5       |
+----+-------+---------+
1 row in set (0.00 sec)
```

Now that the dump is correct, you need to replace the connection inside /home/ec2-user/tomcat.sh:

```
sudo nano /home/ec2-user/tomcat.sh
```

Now find the string in the file:

```
db_url=jdbc:mysql://localhost:3306/
```

Replace this with the following line of code:

```
db_url=jdbc:mysql://demodb.cz4zwh6mj6on.us-east-1.rds.amazonaws.com:3306/
```

Leave everything else untouched:

```
pkill java
systemctl start tomcat
```

You should now see that the output and the application are working again.

It is now convenient to remove the local database with the following command:

```
sudo yum remove mariadb-server
```

Choose the RDS type

If you have a MySQL engine like we saw in the previous example, you can choose between the following instance types:

- MySQL Classic
- Aurora MySQL
- A new type of Serverless Aurora MySQL, found here: https://aws.amazon.com/rds/aurora/serverless/

In most cases, MySQL Classic would be ideal. However, if you know that you will have a big amount of data to manage, Aurora MySQL is ideal. This serverless option is for **infrequently-used**, **variable**, and **unpredictable** workloads instead.

Backup

It is important to enable the backup for your RDS instance and choose the backup as Windows. This is important when you expect a low write load on your database because it is true that the backup will be done without downtime but it can also influence the performance. For more information on best practices for Amazon RDS, refer to https://docs.aws.amazon.com/AmazonRDS/latest/UserGuide/CHAP_BestPractices.html.

You can set up a daily backup and keep a maximum of 35 snapshots. Upon restore you can choose one of these 35 snapshots or any moment inside these 35 days using the new point-in-time recovery feature. For more information on this, refer to https://docs.aws.amazon.com/AmazonRDS/latest/UserGuide/USER_PIT.html.

Multi-AZ

The multi-AZ feature available at `https://aws.amazon.com/rds/details/multi-az/` maintains a second copy of your RDS instance, using the **master-slave** technique in another **availability zone** (**AZ**). If there is an issue with the master instance (or in the whole AZ where the master instance is located), the DNS name is automatically switched to the slave instance. Using this feature, two RDS instances will always be up. In addition, the cost will be doubled. For this reason, it is convenient to only use it in production.

In the following diagram, shown is an multi-AZ architecture:

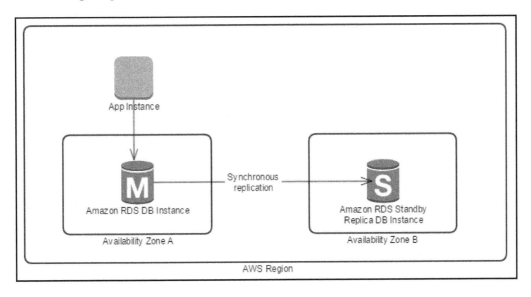

ElastiCache

You can consider inserting a cache for your database in order to reduce the load on your RDS instance. This introduces another piece to your infrastructure and is also necessary for changing the software code in order to make it possible to use the cache instead of the RDS only. Depending on the type of data that you need to save in it, the AWS ElastiCache service available at `https://aws.amazon.com/elasticache/` provides two types: **Redis** and **Memcached**.

Elastic Load Balancer (ELB)

In this section, we are going to replace the Apache with the ELB and also add an SSL certificate as shown in the following diagram:

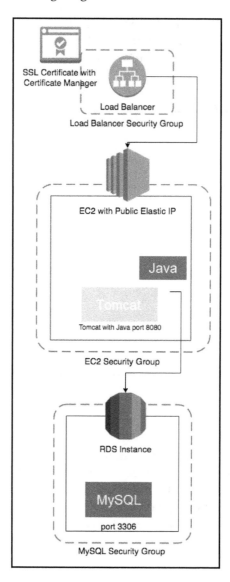

As we did in the previous section for the RDS, it is convenient here to replace a software installed in an EC2 machine with a managed service.

We will benefit from the following features:

- Deploy and reliability on multiple AZs
- A web interface to manage the proxy instead of the Apache configuration files
- A fully manageable service that doesn't need to perform software upgrades
- Scalability to handle requests (pre-warming is requested in some scenarios)
- Ease of storing logs on an S3 bucket

Alternatively, when you use an ELB you need to follow the AWS method and you are not free to customize this as you want. Apache is the Swiss knife of the web server; it has modules that make it possible to do so many different kinds of operations and actions. Using an ELB, it is possible to lose something that may be useful, such as a redirect from HTTP to HTTPS.

Choosing the right ELB

As is well documented on AWS at `https://aws.amazon.com/elasticloadbalancing`, there are 2 versions and 3 types of ELB available:

- Version 1 with **Classic Load Balancer (CLB)**
- Version 2 with **Application Load Balancer (ALB)** and **Network Load Balancer (NLB)**

Each product can be described as follows:

- CLB is the first version of the Elastic Load Balancer and was made available in Spring 2009. For more information on this, refer to `https://aws.amazon.com/blogs/aws/new-aws-load-balancing-automatic-scaling-and-cloud-monitoring-services/`. This is one of the most popular Load Balancer, but it is also the one with the fewest features.
- ALB was made available during summer 2016. For more information, refer to `https://aws.amazon.com/blogs/aws/new-aws-application-load-balancer/`. This extends the CLB version 1 with a lot of features.
- NLB was released in September, 2017. For more information on this, refer to `https://aws.amazon.com/blogs/aws/new-network-load-balancer-effortless-scaling-to-millions-of-requests-per-second/`. This is complementary to the ALB and is more focused on the network level.

If you want a comparison of all the features of each of these three products, you can take a look at the comparison table available at `https://aws.amazon.com/elasticloadbalancing/details/#compare`. However, let's try to summarize these differences as follows:

- You shouldn't create CLB anymore unless you have an EC2 classic network. In this case, you should really consider migrating to the VPC network type as soon as possible. You also need to be familiar with the CLB because it is the most popular product in the AWS Cloud environment.
- If you need to manage HTTP/HTTPS connections - and this applies to most of the web applications - you should use the ALB.
- If you need to manage TCP connections or you need to control the public IP of your balancer instead, the NLB is the right choice. Keep in mind that you cannot use the SSL feature with this type of balancer.

In our example, the right balancer to deploy is the ALB one. This is because we want to use a web application with the HTTP/S protocol and have an SSL certificate in it.

Deploying the balancer

Now that we know what to do, it is time to adapt our application to the balancer according to these steps:

1. Configure the security groups to allow access from the balancer to port `8080` in the EC2 machine. ALB ==> `8080` EC2 (we are referring to the connection from the Application Load Balancer to the EC2 machine). To simplify, we will give access to the whole VPC **Classless Inter-Domain Routing (CIDR)**.
2. Create the ALB, connect to the EC2 machine, and verify that the machine is in Service.
3. Now you can change the DNS record from the public IP of the EC2 machine to the alias of the DNS balancer.
4. Remove the Apache software from the machine; you don't need it anymore.

In every environment, it is convenient to deploy the balancer in more subnets that belong to different AZs. Keep in mind that each zone is like a datacenter and issues can always arise with datacenters. Deployment in multiple zones doesn't increase the cost as it is for RDS instead where the cost is double if you use Multi AZ.

In Chapter 5, *Adding Continuous Integration and Continuous Deployment* we will use Terraform to create ALB. Here, we will perform these changes from the web console in order to understand the details of each step.

Step 1 – open the access for the port 8080 from the whole VPC CIDR

Open the access for the port 8080 from the whole VPC CIDR as follows:

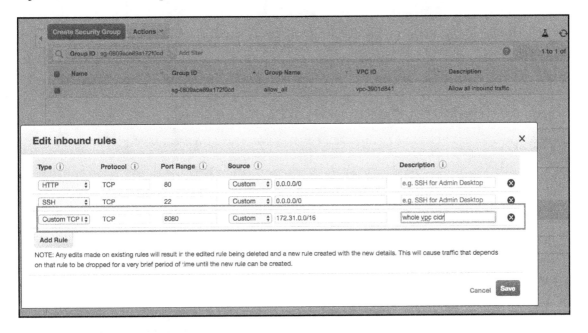

Step 2 – Creating the ALB and associate to the EC2 machine

Create the ALB and associate to the EC2 machine as follows:

Go to **Load Balancers** | **Create Load Balancer** and choose the ALB by clicking the **Create** button on the **Application Load Balancer** section, as shown in the following screenshot:

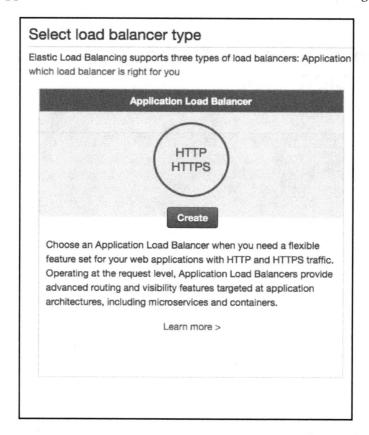

Select the **internet-facing** option from the **Scheme** section. This is important because we want it to be reachable from the world and we also want at least two subnets in two different AZs:

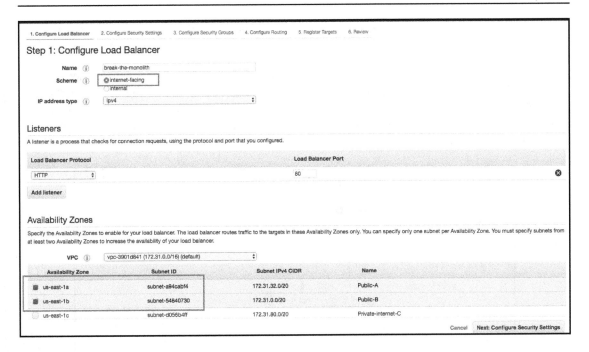

Ignore the following message:

> **Improve your load balancer's security. Your load balancer is not using any secure listener.**

Next, we will add a secure listener.

To do this, click on the **Create a new security group** radio button for this load balancer and open the port 80 for HTTP:

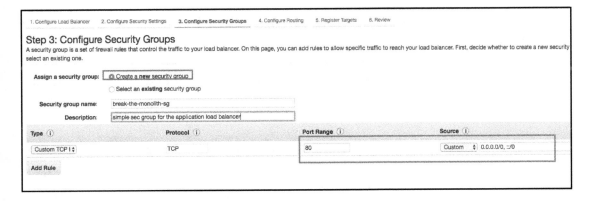

Now create a new target group. In this group, the requests will be rotated and reach the EC2 instance. The port `8080` is the port of the Tomcat software in the EC2 machines.

Our `playground` application has only one URL called `/visits` so we need to insert that one, and this will cause an increment of the counter in the DB every time the health check is performed. In a real environment, you need a health check that performs the control with a read of the DB as opposed to a write as seen in the following example. In this example, it is acceptable to use this method:

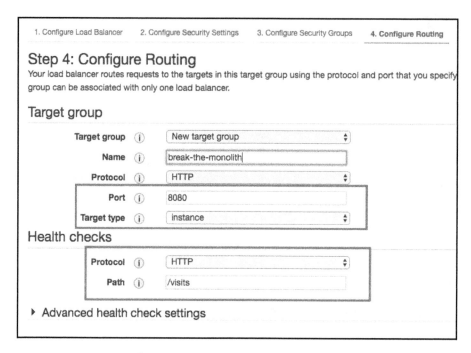

Select the EC2 instance and click on the **Add to registered** button, as shown in the following screenshot:

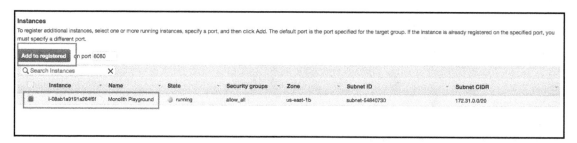

This instance will be added to the **Registered targets** list:

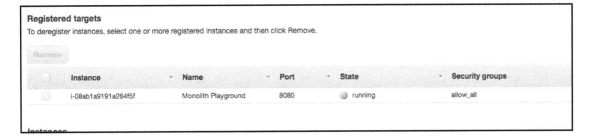

If you check now the target group just created in the **Targets** tab, you can see your instance and the **Status** column. If the status doesn't become **healthy** in half a minute, there is probably an error in the configuration:

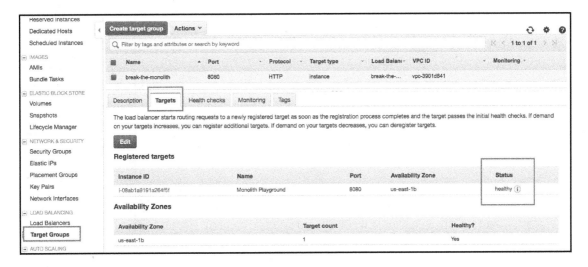

You can now check the load balancer URL as
follows: `http://break-the-monolith-939654549.us-east-1.elb.amazonaws.com/`
`visits`.

 Again, your URL will be different from this one, but at this point, you
should understand how it works.

Step 3 – creating an alias for the ELB

Go to the new Route 53 zone and modify the A record created before with a CNAME alias,
as shown in the following screenshot:

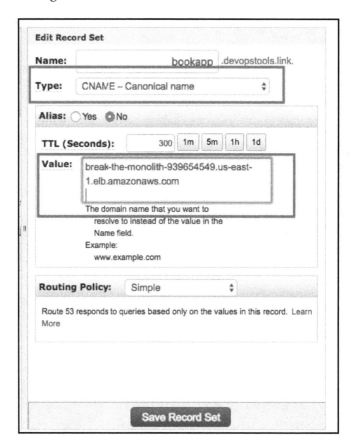

In less than 300 seconds, you should see the change and have the DNS pointing to the new domain.

Step 4 – removing the Apache software from the machine

At this point, we don't need the Apache software in the EC2 machine anymore. To remove it run the following command:

```
sudo yum remove httpd
```

It is also convenient to clean the security group of the EC2 machine by removing the access to port 80:

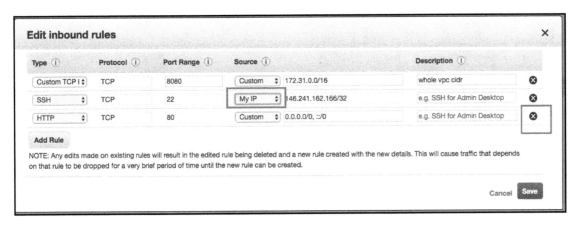

Leave the SSH open to your own IP with the **My IP** source option.

Configuring the SSL certificate

You can configure a single certificate that is valid for one DNS record such as example.devopstools.link or a generic one such as * .devopstools.link which is valid for each subdomain. My advice is to use the * so that you don't need to repeat this certificate procedure every time you have a new resource.

Certificate Manager makes it possible to acquire an SSL certificate for free unless you don't use the private authority. Follow these steps to generate an SSL certificate:

Go to the **AWS Certificate Manager** service and click on the **Provision certificates** section as shown in the following screenshot:

Select the **Request a public certificate** option as shown in the following screenshot:

Now insert the domain name. In my case, this includes the domain name and the domain name with a *:

I decided to use the **DNS validation** option, but the **Email validation** option is also good. In this case, you need to have access to the email address that was used to register the domain:

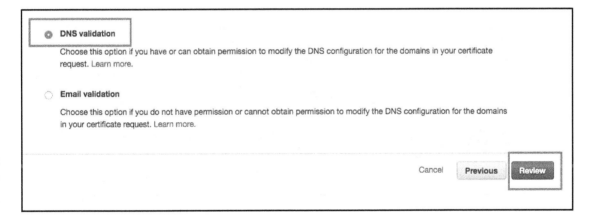

The wizard prompts you to create one DNS record for each domain we inserted at the beginning. In our case, this refers to two domains (`*.devopstools.link` and `devopstools.link`). You can follow the wizard and create it by clicking on the **Create record in Route 53** button, as shown in the following screenshot:

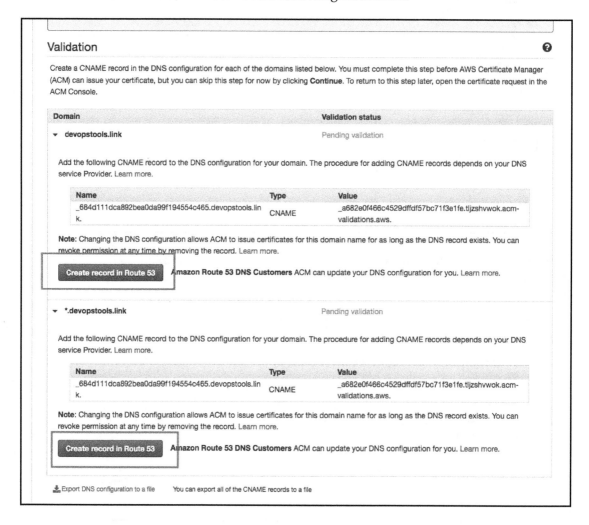

Click on the **Create** button for both DNS records. At this point, the record created will be shown:

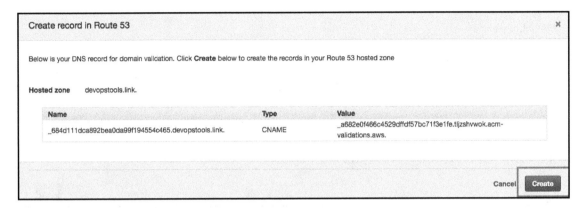

In less than a minute, the status of the new SSL certificate will be **Issued** and will become available for use:

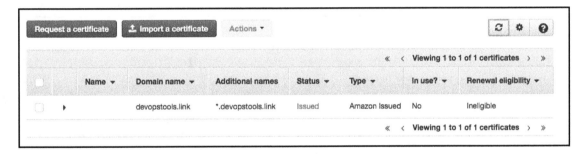

If you have ever created an SSL certificate before, you will know how simple and straightforward this procedure is compared to the classic one. You can now add the new certificate to your balancer and use an SSL listener.

First of all, you need to open the security group of your ALB for the new port 443 as shown in the following screenshot:

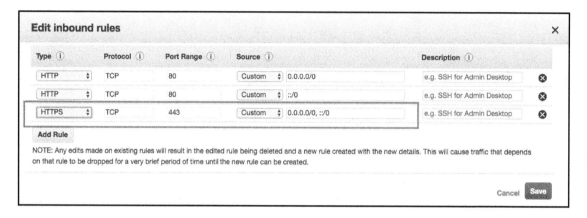

Go to your load balancer, followed by the **Listeners** Tab, and then click on the **Add listener** button as follows:

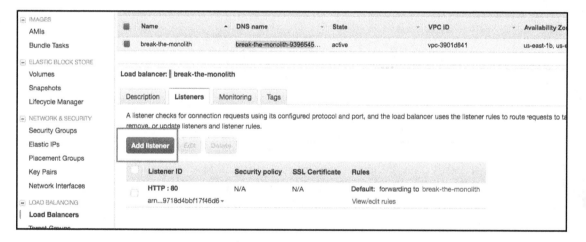

- Select the **HTTPS** protocol and its default port 443
- The rule is to forward to the target already defined at creation time

- Finally, select the certificate created before from the **From ACM (recommended)** drop-down as shown in the following screenshot:

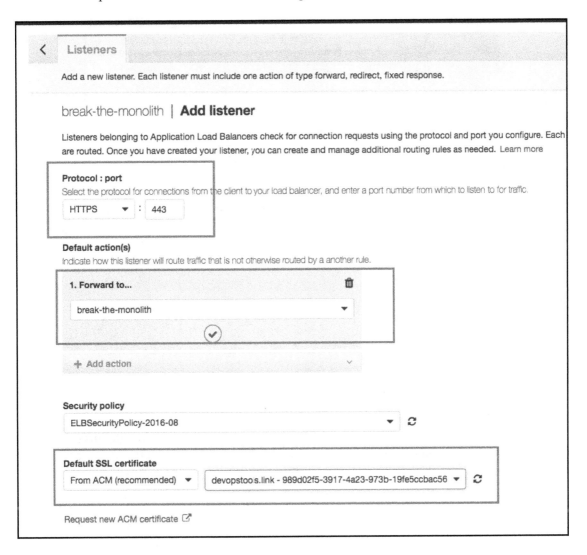

Now you have a secure certificate for your application as shown in the following screenshot:

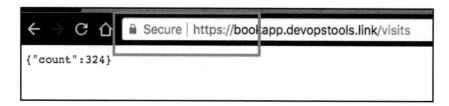

ALB and integration with Auth0

If you want your users are authenticated before gaining access to the content served by your load balancer, then you can integrate the ALB with the Auth0 service available at `https://auth0.com/`. This is a cloud service that is designed to manage users through a different kind of authentication in order to use the words on their home page and provide a universal authentication and authorization platform for web, mobile, and legacy applications.

If you want to try this interesting configuration feature, follow the guidelines at `https://medium.com/@sandrinodm/securing-your-applications-with-aws-alb-built-in-authentication-and-auth0-310ad84c8595`.

Pre-warming a load balancer

A well-known problem in the CLB is that it is necessary to pre-warm in order to manage traffic peak because the system is made to scale up, as you can read in the documentation. We recommend that you increase the load at a rate of no more than 50 percent every five minutes.

The official declaration about this topic is available at `https://aws.amazon.com/articles/best-practices-in-evaluating-elastic-load-balancing/#pre-warming`. This states the following:

> *"Amazon ELB is able to handle the vast majority of use cases for our customers without requiring "pre-warming" (configuring the load balancer to have the appropriate level of capacity based on expected traffic). In certain scenarios, such as when flash traffic is expected, or in the case where a load test cannot be configured to gradually increase traffic, we recommend that you contact us* `https://aws.amazon.com/contact-us/` *to have your load balancer "pre-warmed". We will then configure the load balancer to have the appropriate level of capacity based on the traffic that you expect. We will need to know the start and end dates of your tests or expected flash traffic, the expected request rate per second and the total size of the typical request/response that you will be testing."*

Differences between the ALB and NLB:

- NLB is designed to handle tens of millions of requests per second while maintaining high throughput at ultra-low latency, with no effort on the customer's part. As a result, no pre-warm is needed.
- ALB instead follows the same rules as CLB.
- In short, NLB doesn't require pre-warming. However, CLB and ALB still need it.

Access/error logs

It is a good practice to configure the ELB to store the access/error logs to an S3 bucket:

- **For CLB**: `https://docs.aws.amazon.com/elasticloadbalancing/latest/classic/enable-access-logs.html`
- **For ALB**: `https://docs.aws.amazon.com/elasticloadbalancing/latest/application/load-balancer-access-logs.html`
- **For NLB**: ELBs do not have these kind of logs because it works at network level TPC/IP

The next step

Now that we have the balancer in multi-AZ with an SSL configured as well as a scalable system, the RDS is deployed in multi-AZ. However, the EC2 machine is still in a single AZ so this is consequently a single point of failure which doesn't scale automatically. We need to configure the Auto Scaling feature for the EC2 part, but first of all we need to move the state outside of the machine if it is still there.

Moving the state outside the EC2 machine

If your application has something regarding its state saved on a disk, you need to remove it before applying Auto Scaling. What was previously saved as files in the EC2 machine must be removed and managed by a service. There are two options which are as follows:

- **AWS Elastic File System** (https://aws.amazon.com/efs/): In a few words, this is a network file system that is mounted in your EC2 machine with virtually infinite space where you only pay for the space used by your file.

- **AWS S3** (https://aws.amazon.com/s3/): This was the first AWS service on the market and is an object storage designed to deliver 99.999999999% durability.

In general, the S3 should be your favorite solution, but it is not always applicable because it requires application software change to use it. Consequently, in some cases, you may need an alternative that you can leverage on EFS.

The world is full of software and plugins designed around S3. For example, WordPress saves the files loaded by the users into the disk by default, but with an additional plugin you can save it in AWS S3 and remove the state from the EC2 machine in this way.

Pushing the logs out

Your instance is disposable and can be replaced or destroyed at any time. If you need application-specific logs, you need to use a program to push the logs out to S3 or CloudWatch.

Configure Auto Scaling

The purpose of the couple, **Launch Configurations** and **Auto Scaling Groups** shown below is to ensure scalability and reliability:

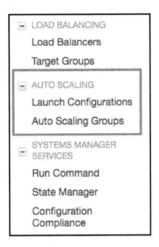

Scalability and reliability are described as follows:

- **Scalability**: if there is an increase of requests/CPU, the system needs to scale up and add instances. In the same way, if the traffic goes down, it is necessary to remove unnecessary resources.
- **Reliability**: if one instance goes down for any reason, the Auto Scaling system automatically replaces it with a new one.

You need to start the instance quickly in order to create an image, so by using the `user_data` option you can also install a software program as we did during the monolith configuration at the beginning of this chapter. However, this results in an additional amount of time in which it is necessary to start a new instance.

When you need to scale up, this is because you need to satisfy an increase in demand and therefore need to do this as soon as possible. For this reason, it is a good idea to create an image with all software and configuration files installed and then insert the parameter or the configuration files that need to be passed at runtime to the `user_data`, if there are any.

Moving our example inside Auto Scaling

Our application is now ready for Auto Scaling. Here, the state is removed from the EC2 and it is only in the RDS database. We tested how reachable it is from the balancer and checked that it can communicate with the database. This is what we are going to create:

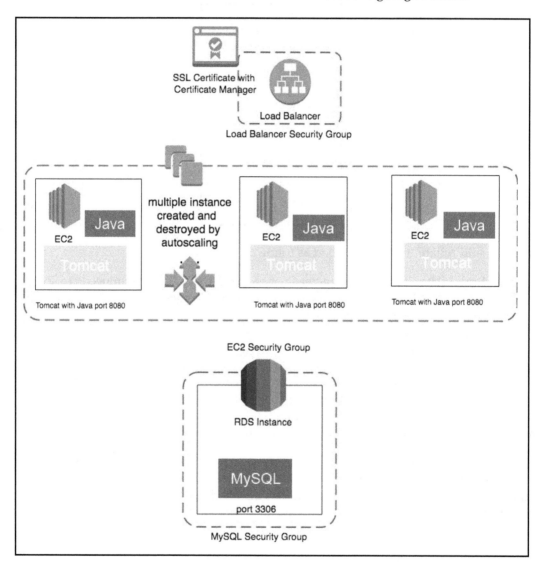

Preparing the image

We need to have an AMI in order to pass as a parameter in the launch configuration. To ensure that you have a good AMI, it is convenient to stop the machine first. When it is stopped, make the AMI. To do this, right-click the **Image** section and then click on the **Create Image** option, as shown in the following screenshot:

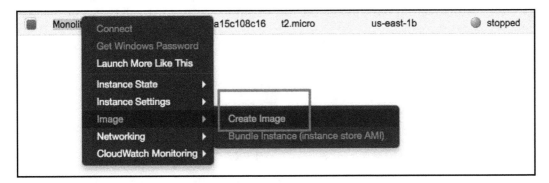

Choose a meaningful name and description before clicking on the **Create Image** button:

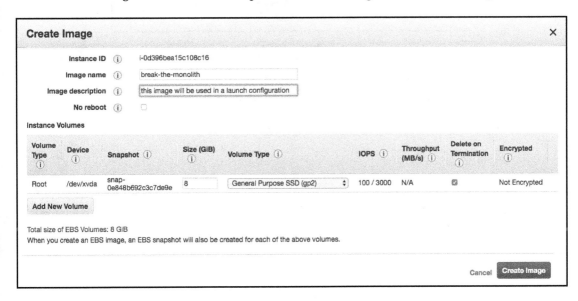

Depending on disk size, the image will be available in a few minutes. In our example with 8 GB of disk, the waiting time will be short.

Using the wizard launch configuration part

To have the Auto Scaling process in place, the following two objects are necessary:

- Launch configuration
- Auto Scaling group

Click on the **Auto Scaling Groups** option and an automatic wizard will then start to create the necessary resources:

Launch configuration is the first step to be followed. Here, select the **My AMIs** option and find the image created in the previous step, as follows:

Now choose the name. Don't modify anything else at this step:

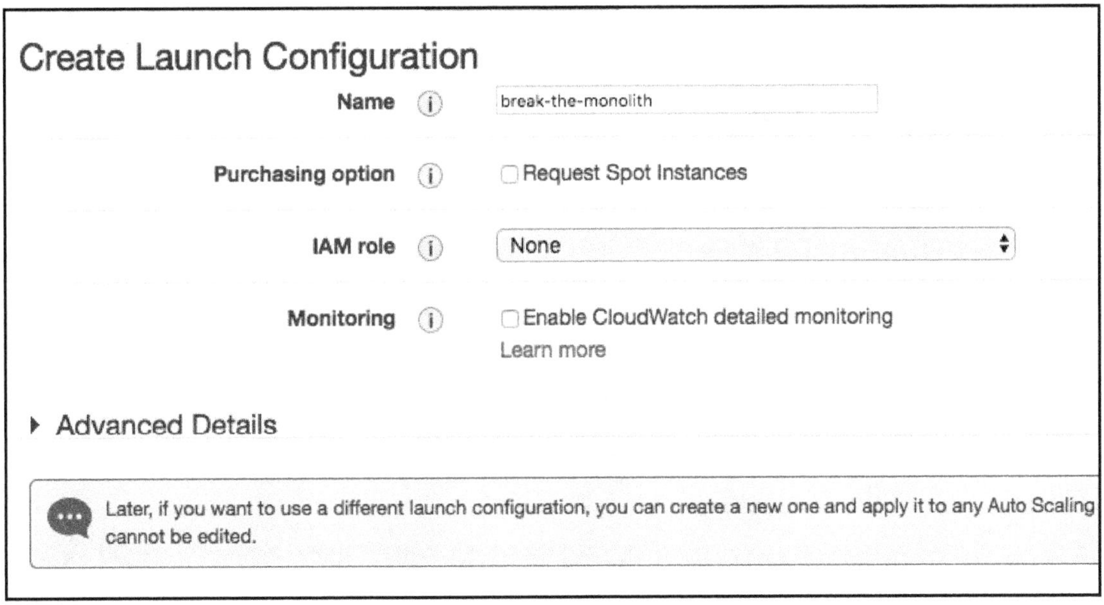

Create Launch Configuration

Name ⓘ	break-the-monolith	
Purchasing option ⓘ	☐ Request Spot Instances	
IAM role ⓘ	None	⬍
Monitoring ⓘ	☐ Enable CloudWatch detailed monitoring Learn more	

▸ **Advanced Details**

💬 Later, if you want to use a different launch configuration, you can create a new one and apply it to any Auto Scaling cannot be edited.

Auto Scaling group part

At this point, the wizard asks us to provide some details for the Auto Scaling part at the beginning of the configuration process. It is okay to start with **1** instance to first check whether or not everything is working well.

VPC and subnets that you specify in the Auto Scaling group can be the same used in the previous example. But keep in mind, for the ALB it is mandatory to choose a public subnet while for the EC2 you can use a private or a public subnet. In Chapter 5, *Adding Continuous Integration and Continuous Deployment* we focus on security, we will explain why it is beneficial to insert the EC2 in private ones.

However, for now, it is okay to use any subnet. The important thing to do is to choose more than one subnets in different AZs:

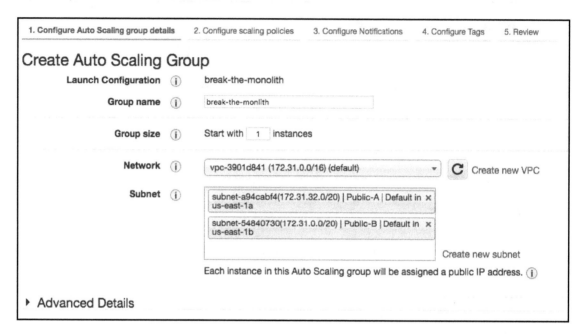

For the security group, choose the one assigned to the EC2 machine in precedence; don't create a new one:

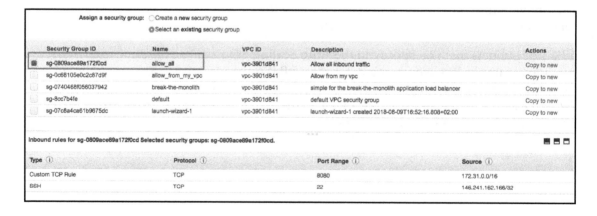

Use a key-pair that you own for a normal EC2. In theory, you don't need to log in to a machine managed by Auto Scaling. You only need a key to log in if there are errors and it is necessary to debug something:

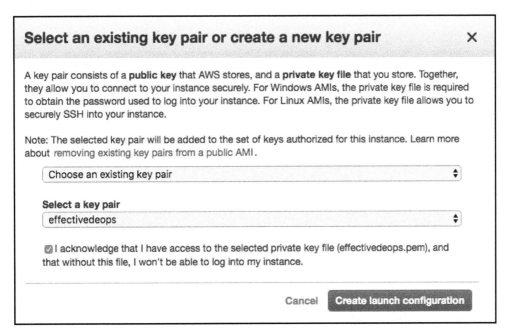

Scaling policies

This is the important part of the wizard, but this is a slightly more difficult stage. Scaling policies decide the condition whether to scale up (adding instances to the Auto Scaling group) and scale down (remove instances from the group). There are many ways to do this; here I have chosen the easiest way, which is through the CPU % usage:

- If the CPU usage is below 70% for more than 5 minutes, add 1 instance
- If the CPU usage is lower than 40% for more than 5 minutes, remove 1 instance

Of course, the chosen metric and values depend on your application, but with this example, you can have an idea:

1. Configure Auto Scaling group details	**2. Configure scaling policies**	3. Configure Notifications	4. Configure Tags	5. Review

Create Auto Scaling Group

You can optionally add scaling policies if you want to adjust the size (number of instances) of your group automatically. A scaling po
CloudWatch alarm that you assign to it. In each policy, you can choose to add or remove a specific number of instances or a percen
triggers, it will execute the policy and adjust the size of your group accordingly. Learn more about scaling policies.

○ **Keep this group at its initial size**

◉ **Use scaling policies to adjust the capacity of this group**

Scale between [1] and [3] instances. These will be the minimum and maximum size of your group.

Scale Group Size

Name:	Scale Group Size
Metric type:	Average CPU Utilization
Target value:	70%
Instances need:	180 seconds to warm up after scaling
Disable scale-in:	☐

Scale the Auto Scaling group using step or simple scaling policies ⓘ

It is necessary to create two alarms (one for each rule) to associate to the Auto Scaling group:

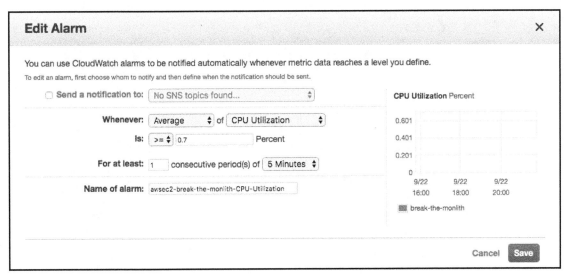

This is the final result:

○ **Keep this group at its initial size**

◉ **Use scaling policies to adjust the capacity of this group**

Scale between [1] and [3] instances. These will be the minimum and maximum size of your group.

Increase Group Size

Name:	[Increase Group Size]
Execute policy when:	awsec2-break-the-monlith-CPU-Utilization Edit Remove
	breaches the alarm threshold: CPUUtilization >= 0.7 for 300 seconds
	for the metric dimensions AutoScalingGroupName = break-the-monlith
Take the action:	[Add ⬍] [1] [instances ⬍]
And then wait:	[180] seconds before allowing another scaling activity

Create a scaling policy with steps ⓘ

Decrease Group Size

Name:	[Decrease Group Size]
Execute policy when:	awsec2-break-the-monlith-High-CPU-Utilization Edit Remove
	breaches the alarm threshold: CPUUtilization >= 0.4 for 300 seconds
	for the metric dimensions AutoScalingGroupName = break-the-monlith
Take the action:	[Remove ⬍] [0] [instances ⬍] when [0.4] <= CPUUtilization < +infinity
	Add step ⓘ

Create a simple scaling policy ⓘ

Scale the Auto Scaling group using a target tracking scaling policy ⓘ

In the next step, add at least the tag name so it is easier to identify the instances created by the Auto Scaling group:

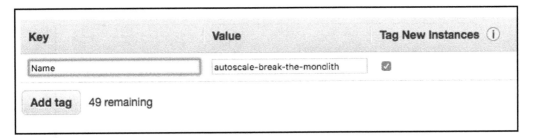

Modifying the Auto Scaling group

If you need to modify the launch configuration, it is mandatory to create a copy and perform the changes at the time of creation because modifications are not allowed. In the Auto Scaling group it is possible to make changes without recreating it.

We need to modify the Auto Scaling group because we want each instance to be registered to the target group associated with our ALB:

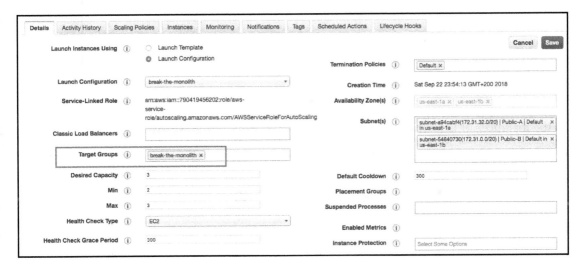

If you want to manually increase the number of instances, it is enough to modify the **Min** size. Keep in mind that the **Desired Capacity** value needs to have a value between **Min** and **Max** sizes:

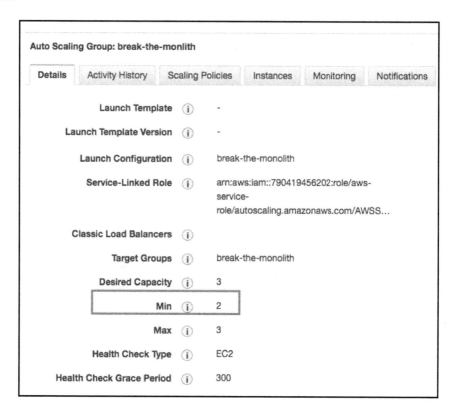

In the instances, it is possible to see the new one created by the Auto Scaling group:

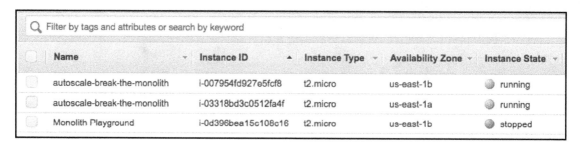

Removing the manually created instance from the balancer

Now that the Auto Scale is working, we can remove the EC2 instance used for configuration from the load balancer and leave the instances that are automatically generated. As you may notice, when you remove the instance it is not immediately removed but goes into a draining state for a short period of time. This occurs in order to avoid poor user experience and manage the possibility that there is still somebody to connect through it:

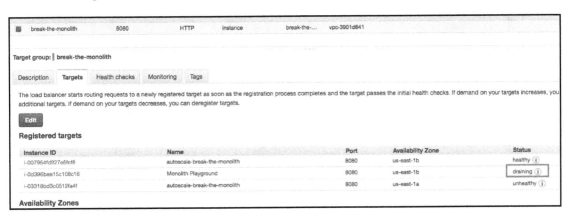

At this point, the configuration of the Auto Scale is complete and you now have an application that satisfies the requirements of scalability and reliability.

Using microservices and serverless

As we tested throughout this whole chapter, breaking the monolith into several pieces produces many advantages but also complicates the whole system.

This concept is amplified when we use a microservices and serverless approach. This is because, if you use these two approaches in the correct way, it is possible to increase scalability, increase reliability, and reduce infrastructure costs. However, you always need to consider that the system will be more complex to build and manage. This leads to increasing the build and operative cost, especially if it is the first time that your team builds and manages a system with this kind of approach.

The following image represents the concept of load and cost with micro services and serverless:

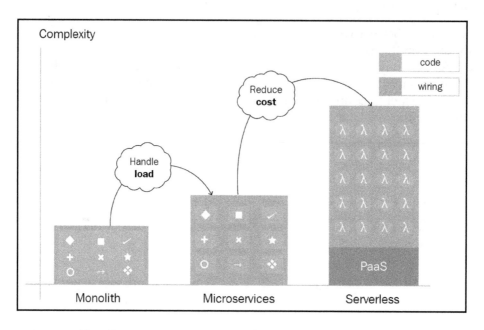

Image source: `https://medium.freecodecamp.org/serverless-is-cheaper-not-simpler-a10c4fc30e49`

Summary

Scaling is a long process that has the potential to be improved. In this chapter, we completed the first step and learned how to break a monolith application into multiple pieces leveraging the AWS services. This approach brings many advantages but also complicates our initial infrastructure, meaning that more time is spent on configuration, bug fixing, and the necessity to study new services. We have explored how powerful and useful all the AWS tools can be for scalability, but it can also sometimes be difficult to use this, especially the first time. Using automation with Terraform modules makes it possible to immediately achieve the result with our knowledge on module creator. In addition, hiding the complexity of a solution cannot help us in understanding what is really happening behind the scenes. This can be necessary during a bug fix. For this reason, some parts of the book, such as the Autos Scale, ALB, and the SSL certification, were completed using the web console and its wizard.

Questions

1. Is it always convenient to break a monolith into a multi-level application?
2. What are the differences between the multi-level approach and the microservices/serverless approach?
3. Can it be difficult moving from software installed in a virtual machine to as a service components?
4. Can a load balancer manage any spike of traffic without any intervention?
5. Can I save money using Certificate Manager instead of a classic SSL certification authority?
6. Why is it important to span the resources in multiple AZs?

Further reading

For more information, read the following articles:

- **Changing the Instance Type**: https://docs.aws.amazon.com/AWSEC2/latest/UserGuide/ec2-instance-resize.html
- **Extending a Linux File System after Resizing the Volume**: https://docs.aws.amazon.com/AWSEC2/latest/UserGuide/recognize-expanded-volume-linux.html
- **Extending a Windows File System after Resizing the Volume**: https://docs.aws.amazon.com/AWSEC2/latest/WindowsGuide/recognize-expanded-volume-windows.html
- **Elastic Load Balancing Documentation**: https://aws.amazon.com/documentation/elastic-load-balancing/
- **Comparison of Elastic Load Balancing Products**: https://aws.amazon.com/elasticloadbalancing/details/#compare
- **Best Practices in Evaluating Elastic Load Balancing**: https://aws.amazon.com/articles/best-practices-in-evaluating-elastic-load-balancing/#pre-warming and https://aws.amazon.com/articles/best-practices-in-evaluating-elastic-load-balancing/
- **Spring Boot, MySQL, JPA, Hibernate Restful CRUD API Tutorial**: https://www.callicoder.com/spring-boot-rest-api-tutorial-with-mysql-jpa-hibernate/ the tutorial used to create our playground.
- **Serverless is cheaper, not simpler**: https://medium.freecodecamp.org/serverless-is-cheaper-not-simpler-a10c4fc30e49

7
Running Containers in AWS

In `Chapter 6`, *Scaling Your Infrastructure*, our architecture changed quite a bit. We explored different ways to scale our applications in AWS, but one of the major technologies that we left out was containers. Containers are at the heart of the **software development life cycle** (**SDLC**) of many major technology companies.

So far, we have used our personal computers to develop our applications. This works well for simple projects, such as our Hello World application. However, when it comes to more complex projects with many dependencies, it's a different story. Have you ever heard of situations in which a certain feature works on a developer's laptop but does not work for the rest of the organization-or-even worse, *does not work in production?* A lot of these issues stem from the differences between environments. When we build our staging and production environments, we rely on CloudFormation, Terraform, and Ansible, to keep those environments consistent. Unfortunately, we can't easily replicate that to our local development environment.

Containers address this issue. With them, we can package an application and include the operating system, the application code, and everything in between. Containers can also help at a later stage, when it's time to break out the monolithic approach.

In this chapter, we will look at **Docker**, the most popular container technology. After a brief explanation of what Docker is and how to use its basic functionalities, we will Dockerize our application. This will help us to understand the value of using Docker as a developer. In this chapter, we will cover the following topics:

- Dockerizing our Hello World application
- Using the EC2 container service
- Updating our CI/CD pipeline to utilize ECS

 This book covers ECS, but also offers further options for using Docker in AWS. You can also take a look at CoreOS Tectonic (`https://tectonic.com/`), Mesosphere DC/OS (`https://mesosphere.com`), or Docker Datacenter (`https://www.docker.com/products/docker-datacenter`).

Technical requirements

The technical requirements for this chapter are as follows:

- Docker
- Dockerfile
- **EC2 Container Registry (ECR)**
- **Elastic Container Service (ECS)**
- **Application Load Balancer (ALB)**
- CodeBuild
- CodePipeline

The GitHub links for the code used in this chapter are as follows:

- `https://github.com/yogeshraheja/helloworld/blob/master/helloworld.js`
- `https://github.com/yogeshraheja/helloworld/blob/master/package.json`
- `https://github.com/yogeshraheja/helloworld/blob/master/Dockerfile`
- `https://github.com/yogeshraheja/EffectiveDevOpsTemplates/blob/master/ecr-repository-cf-template.py`
- `https://github.com/yogeshraheja/EffectiveDevOpsTemplates/blob/master/ecs-cluster-cf-template.py`
- `https://github.com/yogeshraheja/EffectiveDevOpsTemplates/blob/master/helloworld-ecs-alb-cf-template.py`

- https://github.com/yogeshraheja/EffectiveDevOpsTemplates/blob/master/h
elloworld-ecs-service-cf-template.py

- https://github.com/yogeshraheja/EffectiveDevOpsTemplates/blob/master/h
elloworld-codebuild-cf-template.py

- https://raw.githubusercontent.com/yogeshraheja/EffectiveDevOpsTemplate
s/master/helloworld-ecs-service-cf-template.py

- https://github.com/yogeshraheja/EffectiveDevOpsTemplates/blob/master/h
elloworld-codepipeline-cf-template.py

Dockerizing our Hello World application

Docker, and containers in general, are very powerful tools, worth exploring. By combining resource isolation features, including **union capable filesystem** (**UCF**), Docker allows for the creation of packages called **containers**, which include everything that is needed to run an application. Containers, like virtual machines, are self-contained, but they virtualize the OS itself, instead of virtualizing the hardware. In practice, this makes a huge difference. As you have probably noticed by now, starting a virtual machine, such as an EC2 instance, takes time. This comes from the fact that in order to start a virtual machine, the hypervisor (that's the name of the technology that creates and runs virtual machines) has to simulate all of the motions involved in starting a physical server, loading an operating system, and going through the different run-levels. In addition, virtual machines have a much larger footprint on the disk and in the memory. With Docker, the added layer is hardly noticeable, and the size of the containers can stay very small. In order to better illustrate this, we will first install Docker and explore its basic usage a bit.

Getting started with Docker

Before we start to use Docker, it might be useful to better understand Docker's concept and architecture. First, we will discuss Docker's fundamental changes with regards to the SDLC. Following that introduction, we will install Docker on our computers and look at some of the most common commands needed to use Docker.

Docker fundamentals

The best way to understand how Docker works is to compare how using Docker differs from what we've done so far:

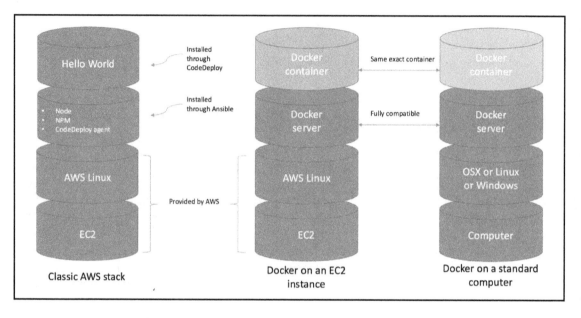

The preceding diagram can be explained as follows:

- The first stack on the left represents what we did so far. Using the EC2 service, we picked an AMI providing AWS Linux, and, with the help of the user data field, we installed Ansible to configure our system. When Ansible kicks in, it installs and configures the system, so that later, CodeDeploy can deploy and run our application.
- The middle stack represents what it means to use Docker on top of EC2. The process starts the same way with an AMI running AWS Linux. However, this time, instead of relying on Ansible and CodeDeploy, we will simply install the Docker server application. After that, we will deploy Docker containers, which will have everything that was previously provided by Ansible and CodeDeploy.
- Finally, the big win of that architecture is what we see on the last stack on the right. No matter what the underlying technology is, as long as we can run a Docker server, we can run the exact same container. This means that we can easily test what we will deploy on EC2. Similarly, if an issue happens in a container running on an EC2 instance, we can pull the exact same container and run it locally to possibly troubleshoot the issue.

In order to make that happen, Docker relies on a couple of key concepts, as shown in the following diagram:

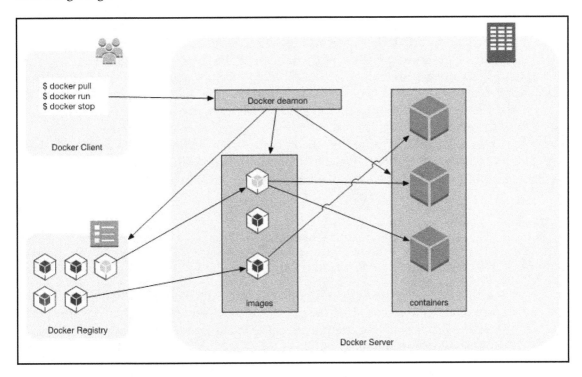

At its core, Docker runs a daemon that loads images (templates describing the stack of the application, including the operating system, application code, and everything in between) and runs them in self-contained directories called containers. When working in Docker, as a developer, your work mostly consists of building new images by layering new commands on top of pre-existing images. Images are stored in external registries. Those registries can be public or private. Finally, all the interaction is done through a RESTful API, usually using the command-line interface.

Docker in action

To see Docker in action, we will start by installing it on our computer. The installation of Docker is very straightforward; you can follow the instructions found at `http://dockr.ly/2iVx6yG` to install and start Docker on Mac, Linux, and Windows. Docker provides two offerings: Docker **Community Edition** (CE) and Docker **Enterprise Edition** (EE). Throughout this book, we are going to focus on open source tools, as well as using Docker CE, which is free of cost. Again, we will be demonstrating the following examples on a Linux based Centos 7.x distribution. If you are also following the same operating system then follow the instructions available at `https://docs.docker.com/install/linux/docker-ce/centos/` to set up Docker locally on your system. When you are done with the installation of Docker CE, verify the installed Docker version using the `docker` utility. At the time of writing this book, `18.06` is the latest version of Docker, although you might see a newer version on your system now:

```
$ docker -version
Docker version 18.06.1-ce, build e68fc7a
```

Once Docker is up and running, we can start using it as follows:

1. The first thing that we will do is pull an image from a registry. By default, Docker points to Docker Hub (`https://hub.docker.com`), which is the official Docker registry from the company Docker Inc. In order to pull an image, we will run the following command:

   ```
   $ docker pull alpine
   ```

   We will use the `latest` default tag, as follows:

   ```
   Using default tag: latest
   latest: Pulling from library/alpine
   8e3ba11ec2a2: Pull complete
   Digest:
   sha256:7043076348bf5040220df6ad703798fd8593a0918d06d3ce30c6c93b
   e117e430
   Status: Downloaded newer image for alpine:latest
   ```

2. In a matter of seconds, Docker will download the image called `alpine` from the registry, which is a minimal Docker image based on Alpine Linux with a complete package index. This is only `4.41 MB` in size:

   ```
   $ docker images
   REPOSITORY    TAG      IMAGE ID      CREATED        SIZE
   alpine        latest   11cd0b38bc3c  2 months ago   4.41 MB
   ```

When working with Docker, the size of a container matters. Consequently, working with smaller base images, such as Alpine Linux, is highly recommended.

3. We can now run our container. In order to do this, we will start with the following simple command:

```
$ docker run alpine echo "Hello World" Hello World
```

4. On the surface, not a lot seems to have happened here, and we were left with the same output as we had when running echo `Hello World` without Docker. What really happened behind the scenes is a lot more interesting; Docker loaded the `alpine` Linux image that we previously pulled, and used the Alpine operating system `echo` command to print `Hello World`. Finally, because the `echo` command completed, the container was terminated.

Containers can also be used in a more interactive way, as follows:

- We can, for example, start a shell and interact with it by using the following command:

```
$ docker run -it alpine /bin/sh
```

The `-i` option means interactive; this allows us to type commands in our container while the `-t` option allocates a pseudo TTY to see what we are typing as well as the output of our commands.

- Containers can also be run in the background by using the `-d` option, which will detach our container from the Terminal:

```
$ docker run -d alpine sleep 1000
c274537aec04d08c3033f45ab723ba90bcb40240d265851b28f39122199b060
0
```

This command returns a 64-bit long ID of the container running the `alpine` image and the sleep `1000` command.

- We can keep track of the different running containers running by using the following command:

```
$ docker ps
```

The output of running the preceding command is as follows:

```
[root@yogeshraheja ~]# docker ps
CONTAINER ID        IMAGE         COMMAND          CREATED            STATUS            PORTS          NAMES
c274537aec04        alpine        "sleep 1000"     About a minute ago Up About a minute                friendly_dijkstra
[root@yogeshraheja ~]# []
```

- Running containers can be stopped using the stop option followed by the container name or ID (adapt the ID and name based on the output of your docker ps command):

  ```
  $ docker stop c274537aec04 c274537aec04
  ```

  You can also use the following command:

  ```
  $ docker stop friendly_dijkstra friendly_dijkstra
  ```

- Stopped containers can be started again with the start option, as follows:

  ```
  $ docker start friendly_dijkstra friendly_dijkstra
  ```

- Finally, containers can be removed by using the the rm command, but always stop the container before removing them:

  ```
  $ docker stop <ID/NAME>
  $ docker rm <ID/NAME>
  ```

The output of the preceding command is as follows:

```
[root@yogeshraheja ~]# docker stop c274537aec04
c274537aec04
[root@yogeshraheja ~]# docker rm c274537aec04
c274537aec04
[root@yogeshraheja ~]# docker ps
CONTAINER ID        IMAGE         COMMAND          CREATED            STATUS            PORTS          NAMES
[root@yogeshraheja ~]# []
```

This brief overview should provide us with the knowledge we need when reading this chapter. We will discover a few more commands along the way, but for a complete list of options, you can use the `docker help` command or consult the Docker CLI documentation at `http://dockr.ly/2jEF8hj`. Running simple commands through containers is sometimes useful but, as we know, the real strength of Docker is its ability to handle any code, including our web application. In order to make that happen, we will use another key concept of Docker: a Dockerfile.

Creating our Dockerfile

Dockerfiles are text files that are usually collocated with applications that instruct Docker on how to build a new Docker image. Through the creation of those files, you have the ability to tell Docker which Docker image to start from, what to copy on the container filesystem, what network port to expose, and so on. You can find the full documentation of the Dockerfile at `http://dockr.ly/2jmoZMw`. We are going to create a Dockerfile for our Hello World application, at the root of the `helloworld` project that we created in our GitHub repository, using the following commands:

```
$ cd helloworld
$ touch Dockerfile
```

The first instruction of a Dockerfile is always a `FROM` instruction. This tells Docker which Docker image to start from. We could use the Alpine image, as we did, but we can also save some time by using an image that has more than just an operating system. Through Docker Hub, the official Docker registry, Docker provides a number of curated sets of Docker repositories called **official**. We know that in order to run our application, we need Node.js and `npm`. We can use the Docker CLI to look for an official `node` image. To do that, we will use the `docker search` command and filter only on official images:

```
$ docker search --filter=is-official=true node
NAME    DESCRIPTION                                     STARS   OFFICIAL
        AUTOMATED
node    Node.js is a JavaScript-based platform for s... 6123    [OK]
```

Alternatively, we can also search for this using our browser. As a result, we would end up with that same image, `https://hub.docker.com/_/node/`. As we can see, the following screenshot comes in a variety of versions:

Supported tags and respective `Dockerfile` links

- `8.11.4-jessie`, `8.11-jessie`, `8-jessie`, `carbon-jessie`, `8.11.4`, `8.11`, `8`, `carbon` (*8/jessie/Dockerfile*)
- `8.11.4-alpine`, `8.11-alpine`, `8-alpine`, `carbon-alpine` (*8/alpine/Dockerfile*)
- `8.11.4-onbuild`, `8.11-onbuild`, `8-onbuild`, `carbon-onbuild` (*8/onbuild/Dockerfile*)
- `8.11.4-slim`, `8.11-slim`, `8-slim`, `carbon-slim` (*8/slim/Dockerfile*)
- `8.11.4-stretch`, `8.11-stretch`, `8-stretch`, `carbon-stretch` (*8/stretch/Dockerfile*)
- `6.14.4-jessie`, `6.14-jessie`, `6-jessie`, `boron-jessie`, `6.14.4`, `6.14`, `6`, `boron` (*6/jessie/Dockerfile*)
- `6.14.4-alpine`, `6.14-alpine`, `6-alpine`, `boron-alpine` (*6/alpine/Dockerfile*)
- `6.14.4-onbuild`, `6.14-onbuild`, `6-onbuild`, `boron-onbuild` (*6/onbuild/Dockerfile*)
- `6.14.4-slim`, `6.14-slim`, `6-slim`, `boron-slim` (*6/slim/Dockerfile*)
- `6.14.4-stretch`, `6.14-stretch`, `6-stretch`, `boron-stretch` (*6/stretch/Dockerfile*)
- `10.9.0-jessie`, `10.9-jessie`, `10-jessie`, `jessie`, `10.9.0`, `10.9`, `10`, `latest` (*10/jessie/Dockerfile*)
- `10.9.0-alpine`, `10.9-alpine`, `10-alpine`, `alpine` (*10/alpine/Dockerfile*)
- `10.9.0-slim`, `10.9-slim`, `10-slim`, `slim` (*10/slim/Dockerfile*)
- `10.9.0-stretch`, `10.9-stretch`, `10-stretch`, `stretch` (*10/stretch/Dockerfile*)
- `chakracore-8.11.1`, `chakracore-8.11`, `chakracore-8` (*chakracore/8/Dockerfile*)
- `chakracore-10.6.0`, `chakracore-10.6`, `chakracore-10`, `chakracore` (*chakracore/10/Dockerfile*)

Docker images are always made up of a name and a tag, using the syntax `name:tag`. If the tag is omitted, Docker will default to `latest`. From the preceding `docker pull` command, we can see how the output says `Using default tag: latest`. When creating a Dockerfile, it is best practice to use an explicit tag that doesn't change over time (unlike the `latest` tag).

If you are trying to migrate an application currently running on AWS Linux and make a certain number of assumptions based on that OS, you may want to look into using the official AWS Docker image. You can read more about this at `http://amzn.to/2jnmklF`.

On the first line of our file, we will add the following:

```
FROM node:carbon
```

This will tell Docker that we want to use that specific version of the node image. This means that we won't have to install node or npm. Since we have the OS and runtime binaries needed by our application, we can start looking into adding our application to this image. First, we will want to create a directory on top of the node:carbon image's filesystem, to hold our code. We can do that using the RUN instruction, as follows:

```
RUN mkdir -p /usr/local/helloworld/
```

We now want to copy our application files onto the image. We will use the COPY directive to do that:

```
COPY helloworld.js package.json /usr/local/helloworld/
```

Make sure that you copy the helloworld.js and package.json files inside the /helloworld project directory where you are locally developing Dockerfile. The files are placed at https://github.com/ yogeshraheja/helloworld/blob/master/helloworld.js and https:// github.com/yogeshraheja/helloworld/blob/master/package.json.

We will now use the WORKDIR instruction to set our new working directory to be that helloworld directory:

```
WORKDIR /usr/local/helloworld/
```

We can now run the npm install command to download and install our dependencies. Because we won't use that container to test our code, we can just install the npm packages needed for production, as follows:

```
RUN npm install --production
```

Our application uses port 3000. We need to make this port accessible to our host. In order to do that, we will use the EXPOSE instruction:

```
EXPOSE 3000
```

Finally, we can start our application. For that, we will use the ENTRYPOINT instruction:

```
ENTRYPOINT [ "node", "helloworld.js" ]
```

We can now save the file. It should look like the template at `https://github.com/ yogeshraheja/helloworld/blob/master/Dockerfile`. We can now build our new image.

Back in the Terminal, we will again use the `docker` command, but this time with the `build` argument. We will also use the `-t` option to provide the name `helloworld` to our image, followed by a (`.`) dot that indicates the location of our Dockerfile:

```
$ docker build -t helloworld .
Sending build context to Docker daemon 4.608kB
Step 1/7 : FROM node:carbon
carbon: Pulling from library/node
f189db1b88b3: Pull complete
3d06cf2f1b5e: Pull complete
687ebdda822c: Pull complete
99119ca3f34e: Pull complete
e771d6006054: Pull complete
b0cc28d0be2c: Pull complete
9bbe77ca0944: Pull complete
75f7d70e2d07: Pull complete
Digest:
sha256:3422df4f7532b26b55275ad7b6dc17ec35f77192b04ce22e62e43541f3d28eb3
Status: Downloaded newer image for node:carbon
 ---> 8198006b2b57
Step 2/7 : RUN mkdir -p /usr/local/helloworld/
 ---> Running in 2c727397cb3e
Removing intermediate container 2c727397cb3e
 ---> dfce290bb326
Step 3/7 : COPY helloworld.js package.json /usr/local/helloworld/
 ---> ad79109b5462
Step 4/7 : WORKDIR /usr/local/helloworld/
 ---> Running in e712a394acd7
Removing intermediate container e712a394acd7
 ---> b80e558dff23
Step 5/7 : RUN npm install --production
 ---> Running in 53c81e3c707a
npm notice created a lockfile as package-lock.json. You should commit this
file.
npm WARN helloworld@1.0.0 No description

up to date in 0.089s
Removing intermediate container 53c81e3c707a
 ---> 66c0acc080f2
Step 6/7 : EXPOSE 3000
 ---> Running in 8ceba9409a63
Removing intermediate container 8ceba9409a63
 ---> 1902103f865c
Step 7/7 : ENTRYPOINT [ "node", "helloworld.js" ]
```

```
   ---> Running in f73783248c5f
Removing intermediate container f73783248c5f
   ---> 4a6cb81d088d
Successfully built 4a6cb81d088d
Successfully tagged helloworld:latest
```

As you can see, each command produces a new intermediary container with the changes triggered by that step.

We can now run our newly created image to create a container with the following command:

```
$ docker run -p 3000:3000 -d helloworld
e47e4130e545e1b2d5eb2b8abb3a228dada2b194230f96f462a5612af521ddc5
```

Here, we are adding the-p option to our command to map the exposed port of our container to a port on our host. There are a few ways to validate that our container is working correctly. We can start by looking at the logs produced by our container (replace the container ID with the output of the previous command):

```
$ docker logs
e47e4130e545e1b2d5eb2b8abb3a228dada2b194230f96f462a5612af521ddc5
Server running
```

We can also use the docker ps command to see the status of our container:

```
$ docker ps
```

The output of the preceding command is as follows:

And, of course, we can simply test the application with the curl command:

```
$ curl localhost:3000
Hello World
```

Also, if your host has a public IP then you can even verify the outputs on the browser with `<ip:exposedport>`, which in my case is `54.205.200.149:3000`:

Finally, kill the container using the `docker kill` command and container ID:

```
$ docker kill e47e4130e545
e47e4130e545
```

Since our image is working correctly, we can commit the code to GitHub:

```
$ git add Dockerfile
$ git commit -m "Adding Dockerfile"
$ git push
```

In addition, you can now create an account (for free) on Docker Hub and upload that new image. If you want to give it a try, you can follow the instructions at `http://dockr.ly/2ki6DQV`.

Having the ability to easily share containers makes a big difference when collaborating on projects. Instead of sharing code and asking people to compile or build packages, you can actually share a Docker image. For instance, this can be done by running the following:

```
docker pull yogeshraheja/helloworld
```

The output of running the preceding command is as follows:

```
[root@yogeshraheja helloworld]# docker pull yogeshraheja/helloworld
Using default tag: latest
latest: Pulling from yogeshraheja/helloworld
Digest: sha256:95906ec13adf9894e4611cd37c8a06569964af0adbb035fcafa6020994675161
Status: Downloaded newer image for yogeshraheja/helloworld:latest
[root@yogeshraheja helloworld]#
```

You can experience the Hello World application, the exact way I see it, no matter what your underlying architecture is. This new way of running applications makes Docker a very strong solution for sharing work or collaborating on projects. Docker's strengths do not end with work collaboration, however. As we are about to see, using containers in production is also a very interesting option. In order to easily implement such solutions, AWS created the EC2 container service. We are going to use it to deploy our newly created `helloworld` image.

Using the EC2 container service

We just went over creating a Docker image for our application. Here, we saw how easy and fast it is to start a container using Docker. This is a very transformative experience compared to using only virtual machine technologies such as EC2. One possibility that we haven't explicitly mentioned so far is that you can start multiple containers with the same image. We can, for example, start our `helloworld` container five times, binding five different ports using the following command (adapt the ID based on the image ID you built. If needed, run Docker images to find its ID):

```
$ for p in {3001..3005}; do docker run -d -p ${p}:3000 4a6cb81d088d; done
```

We can validate that everything is working using the `ps` and `curl` commands:

```
$ docker ps
$ curl localhost:3005
```

The output of running the preceding command is as follows:

```
[root@yogeshraheja helloworld]# for p in {3001..3005}; do docker run -d -p ${p}:3000 4a6cb81d088d; done
90094af21de987618f11f347321fbc3225003736f926d61f0789afc28a0f8214
ff6758efd820890c07fa8f3c961fd0587f6050f78b66766319936cdbe6529616
11f15cfbc88d705d35cc77448d1728b6336ec3ca576b04a4efac8332ffb0db6a
ec27b272835b904c5ccbab3ebc8d063be6be4e63e926b457bda11832b9e1ec7c
cbaca3bb4f18a4510293a72d25c91a30471c095cb88b946217c56d96abc6a065
[root@yogeshraheja helloworld]# docker ps
CONTAINER ID    IMAGE          COMMAND              CREATED         STATUS         PORTS                     NAMES
cbaca3bb4f18    4a6cb81d088d   "node helloworld.js"  30 seconds ago  Up 29 seconds  0.0.0.0:3005->3000/tcp    suspicious_neumann
ec27b272835b    4a6cb81d088d   "node helloworld.js"  30 seconds ago  Up 29 seconds  0.0.0.0:3004->3000/tcp    musing_hamilton
11f15cfbc88d    4a6cb81d088d   "node helloworld.js"  31 seconds ago  Up 30 seconds  0.0.0.0:3003->3000/tcp    wonderful_spence
ff6758efd820    4a6cb81d088d   "node helloworld.js"  31 seconds ago  Up 31 seconds  0.0.0.0:3002->3000/tcp    tender_fermi
90094af21de9    4a6cb81d088d   "node helloworld.js"  32 seconds ago  Up 31 seconds  0.0.0.0:3001->3000/tcp    keen_elbakyan
[root@yogeshraheja helloworld]# curl localhost:3005
Hello World
[root@yogeshraheja helloworld]# curl localhost:3004
Hello World
[root@yogeshraheja helloworld]# curl localhost:3003
Hello World
[root@yogeshraheja helloworld]# curl localhost:3002
Hello World
[root@yogeshraheja helloworld]# curl localhost:3001
Hello World
[root@yogeshraheja helloworld]# []
```

Cleaning up containers:

We can clean up everything by stopping and removing all containers with these two handy one-line commands:

- `$ docker stop $(docker ps -a -q)`
- `$ docker system prune`

The output of running the preceding commands is as follows:

```
[root@yogeshraheja helloworld]# docker stop $(docker ps -a -q)
cbaca3bb4f18
ec27b272835b
11f15cfbc88d
ff6758efd820
90094af21de9
e47e4130e545
0829a984024f
bd5003395c51
874eb1968d49
[root@yogeshraheja helloworld]# docker system prune
WARNING! This will remove:
        - all stopped containers
        - all networks not used by at least one container
        - all dangling images
        - all build cache
Are you sure you want to continue? [y/N] y
Deleted Containers:
cbaca3bb4f18a4510293a72d25c91a30471c095cb88b946217c56d96abc6a065
ec27b272835b904c5ccbab3ebc8d063be6be4e63e926b457bda11832b9e1ec7c
11f15cfbc88d705d35cc77448d1728b6336ec3ca576b04a4efac8332ffb0db6a
ff6758efd820890c07fa8f3c961fd0587f6050f78b66766319936cdbe6529616
90094af21de987618f11f347321fbc3225003736f926d61f0789afc28a0f8214
e47e4130e545e1b2d5eb2b8abb3a228dada2b194230f96f462a5612af521ddc5
0829a984024fcdb9b6330f074bc9d1a8a80fd4985bc536864a0918a813b3844e
bd5003395c51517ac94aea78d5b0e21fddc4730512ba1e79a3fb6829e2861d97
874eb1968d49ee484aecdca25da40bf80f4d88cc1e4e636391400dc2a60f83fe

Total reclaimed space: 10B
[root@yogeshraheja helloworld]# []
```

This ability to start multiple containers on a single host with almost no overhead or latency makes Docker an ideal candidate for production. In addition, more and more companies are deciding to take the service-oriented architecture approach to an all-new level by breaking out each business function into a separate service. This is often called a **microservices** approach. Docker is a natural fit for microservices and for managing microservice architecture. This is because it provides a platform that is language agnostic (you can start any type of application written in any language inside your container), able to scale horizontally and vertically with ease, and a common story around deployment as we deploy containers instead of a variety of services. We will implement our container architecture using the **Infrastructure as Code (IaC)** best practices and use CloudFormation through the intermediary of Troposphere. The first service we are going to look at is AWS's ECR.

Creating an ECR repository to manage our Docker image

In the first part of this chapter, we used the Docker Hub public registry. AWS provides a similar service to this called ECR. This allows you to keep your images in a private registry called a **repository**. ECR is fully compatible with the Docker CLI but also integrates deeply with the remaining ECS services. We are going to use this to store our helloworld images.

As mentioned, we will rely heavily on CloudFormation to make our changes. Unlike what we saw previously, because of its nature, the ECS infrastructure we are going to build needs to be very modular. This is because, in practice, we will want to share some of those components with other services. Consequently, we will create a number of templates and link them to one another. One good way to do that is to rely on CloudFormation's export ability, which allows us to do cross-stack referencing.

One of the added bonuses that export provides is a fail-safe mechanism. You can't delete or edit a stack if another stack references an exported output.

To generate our template, we will create a new Troposphere script. To do this, go to the EffectiveDevOpsTemplates repository and create a new script named ecr-repository-cf- template.py.

We will start by importing a number of modules, including the Export mentioned earlier and the ecr module, in order to create our repository. We will also create our template variable, t, as we did in previous chapters:

```
"""Generating CloudFormation template."""

from troposphere import (
Export,
Join,
Output,
Parameter,
Ref,
Template
)
from troposphere.ecr import Repository
t = Template()
```

Since we are going to create a number of CloudFormation templates in this chapter, we will add a description so that it's easier to understand which template does what when looking at them in the AWS console:

```
t.add_description("Effective DevOps in AWS: ECR Repository")
```

We will create a parameter for the name of the repository so that we will be able to reuse that CloudFormation template for every repository we create:

```
t.add_parameter(Parameter(
        "RepoName",
        Type="String",
        Description="Name of the ECR repository to create"
))
```

We can now create our repository as follows:

```
t.add_resource(Repository(
        "Repository",
        RepositoryName=Ref("RepoName")
))
```

We are keeping the code very simple here and not enforcing any particular permissions. If you need to restrict who can access your repository and see more complex configurations, you can refer to the AWS documentation and, in particular, http://amzn.to/ 2j7hA2P. Lastly, we will output the name of the repository we created and export its value through a template variable t:

```
t.add_output(Output(
    "Repository",
    Description="ECR repository",
    Value=Ref("RepoName"),
    Export=Export(Join("-", [Ref("RepoName"), "repo"])),
))
print(t.to_json())
```

We can save our script now. It should look like this: https://github.com/yogeshraheja/ EffectiveDevOpsTemplates/blob/master/ecr-repository-cf-template.py. We will now generate the CloudFormation template and create our stack as follows:

```
$ python ecr-repository-cf-template.py > ecr-repository-cf.template
$ aws cloudformation create-stack \
    --stack-name helloworld-ecr \
    --capabilities CAPABILITY_IAM \
    --template-body file://ecr-repository-cf.template \
    --parameters \ ParameterKey=RepoName,ParameterValue=helloworld
```

After a few minutes, our stack will be created. We can validate that the repository was correctly created as follows:

```
$ aws ecr describe-repositories
{
    "repositories": [
        {
            "registryId": "094507990803",
            "repositoryName": "helloworld",
            "repositoryArn": "arn:aws:ecr:us-east-
             1:094507990803:repository/helloworld",
            "createdAt": 1536345671.0,
            "repositoryUri": "094507990803.dkr.ecr.us-east-
             1.amazonaws.com/helloworld"
        }
    ]
}
```

We can see our exported output with the following command:

```
$ aws cloudformation list-exports
{
    "Exports": [
        {
            "ExportingStackId": "arn:aws:cloudformation:us-east-
             1:094507990803:stack/helloworld-ecr/94d9ed70-b2cd-11e8-
             b767-50d501eed2b3",
            "Value": "helloworld",
            "Name": "helloworld-repo"
        }
    ]
}
```

Our repository can now be used to store our `helloworld` image. We will use the Docker CLI to do that. The first step of that process is to log in to the `ecr` service. You can do this with the following handy one-line command:

```
$ eval "$(aws ecr get-login --region us-east-1 --no-include-email )"
```

The output of running the preceding command can be shown as follows:

```
[root@yogeshraheja EffectiveDevOpsTemplates]# eval "$(aws ecr get-login --region us-east-1 --no-include-email )"
WARNING! Using --password via the CLI is insecure. Use --password-stdin.
WARNING! Your password will be stored unencrypted in /root/.docker/config.json.
Configure a credential helper to remove this warning. See
https://docs.docker.com/engine/reference/commandline/login/#credentials-store

Login Succeeded
[root@yogeshraheja EffectiveDevOpsTemplates]#
```

Back in our `helloworld` directory where the Dockerfile is, we will tag our image as follows:

```
$ cd helloworld
```

It is a common practice to use the `latest` tag to designate the most recent version of an image. In addition, you need to adapt the following command based on the output of the `aws ecr describe-repositories` output (we assume here that you have already built your image):

```
$ docker tag helloworld:latest 094507990803.dkr.ecr.us-
east-1.amazonaws.com/helloworld:latest
```

We can now push that image to our registry as follows:

```
$ docker push 094507990803.dkr.ecr.us-
east-1.amazonaws.com/helloworld:latest
The push refers to repository [094507990803.dkr.ecr.us-
east-1.amazonaws.com/helloworld]
c7f21f8d59de: Pushed
3c36cf19a914: Pushed
8faa1d9821d6: Pushed
be0fb77bfb1f: Pushed
63c810287aa2: Pushed
2793dc0607dd: Pushed
74800c25aa8c: Pushed
ba504a540674: Pushed
81101ce649d5: Pushed
daf45b2cad9a: Pushed
8c466bf4ca6f: Pushed
latest: digest:
sha256:95906ec13adf9894e4611cd37c8a06569964af0adbb035fcafa6020994675161
size: 2628
```

We can see how each layer of our image is pushed in parallel to our registry. Once the operation completes, we can validate that the new image is present in our registry as follows:

```
$ aws ecr describe-images --repository-name helloworld
{
    "imageDetails": [
        {
            "imageSizeInBytes": 265821145,
            "imageDigest":
"sha256:95906ec13adf9894e4611cd37c8a06569964af0adbb035fcafa6020994675161",
            "imageTags": [
                "latest"
```

```
        ],
        "registryId": "094507990803",
        "repositoryName": "helloworld",
        "imagePushedAt": 1536346218.0
      }
    ]
  }
```

At this point, our image is now available to the rest of our infrastructure. We are going to move on to the next step of our process, which is the creation of the ECS cluster.

Creating an ECS cluster

Creating an ECS cluster is a very similar process to the one in `Chapter 6`, *Scaling Your Infrastructure,* when we created an Auto Scaling Group to run our Hello World application. The main difference is that there is one more level of abstraction. ECS will run a number of services called **task**s.

Each of those tasks may exist multiple times in order to handle the traffic:

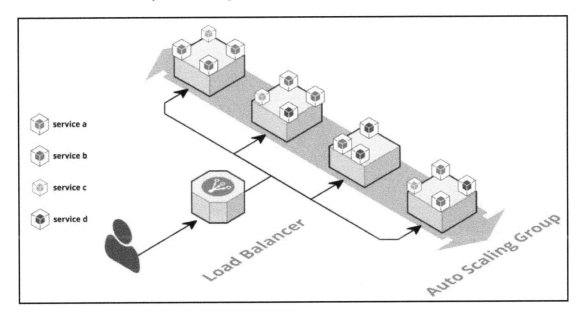

In order to do that, the ECS service provides an orchestration layer. That orchestration layer is in charge of managing the life cycle of containers, including upgrading or downgrading and scaling your containers up or down. The orchestration layer also distributes all containers for every service across all instances of the cluster optimally. Finally, it also exposes a discovery mechanism that interacts with other services such as ALB and ELB to register and deregister containers.

Task placement strategies:

By default, the entire orchestration system is managed by AWS. However, you also have the ability to customize it through the creation of a task placement strategy. This will let you configure the orchestration to optimize for instance count, for load distribution, to add constraints, and make sure that certain tasks are launched on the same instances.

We will create a new script to generate our ECS cluster. The filename will be `ecs-cluster-cf-template.py`. This template starts almost exactly like the template we created in Chapter 6, *Scaling Your Infrastructure*, for the Auto Scaling Group:

```python
"""Generating CloudFormation template."""

from ipaddress import ip_network from ipify import get_ip
from troposphere import (
    Base64,
    Export,
    Join,
    Output,
    Parameter,
    Ref,
    Sub,
    Template,
    ec2
)


from troposphere.autoscaling import (
    AutoScalingGroup,
    LaunchConfiguration,
    ScalingPolicy
)


from troposphere.cloudwatch import (
    Alarm,
    MetricDimension
)
from troposphere.ecs import Cluster
from troposphere.iam import (
    InstanceProfile,
```

```
        Role
    )
```

The only new import is the cluster one from the ECS module. Just like we did in Chapter 6, *Scaling Your Infrastructure*, we will extract our IP address in order to use it later for the SSH security group, create our template variable, and add a description to the stack:

```
    PublicCidrIp = str(ip_network(get_ip()))
    t = Template()
    t.add_description("Effective DevOps in AWS: ECS Cluster")
```

We will now proceed with adding our parameters, which are the the same parameters as used in Chapter 6, *Scaling Your Infrastructure*. This includes the SSH key-pair, the VPC ID, and its subnets:

```
    t.add_parameter(Parameter(
        "KeyPair",
        Description="Name of an existing EC2 KeyPair to SSH",
        Type="AWS::EC2::KeyPair::KeyName",
        ConstraintDescription="must be the name of an existing EC2
        KeyPair.",
    ))

    t.add_parameter(Parameter(
        "VpcId",
        Type="AWS::EC2::VPC::Id",
        Description="VPC"
    ))

    t.add_parameter(Parameter(
        "PublicSubnet",
        Description="PublicSubnet",
        Type="List<AWS::EC2::Subnet::Id>",
        ConstraintDescription="PublicSubnet"
    ))
```

Next, we will look at creating our security group resources:

```
    t.add_resource(ec2.SecurityGroup(
        "SecurityGroup",
        GroupDescription="Allow SSH and private network access",
        SecurityGroupIngress=[
            ec2.SecurityGroupRule(
                IpProtocol="tcp",
                FromPort=0,
                ToPort=65535,
                CidrIp="172.16.0.0/12",
            ),
```

```
        ec2.SecurityGroupRule(
            IpProtocol="tcp",
            FromPort="22",
            ToPort="22",
            CidrIp=PublicCidrIp,
        ),
    ],
    VpcId=Ref("VpcId")
))
```

There is one important difference here. In Chapter 6, *Scaling Your Infrastructure*, we opened up port 3000 since that's what our application is using. Here, we are opening every port to the CIDR 1 72.16.0.0/12, which is the private IP space of our internal network. This will give our ECS cluster the ability to run multiple helloworld containers on the same hosts, binding different ports.

We will now create our cluster resource. This can simply be done with the following command:

```
t.add_resource(Cluster(
    'ECSCluster',
))
```

Next, we will focus on configuring instances of the cluster, starting with their IAM role. Overall, this is one of the more complex resources to create in ECS as the cluster will need to perform a number of interactions with other AWS services. We can create a complete custom policy for it or import the policies AWS created as follows:

```
t.add_resource(Role(
    'EcsClusterRole',
    ManagedPolicyArns=[
        'arn:aws:iam::aws:policy/service-role/AmazonEC2RoleforSSM',
        'arn:aws:iam::aws:policy/AmazonEC2ContainerRegistryReadOnly',
        'arn:aws:iam::aws:policy/service-
role/AmazonEC2ContainerServiceforEC2Role',
        'arn:aws:iam::aws:policy/CloudWatchFullAccess'
    ],
    AssumeRolePolicyDocument={
        'Version': '2012-10-17',
        'Statement': [{
            'Action': 'sts:AssumeRole',
            'Principal': {'Service': 'ec2.amazonaws.com'},
            'Effect': 'Allow',
        }]
    }
))
```

We can now tie our role with the instance profile as follows:

```
t.add_resource(InstanceProfile(
    'EC2InstanceProfile',
    Roles=[Ref('EcsClusterRole')],
))
```

The next step is to create our launch configuration. The following code snippet shows what it looks like:

```
t.add_resource(LaunchConfiguration(
    'ContainerInstances',
    UserData=Base64(Join('', [
        "#!/bin/bash -xe\n",
        "echo ECS_CLUSTER=",
        Ref('ECSCluster'),
        " >> /etc/ecs/ecs.config\n",
        "yum install -y aws-cfn-bootstrap\n",
        "/opt/aws/bin/cfn-signal -e $? ",
        " --stack ",
        Ref('AWS::StackName'),
        " --resource ECSAutoScalingGroup ",
        " --region ",
        Ref('AWS::Region'),
        "\n"])),
    ImageId='ami-04351e12',
    KeyName=Ref("KeyPair"),
    SecurityGroups=[Ref("SecurityGroup")],
    IamInstanceProfile=Ref('EC2InstanceProfile'),
    InstanceType='t2.micro',
    AssociatePublicIpAddress='true',
))
```

In this example, we don't install Ansible like we did before. Instead, we are using an ECS-optimized AMI (you can read more about this at `http://amzn.to/2jX0xVu`) that lets us use the `UserData` field to configure the ECS service, and then starting it. Now that we have our launch configuration, we can create our Auto Scaling Group resources.

When working with ECS, scaling is needed at two levels:

- The containers level, as we will need to run more containers of a given service if the traffic spikes
- The underlying infrastructure level

Containers, through the intermediary of their task definitions, set a requirement for CPU and memory. They will require, for example, 1024 CPU units, which represents one core, and 256 memory units, which means 256 MB of RAM. If the ECS instances are close to being filled up on one of those two constraints, the ECS Auto Scaling Group needs to add more instances:

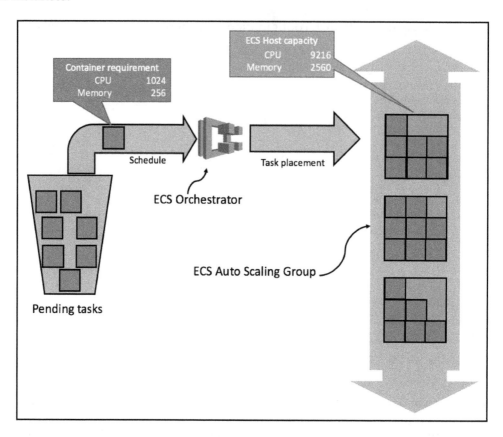

In terms of implementation, the process is very similar to what we did in Chapter 6, *Scaling Your Infrastructure*. Here, we first create the Auto Scaling Group resource, as follows:

```
t.add_resource(AutoScalingGroup(
    'ECSAutoScalingGroup',
    DesiredCapacity='1',
    MinSize='1',
    MaxSize='5',
    VPCZoneIdentifier=Ref("PublicSubnet"),
    LaunchConfigurationName=Ref('ContainerInstances'),
))
```

Next, we will create scaling policies and alarms to monitor the CPU and memory reservation metrics. In order to accomplish that, we will take advantage of Python to generate our stack and create for loops as follows:

```
states = {
    "High": {
        "threshold": "75",
        "alarmPrefix": "ScaleUpPolicyFor",
        "operator": "GreaterThanThreshold",
        "adjustment": "1"
    },
    "Low": {
        "threshold": "30",
        "alarmPrefix": "ScaleDownPolicyFor",
        "operator": "LessThanThreshold",
        "adjustment": "-1"
    }
}

for reservation in {"CPU", "Memory"}:
    for state, value in states.iteritems():
        t.add_resource(Alarm(
            "{}ReservationToo{}".format(reservation, state),
            AlarmDescription="Alarm if {} reservation too {}".format(
                reservation,
                state),
            Namespace="AWS/ECS",
            MetricName="{}Reservation".format(reservation),
            Dimensions=[
                MetricDimension(
                    Name="ClusterName",
                    Value=Ref("ECSCluster")
                ),
            ],
            Statistic="Average",
            Period="60",
            EvaluationPeriods="1",
            Threshold=value['threshold'],
            ComparisonOperator=value['operator'],
            AlarmActions=[
                Ref("{}{}".format(value['alarmPrefix'], reservation))]
        ))
        t.add_resource(ScalingPolicy(
            "{}{}".format(value['alarmPrefix'], reservation),
            ScalingAdjustment=value['adjustment'],
            AutoScalingGroupName=Ref("ECSAutoScalingGroup"),
            AdjustmentType="ChangeInCapacity",
        ))
```

Finally, we will provide a small amount of resource information, namely the stack ID, the VPC ID, and the public subnets:

```
t.add_output(Output(
    "Cluster",
    Description="ECS Cluster Name",
    Value=Ref("ECSCluster"),
    Export=Export(Sub("${AWS::StackName}-id")),
))

t.add_output(Output(
    "VpcId",
    Description="VpcId",
    Value=Ref("VpcId"),
    Export=Export(Sub("${AWS::StackName}-vpc-id")),
))

t.add_output(Output(
    "PublicSubnet",
    Description="PublicSubnet",
    Value=Join(',', Ref("PublicSubnet")),
    Export=Export(Sub("${AWS::StackName}-public-subnets")),
))

print(t.to_json())
```

 CloudFormation provides a number of pseudo-parameters, such as AWS::StackName. Throughout the chapter, we will rely on it to make our template generic enough to be used across different environments and services. In the preceding code, we created an ECR repository for our helloworld container. The name was generated by the stack creation command. If required, we can reuse that exact same template to create another repository for another container.

The script is now complete, and should look like the script at: https://github.com/ yogeshraheja/EffectiveDevOpsTemplates/blob/master/ecs-cluster-cf-template.py.

As before, we can now commit our script and create our stack by first generating our template, as follows:

```
$ git add ecs-cluster-cf-template.py
$ git commit -m "Adding Troposphere script to generate an ECS cluster"
$ git push
$ python ecs-cluster-cf-template.py > ecs-cluster-cf.template
```

To create our stack, we need three parameters; the key-pair, the VPC ID, and the subnets. In the previous chapters, we used the web interface to create those stacks. Here, we will look at how to get that information using the CLI.

To get the VPC ID and the subnet IDs, we can use the following commands:

```
$ aws ec2 describe-vpcs --query 'Vpcs[].VpcId'
[
    "vpc-4cddce2a"
]
$ aws ec2 describe-subnets --query 'Subnets[].SubnetId'
[
    "subnet-e67190bc",
    "subnet-658b6149",
    "subnet-d890d3e4",
    "subnet-6fdd7927",
    "subnet-4c99c229",
    "subnet-b03baebc"
]
```

We can now create our stack by combining the preceding outputs. Since ECS clusters can run a variety of containers and a number of applications and services, we will aim for one ECS cluster per environment, starting with staging. In order to differentiate each environment, we will rely on the stack names. Consequently, it is important to call your `staging-cluster` stack, as shown here:

```
$ aws cloudformation create-stack \
    --stack-name staging-cluster \
    --capabilities CAPABILITY_IAM \
    --template-body file://ecs-cluster-cf.template \
    --parameters \
    ParameterKey=KeyPair,ParameterValue=EffectiveDevOpsAWS \
    ParameterKey=VpcId,ParameterValue=vpc-4cddce2a \
    ParameterKey=PublicSubnet,ParameterValue=subnet-e67190bc\\,subnet-
    658b6149\\,subnet-d890d3e4\\,subnet-6fdd7927\\,subnet-
    4c99c229\\,subnet-b03baebc
{
    "StackId": "arn:aws:cloudformation:us-east-
    1:094507990803:stack/staging-cluster/581e30d0-b2d2-11e8-b48f-
    503acac41e99"
}
```

We will now add a load balancer. In the previous chapter, we used an ELB for our Auto Scaling Group. Later, we also mentioned the existence of the ALB service. This time, we will create an ALB instance to proxy our application traffic.

Creating an ALB

As mentioned previously, ECS provides an orchestrator that takes care of allocating the containers across our Auto Scaling Group. It also keeps track of which port each container uses and integrates with ALB so that our load balancer can correctly route the incoming traffic to all containers running a given service. ECS supports both the ELB and ALB services but the ALB gives more flexibility when working with containers. We will demonstrate how to create an ALB using CloudFormation through Troposphere.

We will start by creating a new file and calling it `helloworld-ecs-alb-cf-template.py`. We will then put our usual import, and will create our template variable and add a description, as follows:

```
"""Generating CloudFormation template."""

from troposphere import elasticloadbalancingv2 as elb

from troposphere import (
    Export,
    GetAtt,
    ImportValue,
    Join,
    Output,
    Ref,
    Select,
    Split,
    Sub,
    Template,
    ec2
)

t = Template()

t.add_description("Effective DevOps in AWS: ALB for the ECS Cluster")
```

We are now going to create our security group. No surprises here; we are opening `TCP/3000` to the world, as we did in Chapter 6, *Scaling Your Infrastructure*, with the ELB:

```
t.add_resource(ec2.SecurityGroup(
    "LoadBalancerSecurityGroup",
    GroupDescription="Web load balancer security group.",
    VpcId=ImportValue(
        Join(
            "-",
            [Select(0, Split("-", Ref("AWS::StackName"))),
                "cluster-vpc-id"]
```

```
            )
        ),
        SecurityGroupIngress=[
            ec2.SecurityGroupRule(
                IpProtocol="tcp",
                FromPort="3000",
                ToPort="3000",
                CidrIp="0.0.0.0/0",
            ),
        ],
    ))
```

The main difference from what we did previously is that instead of starting with a
parameter section and requesting, yet again, to provide the VPC ID and public subnets, we
are taking advantage of the value that we exported before. When we launch this stack, we
will call it staging-alb. The block of code inside the ImportValue parameter does the
following:

1. First, we get the name of our stack. We will launch that stack under the name
   staging-alb.
2. The Split function breaks the stack name on the character –, meaning that we
   end up with [staging, alb].
3. The Select function takes the first element of the list: staging.
4. The Join function concatenates that element with the string cluster-vpc-id.
   In the end, we get Import ("staging-cluster-vpc-id"), which is the name
   of the key we defined to export the VPC ID when we created our ECS cluster:

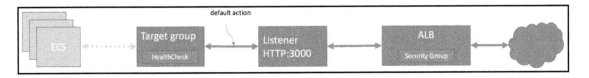

We will now create our ALB. ALB, being more flexible and feature-rich than ELB, requires a
bit more effort when it comes to configuration. ALB works through the intermediary of
three different resources. The first one is the ALB resource, which handles incoming
connections. On the opposite side, we can find the target groups, which are the resources
used by the ECS clusters registered to those ALBs. Finally, in order to tie the two, we find
the listener's resources. We will first define our load balancer resource, as follows:

```
t.add_resource(elb.LoadBalancer(
    "LoadBalancer",
    Scheme="internet-facing",
    Subnets=Split(
```

```
        ',',
        ImportValue(
            Join("-",
                [Select(0, Split("-", Ref("AWS::StackName")))),
                 "cluster-public-subnets"]
                )
            )
        ),
        SecurityGroups=[Ref("LoadBalancerSecurityGroup")],
    ))
```

> We use a very similar series of calls to the function to import our subnet as we did just before for the VPC ID.

We will now create our target group and configure our health check, as follows:

```
t.add_resource(elb.TargetGroup(
    "TargetGroup",
    DependsOn='LoadBalancer',
    HealthCheckIntervalSeconds="20",
    HealthCheckProtocol="HTTP",
    HealthCheckTimeoutSeconds="15",
    HealthyThresholdCount="5",
    Matcher=elb.Matcher(
        HttpCode="200"),
    Port=3000,
    Protocol="HTTP",
    UnhealthyThresholdCount="3",
    VpcId=ImportValue(
        Join(
            "-",
            [Select(0, Split("-", Ref("AWS::StackName")))),
                "cluster-vpc-id"]
            )
        ),
    ))
```

Finally, we will add the listener to connect our target group to our load balancer:

```
t.add_resource(elb.Listener(
    "Listener",
    Port="3000",
    Protocol="HTTP",
    LoadBalancerArn=Ref("LoadBalancer"),
    DefaultActions=[elb.Action(
        Type="forward",
```

```
            TargetGroupArn=Ref("TargetGroup")
      )]
))
```

Lastly, we will want to create two outputs. The first output is the target group. We will export its value so that our application can register to the group. The second output is the DNS record of the ALB. This will be the entry point to our application:

```
t.add_output(Output(
    "TargetGroup",
    Description="TargetGroup",
    Value=Ref("TargetGroup"),
    Export=Export(Sub("${AWS::StackName}-target-group")),
))

t.add_output(Output(
    "URL",
    Description="Helloworld URL",
    Value=Join("", ["http://", GetAtt("LoadBalancer", "DNSName"), ":3000"])
))

print(t.to_json())
```

The file is now ready, and should look like the file at: https://github.com/yogeshraheja/ EffectiveDevOpsTemplates/blob/master/helloworld-ecs-alb-cf-template.py. We can now generate our template and create our stack, as follows:

```
$ git add helloworld-ecs-alb-cf-template.py
$ git commit -m "Adding a Load balancer template for our helloworld
application on ECS"
$ git push
$ python helloworld-ecs-alb-cf-template.py > helloworld-ecs-alb-cf.template
$ aws cloudformation create-stack \
    --stack-name staging-alb \
    --capabilities CAPABILITY_IAM \
    --template-body file://helloworld-ecs-alb-cf.template
  {
    "StackId": "arn:aws:cloudformation:us-east-
    1:094507990803:stack/staging-alb/4929fee0-b2d4-11e8-825f-
    50fa5f2588d2"
  }
```

As mentioned, it is important to call the stack `staging-alb`, and that first word is used to import the VPC ID and subnets. The last stack we need is the creation of our container service.

Creating our ECS hello world service

We have an ECS cluster and a load balancer ready to take on traffic on one side and an ECR repository containing the image of our application on the other side. We now need to tie the two together. This is done by creating an ECS service resource. We will create a new file called `helloworld-ecs-service-cf-template.py` and start as usual with its imports, template variable creation, and template description:

```python
"""Generating CloudFormation template."""

from troposphere.ecs import (
    TaskDefinition,
    ContainerDefinition
)
from troposphere import ecs
from awacs.aws import (
    Allow,
    Statement,
    Principal,
    Policy
)
from troposphere.iam import Role

from troposphere import (
    Parameter,
    Ref,
    Template,
    Join,
    ImportValue,
    Select,
    Split,
)

from awacs.sts import AssumeRole

t = Template()

t.add_description("Effective DevOps in AWS: ECS service - Helloworld")
```

Our template will take one argument, which is the tag of the image we want to deploy. Our repository currently only has one image tagged as the latest, but in the next section we will update our deployment pipeline and automatize the deployment of our service to ECS:

```
t.add_parameter(Parameter(
    "Tag",
    Type="String",
    Default="latest",
    Description="Tag to deploy"
))
```

In ECS, applications are defined by their task definitions. This is where we declare which repository to use to get our image, how much CPU and memory the application needs, and all other system properties such as port mapping, environment variables, mount points, and so on. We will keep our task definition minimal; in order to select the proper image, we will utilize the `ImportValue` function (we previously exported the repository name) combined with a `Join` function to craft the repository URL. We will require 32 MB of RAM and one-quarter of a core to run our application. Finally, we will specify that port 3000 needs to be mapped onto the system:

```
t.add_resource(TaskDefinition(
    "task",
    ContainerDefinitions=[
        ContainerDefinition(
            Image=Join("", [
                Ref("AWS::AccountId"),
                ".dkr.ecr.",
                Ref("AWS::Region"),
                ".amazonaws.com",
                "/",
                ImportValue("helloworld-repo"),
                ":",
                Ref("Tag")]),
            Memory=32,
            Cpu=256,
            Name="helloworld",
            PortMappings=[ecs.PortMapping(
                ContainerPort=3000)]
        )
    ],
))
```

As for most of the AWS managed services, the ECS service needs a certain set of permissions provided by the intermediary of a role. We will create that role and use the vanilla policy for the ECS service role, as follows:

```
t.add_resource(Role(
    "ServiceRole",
    AssumeRolePolicyDocument=Policy(
        Statement=[
            Statement(
                Effect=Allow,
                Action=[AssumeRole],
                Principal=Principal("Service", ["ecs.amazonaws.com"])
            )
        ]
    ),
    Path="/",
    ManagedPolicyArns=[
        'arn:aws:iam::aws:policy/service-
role/AmazonEC2ContainerServiceRole']
))
```

We will complete the creation of our template with the addition of the ECS service resource, which ties the task definition, the ECS cluster, and the ALB together:

```
t.add_resource(ecs.Service(
    "service",
    Cluster=ImportValue(
        Join(
            "-",
            [Select(0, Split("-", Ref("AWS::StackName"))),
                "cluster-id"]
        )
    ),
    DesiredCount=1,
    TaskDefinition=Ref("task"),
    LoadBalancers=[ecs.LoadBalancer(
        ContainerName="helloworld",
        ContainerPort=3000,
        TargetGroupArn=ImportValue(
            Join(
                "-",
                [Select(0, Split("-", Ref("AWS::StackName"))),
                    "alb-target-group"]
            ),
        ),
    )],
    Role=Ref("ServiceRole")
))
```

Finally, as always, we will output the template generated by our code using the following command:

```
print(t.to_json())
```

The script is now ready and should look like the script at: `https://github.com/yogeshraheja/EffectiveDevOpsTemplates/blob/master/helloworld-ecs-service-cf-template.py`.

We will now generate the template and create our stack, as follows:

```
$ git add helloworld-ecs-service-cf-template.py
$ git commit -m "Adding helloworld ECS service script"
$ git push
$ python helloworld-ecs-service-cf-template.py > helloworld-ecs-service-
cf.template
$ aws cloudformation create-stack \
    --stack-name staging-helloworld-service \
    --capabilities CAPABILITY_IAM \
    --template-body file://helloworld-ecs-service-cf.template \
    --parameters \ ParameterKey=Tag,ParameterValue=latest
```

After a few minutes, the stack should be created. We can circle back to the output of the ALB stack to get the URL of our newly deployed application and test its output, as follows:

```
$ aws cloudformation describe-stacks \
    --stack-name staging-alb \
    --query 'Stacks[0].Outputs'

[
    {
        "Description": "TargetGroup",
        "ExportName": "staging-alb-target-group",
        "OutputKey": "TargetGroup",
        "OutputValue": "arn:aws:elasticloadbalancing:us-east-
        1:094507990803:targetgroup/stagi-Targe-
        ZBW30U7GT7DX/329afe507c4abd4d"
    },
    {
        "Description": "Helloworld URL",
        "OutputKey": "URL",
        "OutputValue": "http://stagi-LoadB-122Z9ZDMCD68X-1452710042.us-
        east-1.elb.amazonaws.com:3000"
    }
]

$ curl
http://stagi-LoadB-122Z9ZDMCD68X-1452710042.us-east-1.elb.amazonaws.com:300
```

```
0
Hello World
Also the same can be confirmed from the browser.
```

This can also be confirmed from the browser, as shown in the following screenshot:

We have completed the creation of our staging ECS environment. At this point, we can easily manually deploy new code to our staging, as follows:

1. Make the changes in the `helloworld` code, locally. For example, change `Hello World` to `Hello From Yogesh Raheja`, as shown in the following screenshot:

```
[root@yogeshraheja helloworld]# cat helloworld.js
var http = require("http")

http.createServer(function (request, response) {

    // Send the HTTP header
    // HTTP Status: 200 : OK
    // Content Type: text/plain
    response.writeHead(200, {'Content-Type': 'text/plain'})

    // Send the response body as "Hello World"
    response.end('Hello From Yogesh Raheja\n')
}).listen(3000)

// Console will print the message
console.log('Server running')
```

2. Log in to the `ecr` registry, as follows:

```
$ eval "$(aws ecr get-login --region us-east-1 --no-include-email)"
```

3. Build your Docker container, as follows:

```
$ docker build -t helloworld
```

4. Pick a new unique tag, and use it to tag your image. For example, let's suppose that your new tag is `foobar`, as shown in the following code:

```
$ docker tag helloworld 094507990803.dkr.ecr.us-
east-1.amazonaws.com/helloworld:foobar
```

5. Push the image to the `ecr` repository, as follows:

```
$ docker push 094507990803.dkr.ecr.us-
east-1.amazonaws.com/helloworld:foobar
```

6. Update the ECS service CloudFormation stack, as follows:

```
$ aws cloudformation update-stack \
    --stack-name staging-helloworld-service \
    --capabilities CAPABILITY_IAM \
    --template-body file://helloworld-ecs-service-cf.template \
    --parameters \
      ParameterKey=Tag,ParameterValue=foobar
```

7. Check the outputs after it updates, as follows:

```
$ curl
http://stagi-LoadB-122Z9ZDMCD68X-1452710042.us-east-1.elb.amazo
naws.com:3000

Hello From Yogesh Raheja
```

The browser output also reflects the updated image response:

Using this sequence of events, we are going to automate the deployment process and create a new continuous integration/continuous deployment pipeline.

Creating a CI/CD pipeline to deploy to ECS

As we know, having the ability to continuously deploy code across our environments is a very powerful tool as it helps to break out those traditional Dev versus Ops silos and improve the velocity at which new code is being released. We created a pipeline that allows us to automatically deploy new changes from our Hello World application to our Auto Scaling Groups for staging and production. We will create a similar pipeline but, this time, it will deploy changes to ECS. Our ECS infrastructure will be as follows:

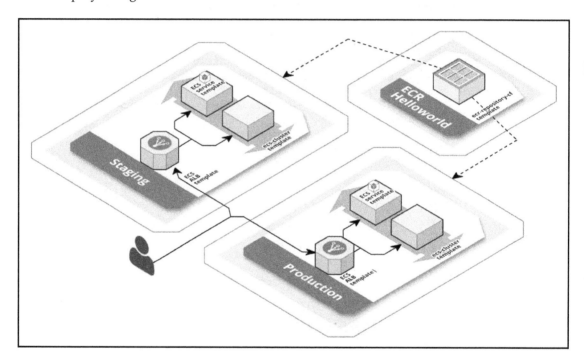

Reusing the CloudFormation templates produced in the previous section will create a production environment identical to the staging one. Note that the ecr repository is meant to be unique for a given application, and therefore will share it across our environments. In addition, we will follow the best practices learned in chapter 3, *Treating Your Infrastructure As Code*, and create our pipeline through a CloudFormation stack. Our first step will be to create an ECS cluster for production.

Creating our production ECS cluster

Thanks to the upfront work we did with our CloudFormation templates, adding a new environment will be trivial. We will start by launching a production ECS cluster:

```
$ aws cloudformation create-stack \
    --stack-name production-cluster \
    --capabilities CAPABILITY_IAM \
    --template-body file://ecs-cluster-cf.template \
    --parameters \
      ParameterKey=KeyPair,ParameterValue=EffectiveDevOpsAWS \
      ParameterKey=VpcId,ParameterValue=vpc-4cddce2a \
      ParameterKey=PublicSubnet,ParameterValue=subnet-
      e67190bc\\,subnet-658b6149\\,subnet-d890d3e4\\,subnet-
      6fdd7927\\,subnet-4c99c229\\,subnet-b03baebc
{
    "StackId": "arn:aws:cloudformation:us-east-
    1:094507990803:stack/production-cluster/1e1a87f0-b2da-11e8-8fd2-
    503aca4a58d1"
}
```

We need to wait for the creation of the stack to complete as we need to get some of the exported values from the cluster creation. We can run the following command to get our Terminal to hang until we can create our next stack:

```
$ aws cloudformation wait stack-create-complete \
    --stack-name production-cluster
```

In the meantime, we create our ALB and wait for the creation process to complete:

```
$ aws cloudformation create-stack \
    --stack-name production-alb \
    --capabilities CAPABILITY_IAM \
    --template-body file://helloworld-ecs-alb-cf.template
{
    "StackId": "arn:aws:cloudformation:us-east-
    1:094507990803:stack/production-alb/bea35530-b2da-11e8-a55e-
    500c28903236"
}

$ aws cloudformation wait stack-create-complete --stack-name production-alb
```

Finally, we can create our service with the following code:

```
$ aws cloudformation create-stack \
    --stack-name production-helloworld-service \
    --capabilities CAPABILITY_IAM \
    --template-body file://helloworld-ecs-service-cf.template \
    --parameters \ ParameterKey=Tag,ParameterValue=latest
{
    "StackId": "arn:aws:cloudformation:us-east-
    1:094507990803:stack/production-helloworld-service/370a3d40-b2db-
    11e8-80a8-503f23fb5536"
}

$ aws cloudformation wait stack-create-complete \
    --stack-name production-helloworld-service
```

At this point, our production environment should be working. We can get its URL by looking at the output of the ALB stack creation, and we can CURL the endpoint to ensure that the application is up and running:

```
$ aws cloudformation describe-stacks \
    --stack-name production-alb \
    --query 'Stacks[0].Outputs'
[
    {
        "Description": "TargetGroup",
        "ExportName": "production-alb-target-group",
        "OutputKey": "TargetGroup",
        "OutputValue": "arn:aws:elasticloadbalancing:us-east-
        1:094507990803:targetgroup/produ-Targe-
        LVSNKY9T8S6E/83540dcf2b5a5b54"
    },
    {
        "Description": "Helloworld URL",
        "OutputKey": "URL",
        "OutputValue": "http://produ-LoadB-40X7DRUNEBE3-676991098.us-
        east-1.elb.amazonaws.com:3000"
    }
]

$ curl
http://produ-LoadB-40X7DRUNEBE3-676991098.us-east-1.elb.amazonaws.com:3000
Hello World
```

The output will be as follows:

```
←  →  C    ⓘ Not secure  │  produ-loadb-40x7drunebe3-676991098.us-east-1.elb.amazonaws.com:3000

Hello World
```

Now that our production environment is ready, we will look into automating the creation of containers. In order to accomplish that, we will rely on the CodeBuild service.

Automating the creation of containers with CodeBuild

AWS CodeBuild is a managed service geared toward compiling source code. It is comparable to Jenkins but since it's a managed service that conforms to AWS standards, it presents a different set of features and benefits. In our case, using CodeBuild over Jenkins will allow us to create containers without needing to spin up and manage an extra EC2 instance. The service also integrates well with CodePipeline, which, as before, will drive our process.

We will use CloudFormation through the intermediary of Troposphere to create our CodeBuild project.

We will also create a new script and call it `helloworld-codebuild-cf-template.py`. We will start with our usual import, template variable creation, and description, shown as follows:

```
"""Generating CloudFormation template."""

from awacs.aws import (
    Allow,
    Policy,
    Principal,
    Statement
)

from awacs.sts import AssumeRole

from troposphere import (
    Join,
    Ref,
```

```
        Template
    )

from troposphere.codebuild import (
    Artifacts,
    Environment,
    Project,
    Source
)
from troposphere.iam import Role

t = Template()

t.add_description("Effective DevOps in AWS: CodeBuild - Helloworld
container")
```

We will now define a new role to grant the proper permissions to our CodeBuild project. The CodeBuild project will interact with a number of AWS services such as ECR, CodePipeline, S3, and CloudWatch logs. To speed up the process, we will rely on the AWS vanilla policies to configure the permissions. This gives us the following code:

```
t.add_resource(Role(
    "ServiceRole",
    AssumeRolePolicyDocument=Policy(
        Statement=[
            Statement(
                Effect=Allow,
                Action=[AssumeRole],
                Principal=Principal("Service", ["codebuild.amazonaws.com"])
            )
        ]
    ),
    Path="/",
    ManagedPolicyArns=[
        'arn:aws:iam::aws:policy/AWSCodePipelineReadOnlyAccess',
        'arn:aws:iam::aws:policy/AWSCodeBuildDeveloperAccess',
        'arn:aws:iam::aws:policy/AmazonEC2ContainerRegistryPowerUser',
        'arn:aws:iam::aws:policy/AmazonS3FullAccess',
        'arn:aws:iam::aws:policy/CloudWatchLogsFullAccess'
    ]
))
```

CodeBuild projects require defining a number of elements. The first one we will define is the environment. This tells CodeBuild what type of hardware and OS we need to build our project, and what needs to be preinstalled. It will also let us define extra environment variables. We will use a Docker image provided by AWS, which will give us everything we need to get our work done. The Docker image comes with the AWS and Docker CLI preinstalled and configured. We will also define an environment variable to find our `ecr` repository endpoint:

```
environment = Environment(
    ComputeType='BUILD_GENERAL1_SMALL',
    Image='aws/codebuild/docker:1.12.1',
    Type='LINUX_CONTAINER',
    EnvironmentVariables=[
        {'Name': 'REPOSITORY_NAME', 'Value': 'helloworld'},
        {'Name': 'REPOSITORY_URI',
            'Value': Join("", [
                Ref("AWS::AccountId"),
                ".dkr.ecr.",
                Ref("AWS::Region"),
                ".amazonaws.com",
                "/",
                "helloworld"])},
    ],
)
```

In CodeBuild, most of the logic is defined in a resource called a `buildspec`. The `buildspec` section defines the different phases of the build and what to run during those phases. It is very similar to the Jenkins file we created in Chapter 5, *Adding Continuous Integration and Continuous Deployment*. The `buildspec` section can be created as part of the CodeBuild project or added as a YAML file to the root directory of the projects that are being built. We will opt for the first option and define `buildspec` inside our CloudFormation template. We will create a variable and store a YAML string into it. Since it's going to be a multiline variable, we will use the Python triple quote syntax.

The first key-pair we need to specify is the version of the template. The current version of CodeBuild templates is `0.1`:

```
buildspec = """version: 0.1
```

The goal of our build process is to generate a new container image, tag it, and push it to the `ecr` repository. This will be done in three phases:

- **Pre-build**: This will generate the container image tag and log in to ECR
- **Build**: This will build the new container image
- **Post-build**: This will push the new container image to ECR and update the `latest` tag to point to the new container

In order to easily understand what is in each container, we will tag them with the SHA of the most recent Git commit in the `helloworld` project. This will help in understanding what is in each container, as we will be able to run commands such as `git checkout <container tag>` or `git log <container tag>`. Due to how CodeBuild and CodePipeline are architected, getting this tag in CodeBuild requires a bit of work. We will need to run two complex commands as follows:

- The first one will extract the execution ID of the current code pipeline execution. This is achieved by combining the AWS CLI and the environment variables `CODEBUILD_BUILD_ID` and `CODEBUILD_INITIATOR`, which are defined by the CodeBuild service when a build starts.
- Next, we will use that execution ID to extract the artifact revision ID, which happens to be the commit SHA we are looking for.

These commands use some of the most advanced features of the `--query` filter option. You can read more about this at the following link: `http://amzn.to/2k7SoLE`.

 In CodeBuild, each command runs in its own environment, and therefore the easiest way to share data across steps is to use temporary files.

Right after the `buildspec` version definition, add the following to generate the first part of our pre-build phase and extract the tag:

```
phases:
  pre_build:
    commands:
      - aws codepipeline get-pipeline-state --name
"${CODEBUILD_INITIATOR##*/}" --query
stageStates[?actionStates[0].latestExecution.externalExecutionId==\`$CODEBU
ILD_BUILD_ID\`].latestExecution.pipelineExecutionId --output=text >
/tmp/execution_id.txt
      - aws codepipeline get-pipeline-execution --pipeline-name
"${CODEBUILD_INITIATOR##*/}" --pipeline-execution-id $(cat
/tmp/execution_id.txt) --query
'pipelineExecution.artifactRevisions[0].revisionId' --output=text >
/tmp/tag.txt
```

Our tag is now present in the `/tmp/tag.txt` file. We now need to generate two files as follows:

- The first one will contain the argument for the `docker tag` command (this will be something like `<AWS::AccountId>.dkr.ecr.us-east-1.amazonaws.com/helloworld:<tag>`). To do that, we will take advantage of the environment variable defined earlier in our template.
- The second file will be a JSON file that will define a key-value pair with the tag. We will use that file a bit later when we work on deploying our new containers to ECS.

After the previous commands, add the following commands to generate those files:

```
printf "%s:%s" "$REPOSITORY_URI" "$(cat /tmp/tag.txt)" > /tmp/build_tag.txt
      - printf '{"tag":"%s"}' "$(cat /tmp/tag.txt)" > /tmp/build.json
```

To conclude the `pre_build` section, we will log in to our `ecr` repository:

```
      - $(aws ecr get-login --no-include-email)
```

We will now define our build phase. Thanks to the `build_tag` file created earlier, the build phase will be straightforward. We will call the `docker build` command in a similar way to how we did in the first section of this chapter:

```
build:
  commands:
    - docker build -t "$(cat /tmp/build_tag.txt)" .
```

We will now add the `post_build` phase to complete the build. In this section, we will push the newly built container to our `ecr` repository as follows:

```
post_build:
    commands:
      - docker push "$(cat /tmp/build_tag.txt)"
      - aws ecr batch-get-image --repository-name $REPOSITORY_NAME --image-
ids imageTag="$(cat /tmp/tag.txt)" --query 'images[].imageManifest' --
output text | tee /tmp/latest_manifest.json
      - aws ecr put-image --repository-name $REPOSITORY_NAME --image-tag
latest --image-manifest "$(cat /tmp/latest_manifest.json)"
```

In addition to the phases, one of the sections that is also defined in a `buildspec` is the `artifacts` section. This section is used to define what needs to be uploaded to S3 after the build succeeds, as well as how to prepare it. We will export the `build.json` file and set the `discard-paths` variable to true so we don't preserve the `/tmp/` directory information. Finally, we will close our triple quote string as follows:

```
artifacts:
  files: /tmp/build.json
  discard-paths: yes
"""
```

Now that our `buildspec` variable is defined, we can add our CodeBuild project resource. Through the instantiation of the project, we will set a name for our project, set its environment by calling the variable previously defined, set the service role, and configure the source and artifact resources, which define how to handle the build process and its output:

```
t.add_resource(Project(
    "CodeBuild",
    Name='HelloWorldContainer',
    Environment=environment,
    ServiceRole=Ref("ServiceRole"),
    Source=Source(
        Type="CODEPIPELINE",
        BuildSpec=buildspec
    ),
    Artifacts=Artifacts(
        Type="CODEPIPELINE",
        Name="output"
    ),
))
```

As always, we will conclude the creation of the script with the following `print` command:

```
print(t.to_json())
```

Our script is now complete and should look like this: `https://github.com/yogeshraheja/EffectiveDevOpsTemplates/blob/master/helloworld-codebuild-cf-template.py`.

We can save the file, add it to git, generate the CloudFormation template, and create our stack as follows:

```
$ git add helloworld-codebuild-cf-template.py
$ git commit -m "Adding CodeBuild Template for our helloworld application"
$ git push
$ python helloworld-codebuild-cf-template.py > helloworld-codebuild-
cf.template
$ aws cloudformation create-stack \
    --stack-name helloworld-codebuild \
    --capabilities CAPABILITY_IAM \
    --template-body file://helloworld-codebuild-cf.template
```

In a matter of minutes, our stack will be created. We will now want to take advantage of it. To do so, we will turn to CodePipeline once again and create a brand new, container-aware pipeline.

Creating our deployment pipeline with CodePipeline

We will use AWS CodePipeline to build a pipeline very similar to the one we created in Chapter 5, *Adding Continuous Integration and Continuous Deployment*:

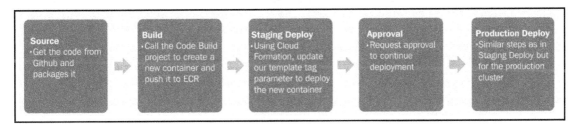

We will start with a Source step where we will connect to GitHub and trigger new pipelines that run automatically when the code changes. After this, we will build a new container and push it to our `ecr` repository rely upon the CodeBuild project we just created. We will then deploy the new container to staging. To do that, we will use the CloudFormation integration provided by CodePipeline, combined with the `build.json` file produced in the `buildspec` section of our CodeBuild project. You may recall that our `helloworld` service templates take the tag to deploy as an argument. We will trigger a stack update action and override the default value for that parameter with what's defined in the `build.json` file. After that, we will add a manual approval step before triggering the same deployment again, but this time for production.

Deploying and updating CloudFormation templates through CodePipeline will require specifying the location of the template within the inputs. In order to easily provide it, we will first start by adding the CloudFormation template to our source.

Adding the CloudFormation template to our code base

ECS changes are driven by the task definition present in our `helloworld-ecs-service-cf.template` file. So far we have only stored our Python script in GitHub. We will have to make a special case for that template and store the JSON output of it so that CodePipeline can interact with our stack. We will add this file to our Git repository in a new directory as follows:

```
$ cd helloworld
$ mkdir templates
$ curl -L
https://raw.githubusercontent.com/yogeshraheja/EffectiveDevOpsTemplates/mas
ter/helloworld-ecs-service-cf-template.py | python > templates/helloworld-
ecs-service-cf.template
$ git add templates
$ git commit -m "Adding CloudFormation template for the helloworld task"
$ git push
```

Now that our template is present in our source, we can create our CloudFormation template for our pipeline.

Creating a CloudFormation template for CodePipeline

We will start by creating a file called `helloworld-codepipeline-cf- template.py` inside EffectiveDevOpsTemplates locally.

We will start the script with our boilerplates:

```python
"""Generating CloudFormation template."""

from awacs.aws import (
    Allow,
    Policy,
    Principal,
    Statement,
)
from awacs.sts import AssumeRole
from troposphere import (
    Ref,
    GetAtt,
    Template,
)
from troposphere.codepipeline import (
    Actions,
    ActionTypeId,
    ArtifactStore,
    InputArtifacts,
    OutputArtifacts,
    Pipeline,
    Stages
)
from troposphere.iam import Role
from troposphere.iam import Policy as IAMPolicy

from troposphere.s3 import Bucket, VersioningConfiguration

t = Template()

t.add_description("Effective DevOps in AWS: Helloworld Pipeline")
```

The first resource we will create is the S3 bucket that the pipeline will use to store all the artifacts produced by each stage. We will also turn on versioning on that bucket:

```
t.add_resource(Bucket(
    "S3Bucket",
    VersioningConfiguration=VersioningConfiguration(
        Status="Enabled",
    )
))
```

We will now create the IAM roles needed as follows:

1. The first role we are going to define will be for the CodePipeline service:

```
t.add_resource(Role(
    "PipelineRole",
    AssumeRolePolicyDocument=Policy(
        Statement=[
            Statement(
                Effect=Allow,
                Action=[AssumeRole],
                Principal=Principal("Service",
["codepipeline.amazonaws.com"])
            )
        ]
    ),
    Path="/",
    Policies=[
        IAMPolicy(
            PolicyName="HelloworldCodePipeline",
            PolicyDocument={
                "Statement": [
                    {"Effect": "Allow", "Action":
"cloudformation:*", "Resource": "*"},
                    {"Effect": "Allow", "Action":
"codebuild:*", "Resource": "*"},
                    {"Effect": "Allow", "Action":
"codepipeline:*", "Resource": "*"},
                    {"Effect": "Allow", "Action": "ecr:*",
"Resource": "*"},
                    {"Effect": "Allow", "Action": "ecs:*",
"Resource": "*"},
                    {"Effect": "Allow", "Action": "iam:*",
"Resource": "*"},
                    {"Effect": "Allow", "Action": "s3:*",
"Resource": "*"},
                ],
            }
```

```
                ),
            ]
    ))
```

2. The second role will be used by the deploy stages to perform CloudFormation changes:

```
t.add_resource(Role(
    "CloudFormationHelloworldRole",
    RoleName="CloudFormationHelloworldRole",
    Path="/",
    AssumeRolePolicyDocument=Policy(
        Statement=[
            Statement(
                Effect=Allow,
                Action=[AssumeRole],
                Principal=Principal(
                    "Service",
["cloudformation.amazonaws.com"])
            ),
        ]
    ),
    Policies=[
        IAMPolicy(
            PolicyName="HelloworldCloudFormation",
            PolicyDocument={
                "Statement": [
                    {"Effect": "Allow", "Action":
"cloudformation:*", "Resource": "*"},
                    {"Effect": "Allow", "Action": "ecr:*",
"Resource": "*"},
                    {"Effect": "Allow", "Action": "ecs:*",
"Resource": "*"},
                    {"Effect": "Allow", "Action": "iam:*",
"Resource": "*"},
                ],
            }
        ),
    ]
))
```

3. We can now create our pipeline resource. We will first configure its name and specify the role **Amazon Resource Name (ARN)** of the role we just created:

```
t.add_resource(Pipeline(
    "HelloWorldPipeline",
    RoleArn=GetAtt("PipelineRole", "Arn"),
```

4. After this, we will reference the S3 bucket created earlier so that we have a place to store the different artifacts produced through the pipeline execution:

```
ArtifactStore=ArtifactStore(
    Type="S3",
    Location=Ref("S3Bucket")
```

5. We will now define each stage of the pipeline. The CloudFormation structure reflects what we did previously using the web interface. Each stage has a unique name and is composed of actions. Each action is defined by a name, a category, a configuration, and, optionally, input and output artifacts:

Our first stage will be the GitHub stage, as follows:

```
Stages=[
        Stages(
            Name="Source",
            Actions=[
                Actions(
                    Name="Source",
                    ActionTypeId=ActionTypeId(
                        Category="Source",
                        Owner="ThirdParty",
                        Version="1",
                        Provider="GitHub"
                    ),
                    Configuration={
                        "Owner": "ToBeConfiguredLater",
                        "Repo": "ToBeConfiguredLater",
                        "Branch": "ToBeConfiguredLater",
                        "OAuthToken": "ToBeConfiguredLater"
                    },
                    OutputArtifacts=[
                        OutputArtifacts(
                            Name="App"
                        )
                    ],
                )
            ]
        ),
```

6. We will create a first artifact called `App` with the content of the repository. In order to avoid hardcoding any `OAuthToken`, we will configure the GitHub integration after creating the CloudFormation stack.

Our next step will be to configure our build. As mentioned, we will simply call out to the CodeBuild stack we spawned up in the last section. We will store the output artifact under the name `BuildOutput`, meaning that we now have two artifacts: the `App` artifact and `BuildOutput`, which contains the `tag.json` file produced by CodeBuild:

```
Stages(
            Name="Build",
            Actions=[
                Actions(
                    Name="Container",
                    ActionTypeId=ActionTypeId(
                        Category="Build",
                        Owner="AWS",
                        Version="1",
                        Provider="CodeBuild"
                    ),
                    Configuration={
                        "ProjectName": "HelloWorldContainer",
                    },
                    InputArtifacts=[
                        InputArtifacts(
                            Name="App"
                        )
                    ],
                    OutputArtifacts=[
                        OutputArtifacts(
                            Name="BuildOutput"
                        )
                    ],
                )
            ]
        ),
```

7. We will now create our staging deployment. Unlike before, we won't use CodeDeploy but will directly update our CloudFormation template. In order to accomplish that, we will need to provide the location of the template to the configuration of our action. Since we added it to our `helloworld` GitHub repository, we can reference it with the help of the App artifact. Our template is present under `<directory root>/templates/helloworld-ecs-service-cf.template`, which in turn means for CodePipeline `App::templates/helloworld-ecs-service-cf.template`.

The next trick in configuring our CloudFormation action relies on the fact that we can override the parameters provided for the stack. CloudFormation provides a couple of functions to help with dynamic parameters. You can read more about those at `http://amzn.to/2kTgIUJ`. We will focus on a particular one here: `Fn::GetParam`. This function returns a value from a key-value pair file present in an artifact. This is where we take advantage of the file we created in CodeBuild, as it will contain a JSON string in the format `{ "tag": "<latest git commit sha>" }`:

```
        Stages(
                Name="Staging",
                Actions=[
                    Actions(
                        Name="Deploy",
                        ActionTypeId=ActionTypeId(
                            Category="Deploy",
                            Owner="AWS",
                            Version="1",
                            Provider="CloudFormation"
                        ),
                        Configuration={
                            "ChangeSetName": "Deploy",
                            "ActionMode": "CREATE_UPDATE",
                            "StackName": "staging-helloworld-ecs-
service",
                            "Capabilities": "CAPABILITY_NAMED_IAM",
                            "TemplatePath":
"App::templates/helloworld-ecs-service-cf.template",
                            "RoleArn":
GetAtt("CloudFormationHelloworldRole", "Arn"),
                            "ParameterOverrides": """{"Tag" : {
"Fn::GetParam" : [ "BuildOutput", "build.json", "tag" ] } }"""
                        },
                        InputArtifacts=[
                            InputArtifacts(
```

```
                            Name="App",
                        ),
                        InputArtifacts(
                            Name="BuildOutput"
                        )
                    ],
                )
            ]
        ),
```

8. After the staging deployment completes, we will request a manual approval, as follows:

```
    Stages(
                Name="Approval",
                Actions=[
                    Actions(
                        Name="Approval",
                        ActionTypeId=ActionTypeId(
                            Category="Approval",
                            Owner="AWS",
                            Version="1",
                            Provider="Manual"
                        ),
                        Configuration={},
                        InputArtifacts=[],
                    )
                ]
            ),
```

9. Finally, we will create a last stage to run the production deployment. The code is exactly the same here as it is for staging, except for the name of the stage and the stack targeted by our configuration:

```
    Stages(
                Name="Production",
                Actions=[
                    Actions(
                        Name="Deploy",
                        ActionTypeId=ActionTypeId(
                            Category="Deploy",
                            Owner="AWS",
                            Version="1",
                            Provider="CloudFormation"
                        ),
                        Configuration={
                            "ChangeSetName": "Deploy",
                            "ActionMode": "CREATE_UPDATE",
```

```
                                    "StackName": "production-helloworld-
        ecs-service",

                                    "Capabilities": "CAPABILITY_NAMED_IAM",
                                    "TemplatePath":
        "App::templates/helloworld-ecs-service-cf.template",
                                    "RoleArn":
        GetAtt("CloudFormationHelloworldRole", "Arn"),
                                    "ParameterOverrides": """{"Tag" : {
        "Fn::GetParam" : [ "BuildOutput", "build.json", "tag" ] } }"""
                              },
                              InputArtifacts=[
                                    InputArtifacts(
                                        Name="App",
                                    ),
                                    InputArtifacts(
                                        Name="BuildOutput"
                                    )
                              ],
                         )
                    ]
               )
          ],
    ))
```

10. Our pipeline resource has now been created. We can conclude the creation of our script by printing out our template:

```
print(t.to_json())
```

The script is now ready to be used. It should look like the script at: https://github.com/yogeshraheja/EffectiveDevOpsTemplates/blob/master/helloworld-codepipeline-cf-template.py.

We can now create our pipeline.

Starting and configuring our CloudFormation stack

We will proceed as usual for the first part of our pipeline's creation, as follows:

```
$ git add helloworld-codepipeline-cf-template.py
$ git commit -m "Adding Pipeline to deploy our helloworld application using
ECS"
$ git push
$ python helloworld-codepipeline-cf-template.py > helloworld-codepipeline-
cf.template
$ aws cloudformation create-stack \
    --stack-name helloworld-codepipeline \
    --capabilities CAPABILITY_NAMED_IAM \
    --template-body file://helloworld-codepipeline-cf.template
```

 We are using the `CAPABILITY_NAMED_IAM` capability in this case, as we are defining custom names at the IAM level.

This will create our pipeline. However, a small catch is that we didn't specify the GitHub credentials in the pipeline. This is because we don't want to store it in clear text in GitHub. AWS offers a service within IAM to do encryption, but we won't cover that in this book. Consequently, we will simply edit the pipeline the first time around, as follows:

1. Open `https://console.aws.amazon.com/codepipeline` in your browser
2. Select your newly created pipeline
3. Click on **Edit** at the top
4. Click on the pen icon on the **GitHub** action:

5. Click on **Connect to GitHub** on the right-hand-side menu and follow the steps to authorize AWS CodePipeline
6. Select your `helloworld` project in the repository step and the master branch
7. Click on **Update**, save the pipeline changes, and finally, **Save and Continue**

After a few seconds, your pipeline will trigger, and you should see your first deployment going through. This concludes the creation of our CI/CD pipeline:

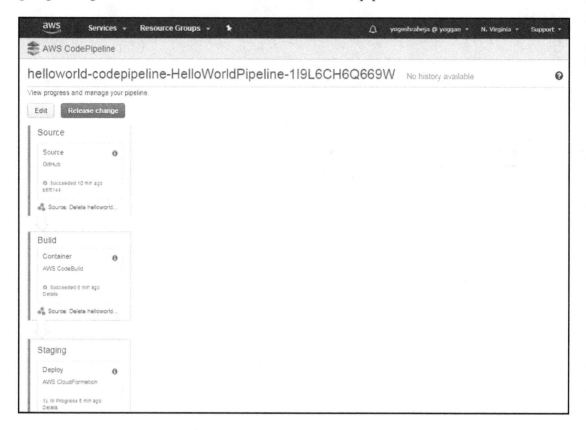

You will also be able to see all of the CloudFormation stack details on the AWS console with the CREATE_COMPLETE status, as shown in the following screenshot:

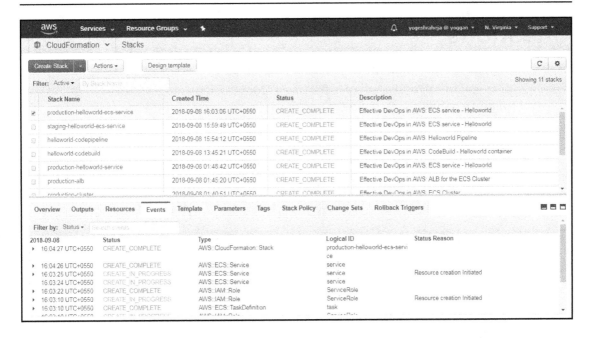

Summary

In this chapter, we explored the concept of containers, using Docker and ECS. After exploring the basics of how Docker works, we created a container for our application. After running it locally, we created a new set of resources to run Docker containers on AWS. We did that using the DevOps best practices and used CloudFormation to generate our resources, treating our infrastructure as code. This allows us to keep those changes under source control. Resource-wise, we created an ECR repository to manage the different revisions of our containers. We also created two ECS clusters with auto scaling capabilities for staging and production, two ALBs to proxy the traffic to our containers, a set of tasks, and an ECS service, to configure and deploy our application.

Finally, we re-implemented a CI/CD pipeline. We did that by using CodeBuild, CodePipeline, and their integrations with CloudFormation.

We will continue improving our systems and we will implement one of the last key characteristics of DevOps; measuring everything. By taking advantage of a number of features that are present in the different services that we use, and by coupling them with other AWS services (such as CloudWatch), we will be able to implement a monitoring strategy for our infrastructure and services.

Questions

1. What is Docker? List the important components of Docker Engine.
2. Can you install and configure the latest Docker CE on any supported platform/OS of your choice?
3. Can you create a Docker image and use the same image to create a web server container?
4. Can you create ECR and ECS using AWS webconsole to get familiar with ECS terminologies?

Further reading

Refer to the following links for further information:

- **Docker Documentation**: https://docs.docker.com
- **Docker Hub**: https://hub.docker.com
- **AWS CodeBuild**: https://aws.amazon.com/codebuild/
- **AWS CodePipeline**: https://aws.amazon.com/codepipeline/
- **AWS Elastic Container Service**: https://aws.amazon.com/ecs/

8
Hardening the Security of Your AWS Environment

In this chapter, we will focus on how to secure our AWS account and application. The cloud and security are two concepts that don't always go together. This is not because of the cloud's nature, but because of the idea that a server on the premises is more secure than a server on the cloud. This is because you know exactly where an on-premise server is, and how the connections to it reach there. The purpose of this chapter is to look at some practical tools and information to demonstrate that a well-managed AWS cloud can be more secure than an on-premise environment.

First we will look at how to secure access for our IAM users. Then, we will look at how to enable logging on for IAM usage with CloudTrail, and, at the network level, with VPC Flow Logs. Creating the right subnets is a crucial step to undertake before placing our application and infrastructure in the cloud. Finally, we will explore the power of a wonderful tool provided by AWS—the **web application firewall (WAF)**.

One of the most important security principles is that of the *least privilege*. This refers to limiting the access rights of users to the minimum permissions that they need in order to complete their work in the correct way.

In this chapter, we will implement this at many levels in the AWS infrastructure. Moving forward, we will take a closer look at the following topics:

- **Identity Access Management (IAM)** security
- CloudTrail
- **Virtual Private Cloud (VPC)** subnets
- AWS WAF

Technical requirements

The code files included within the chapter can be found on GitHub at link: `https://github.com/giuseppeborgese/effective_devops_with_aws__second_edition`.

IAM security

IAM enables you to securely control access to AWS services. Here, we need to implement the least privilege principle, and monitor who does what by recording all of the users' actions.

Root account

When you create an AWS account and log in with the root account, you will see something like the following screenshot:

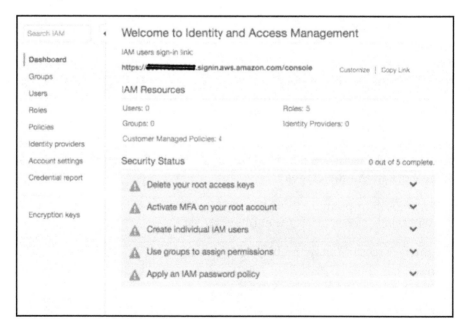

It is important to perform all of the actions suggested by the IAM web console, and also, to change the root account's password.

Root account password

First, change the root account's password. At the top right of the page, between the bell icon and the **Global** drop-down menu, you will find your AWS alias or account number. Click on this, and then click on the **My Account** option:

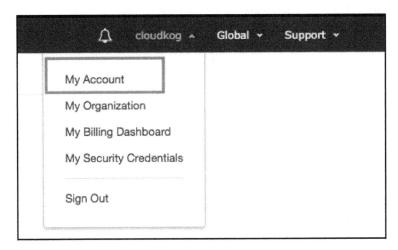

Next, click on the **Edit** button. The others steps are more straightforward and logical, as follows:

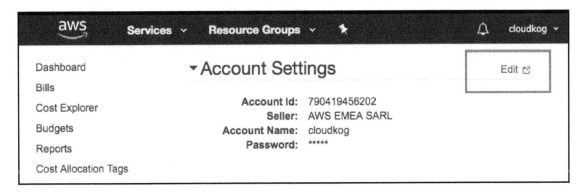

For security reasons, the web page will request that you provide your login information again. Password protection is never enough, especially for the root account; you should absolutely activate **multi-factor authentication** (**MFA**), whether you have a virtual or hardware device. Plenty of solutions are available on the market. Just to provide some examples, Google Authenticator is one of the most well-known apps for Android devices. I have also used a physical dongle made by Yubico (https://www.yubico.com/).

Delete your root access keys

Access keys have the same permissions as those given following access with a password, so a more secure environment is created when this kind of access is removed from the root account, leaving only password access for use (except in some special cases). Don't worry about the message shown in the following screenshot:

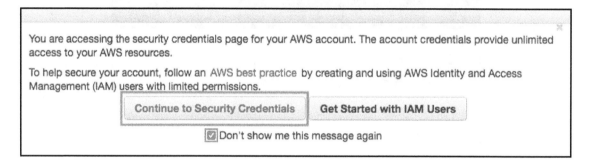

If you created an access key for the root account and find that it was deleted, you will be shown the following message:

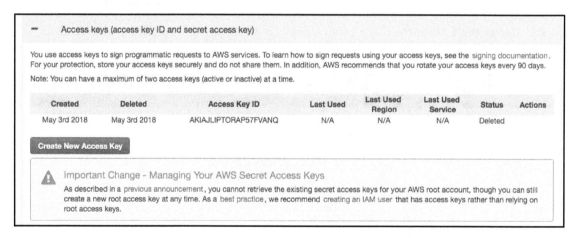

Setting up a password policy for IAM users

The password policy that you should apply depends on the level of security that you want to apply to your IAM users passwords. I would suggest something like the following, but it will depend on your use case:

▾ Password Policy

A password policy is a set of rules that define the type of password an IAM user can set. For more information about password policies, go to Managing Passwords in Using IAM.

Currently, this AWS account does not have a password policy. Specify a password policy below.

Minimum password length: `10`

☑ Require at least one uppercase letter ❶
☑ Require at least one lowercase letter ❶
☑ Require at least one number ❶
☑ Require at least one non-alphanumeric character ❶
☑ Allow users to change their own password ❶
☑ Enable password expiration ❶
   Password expiration period (in days): `90`
☑ Prevent password reuse ❶
   Number of passwords to remember: `10`
☐ Password expiration requires administrator reset ❶

Apply password policy   **Delete password policy**

Creating an administrator group and a personal IAM user

To operate with the root account, it is more secure to create a personal IAM user and operate through that. It is also a best practice to assign permissions to the group, and not directly to the IAM users. Do this as follows:

1. Create a group called `admins` or something similiar.
2. Assign the administrator policy to this group.
3. Create a personal IAM user with some kind of criteria. In my case, I would choose `myname.mysurname giuseppe.borgese`.
4. Insert the new IAM user in to the `admins` group.

This allows other IAM users to evaluate whether to create groups with fewer privileges than the administrator. It also allows them to assign the necessary rights, but not more than are required. For example, if an IAM user needed to manage EC2 machines, we could give them the predefined **AmazonEC2FullAccess** policy, and, correspondingly, if they needed to manage an RDS environment, they could be given an **AmazonRDSFullAccess** policy.

AmazonEC2FullAccess policy

The tasks that require root account access are listed clearly on the AWS documentation page at `https://docs.aws.amazon.com/general/latest/gr/aws_tasks-that-require-root.html`. To follow is a list of these tasks:

- Modifying root user details
- Changing your AWS support plan
- Closing an AWS account
- Signing up for GovCloud
- Submiting a reverse DNS for Amazon EC2 requests
- Creating a CloudFront key pair
- Creating an AWS created X.509 signing certificate
- Transfering a route 53 domain to another AWS account
- Changing the Amazon EC2 setting for longer resource IDs
- Requesting the removal of the port 25 email throttle on your EC2 instance
- Finding your AWS account canonical user ID

All of these operations are very rare, so it would be unusual for you to find one of these events cropping up among your everyday tasks.

Final security status

Now that all of your tasks have been accomplished, you can log out from the root user and start to use the IAM user with the administrator rights that you have created, as follows:

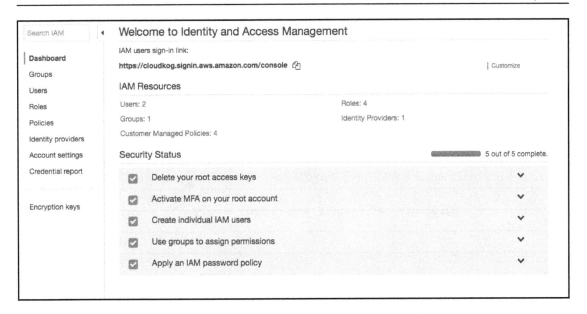

If you are completely new to the cloud approach, it is worth spending some time reading the *AWS Shared Responsibility Model* at `https://aws.amazon.com/compliance/shared-responsibility-model/`. On the page, there is a clear definition of what AWS's responsibility is (*security of the cloud*), and also, what our responsibility is (*security in the cloud*). In a few words, it is our responsibility to ensure that what we create inside of the cloud, and all of the tools that we use to create it, are AWS-secure.

In the past, there were many security breaches in the famous AWS S3 service, because people configured the service to be readable/writable from anywhere in the world. AWS guarantees that the service is always updated and patched, but the permissions we give when accessing it are left in our court.

On YouTube, it is possible to listen to a very nice song by Kate Turchin, located at `https://www.youtube.com/watch?v=tIb5PGW_t1o`. This song explains the shared responsibility model in an accessible way:

AWS Shared Responsibility Model: EXPLAINED (song)
Kate Turchin • 4555 visualizzazioni • 11 mesi fa

A musical explanation of the Amazon Shared Responsibility Model. Written and performed by Kate Turchin, "The Cloud Security ...

CloudTrail

We have enabled IAM personal users and have avoided the root account. We have also assigned the necessary IAM policy to our groups, and have assigned each user to the right group. However, we also need to record all of their actions. To fulfill this purpose, the AWS service to enable is CloudTrail.

Each event performed over the AWS infrastructure by an IAM user or a resource with an IAM role assigned to it will be recorded in an S3 bucket and/or in a CloudWatch log group. My advice is to follow the AWS documentation at: `https://docs.aws.amazon.com/awscloudtrail/latest/userguide/cloudtrail-create-a-trail-using-the-console-first-time.html`. Creating a trail from the web console will be very straightforward, if you read this document.

VPC Flow Logs

An **intrusion detection system** (**IDS**) and an **intrusion prevention system** (**IPS**) are common tools in a secure network. In an on-premise environment, they are not so easy or cheap to implement, because you need dedicated hardware, and also a network structure that accommodates this feature. By contrast, in AWS, using only one feature of the VPC service, you can enable and disable these tools whenever and wherever you consider appropriate. You can have these tools at three levels of your network:

- The VPC level
- The subnet level
- The **elastic network interface** (**ENI**) level

As you know, a network interface belongs to one subnet, and one subnet belongs to a VPC. So, if you enable tools at the subnet level, you don't have to apply them at the network interface level, and if you enable them at the VPC level, you don't need to apply them at the subnet level. Before you activate this feature, you need to create the following three resources:

- An empty CloudWatch group, where the data will be stored
- An AWS role to perform the VPC Flow Log operation
- A policy associated with the role, with the necessary permissions

Of course, you can create these resources manually, and all of the instructions to do this are available on the flow logs documentation page at `https://docs.aws.amazon.com/AmazonVPC/latest/UserGuide/flow-logs.html`. However, to take a more DevOps/automated approach, we can use a Terraform module. In this case, we use a remote module created on GitHub. As you can see in the official Terraform documentation about module sources at `https://www.terraform.io/docs/modules/sources.html#github`, GitHub is a supported source type. However, if you want to use your own GitHub repository, you can use `ssh` or `https` as module sources. For more information, refer to `https://www.terraform.io/docs/modules/sources.html#github`.

The code to call the module is very simple, and requires only two parameters—the `source` and the `prefix`. The `prefix` will be used to name all the module resources. You can download or look into the GitHub repository link given in the *Technical requirement* section to see what this module does, in detail. However, to use it, the following few lines are enough:

```
module "flow-log-prerequisite" {
    source =
"github.com/giuseppeborgese/effective_devops_with_aws__second_edition//terr
aform- modules//vpc-flow-logs-prerequisite"
    prefix = "devops2nd"
  }
output "role" { value = "${module.flow-log-prerequisite.rolename}" }
output "loggroup" { value = "${module.flow-log-
prerequisite.cloudwatch_log_group_arn}" }
```

The names in the output are useful to use in the web console after that.

After you have added the module lines to any of your existing files, or to a new one with a `.tf` extension, it is necessary to initialize them with `terraform init`.

The following is the output of the `terraform init` command:

```
terraform init -upgrade
 Upgrading modules...
 - module.flow-log-prerequisite
 Updating source
"github.com/giuseppeborgese/effective_devops_with_aws__second_edition//terr
aform-modules//vpc-flow-logs-prerequisite"
Initializing the backend...
Initializing provider plugins...
 ....
```

The `terraform` binary has just downloaded the module code. At this point, if it wasn't been done beforehand, download the AWS provider information from the latest available version. The `-upgrade` option forces you to use the latest available version, so that is usually a good idea.

Now, with a `terraform plan`, we can see which three objects will be created:

```
terraform plan -out /tmp/tf11.out
Refreshing Terraform state in-memory prior to plan...
The refreshed state will be used to calculate this plan, but will not
be persisted to local or remote state storage.
...
...
An execution plan has been generated and is shown below.
Resource actions are indicated with the following symbols:
+ create
Terraform will perform the following actions:
+ module.flow-log-prerequisite.aws_cloudwatch_log_group.flow_log
id: <computed>
arn: <computed>
name: "devops2nd_flowlogs"
retention_in_days: "0"
+ module.flow-log-prerequisite.aws_iam_role.flow_role
id: <computed>
arn: <computed>
assume_role_policy: "{\n \"Version\": \"2012-10-17\",\n \"Statement\": [\n
{\n \"Sid\": \"\",\n \"Effect\": \"Allow\",\n \"Principal\": {\n
\"Service\": \"vpc-flow-logs.amazonaws.com\"\n },\n \"Action\":
\"sts:AssumeRole\"\n }\n ]\n}\n"
create_date: <computed>
force_detach_policies: "false"
max_session_duration: "3600"
name: "devops2nd_flowlogs"
path: "/"
unique_id: <computed>
+ module.flow-log-prerequisite.aws_iam_role_policy.flow_policy
id: <computed>
name: "devops2nd_flowlogs"
policy: "{\n \"Version\": \"2012-10-17\",\n \"Statement\": [\n {\n
\"Action\": [\n \"logs:CreateLogGroup\",\n \"logs:CreateLogStream\",\n
\"logs:PutLogEvents\",\n \"logs:DescribeLogGroups\",\n
\"logs:DescribeLogStreams\"\n ],\n \"Effect\": \"Allow\",\n \"Resource\":
\"*\"\n }\n ]\n}\n"
role: "${aws_iam_role.flow_role.id}"

Plan: 3 to add, 0 to change, 0 to destroy.
```

This plan was saved to: /tmp/tf11.out.

To apply these actions, run the following command:

```
terraform apply /tmp/tf11.out
```

Then, create them with a terraform apply command:

```
tf11 apply /tmp/tf11.out
 module.flow-log-prerequisite.aws_cloudwatch_log_group.flow_log:
Creating...
 arn: "" => "<computed>"
 name: "" => "devops2nd_flowlogs"
 retention_in_days: "" => "0"
 module.flow-log-prerequisite.aws_iam_role.flow_role: Creating...
 arn: "" => "<computed>"
 assume_role_policy: "" => "{\n \"Version\": \"2012-10-17\",\n
\"Statement\": [\n {\n \"Sid\": \"\",\n \"Effect\": \"Allow\",\n
\"Principal\": {\n \"Service\": \"vpc-flow-logs.amazonaws.com\"\n },\n
\"Action\": \"sts:AssumeRole\"\n }\n ]\n}\n"
 create_date: "" => "<computed>"
 force_detach_policies: "" => "false"
 max_session_duration: "" => "3600"
 name: "" => "devops2nd_flowlogs"
 path: "" => "/"
 unique_id: "" => "<computed>"
 module.flow-log-prerequisite.aws_iam_role.flow_role: Creation complete
after 2s (ID: devops2nd_flowlogs)
 module.flow-log-prerequisite.aws_iam_role_policy.flow_policy: Creating...
 name: "" => "devops2nd_flowlogs"
 policy: "" => "{\n \"Version\": \"2012-10-17\",\n \"Statement\": [\n {\n
\"Action\": [\n \"logs:CreateLogGroup\",\n \"logs:CreateLogStream\",\n
\"logs:PutLogEvents\",\n \"logs:DescribeLogGroups\",\n
\"logs:DescribeLogStreams\"\n ],\n \"Effect\": \"Allow\",\n \"Resource\":
\"*\"\n }\n ]\n}\n"
 role: "" => "devops2nd_flowlogs"
 module.flow-log-prerequisite.aws_cloudwatch_log_group.flow_log: Creation
complete after 3s (ID: devops2nd_flowlogs)
 module.flow-log-prerequisite.aws_iam_role_policy.flow_policy: Creation
complete after 1s (ID: devops2nd_flowlogs:devops2nd_flowlogs)
Apply complete! Resources: 3 added, 0 changed, 0 destroyed.
 Outputs:
loggroup = arn:aws:logs:us-east-1:790419456202:log-
group:devops2nd_flowlogs:*
 role = devops2nd_flowlogs
```

Take a note of these last two pieces of output as we need to activate the flow log.

Creating the flow log for one subnet

Now, with all of the prerequisites satisfied, we are going to create a flow log for one subnet that is open in the AWS web console for the VPC service:

1. Select one subnet. Now, select the **Flow Logs** tab, and click on the **Create flow log** button, as shown in the following screenshot:

2. Insert the information as it is given in the following screenshot. The log group and the role are the ones created with the Terraform module. In this example, we are interested in seeing the traffic that is accepted, so we select the **Accept** option in the **Filter** drop-down menu:

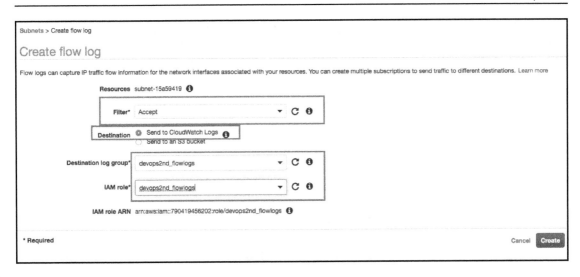

Now that you have a situation like this in your AWS web console, take note of the subnet number, because we will need it when it comes to verification. Of course, your subnet ID will be different from mine, which is `subnet-15a59419`.

Verifying the flow logs

In order to verify whether a flow log is working, and to get practice with the flow log, we are going to create an EC2 machine for the subnet login in SSH, and we will analyze the traffic for that SSH login.

We won't cover the full process of creating an EC2 machine here because it is a basic task. If you are at this point in the book, you should already know how to do it. What I suggest is to use a `t2.micro` that is a free-tier eligible type. Also, it is very important to create the machine in the subnet where you just activated the flow log, and to allow the SSH to have access from your location.

After a short period of time, you can go into the CloudWatch service, click on the **Logs** option, and select the log group, `devops2nd_flowlogs`, created with Terraform:

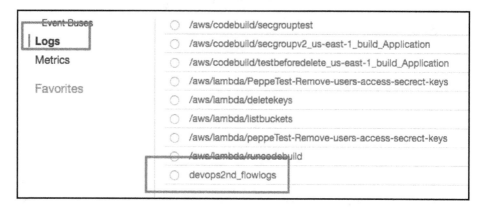

Inside of that, you will find the name of the network interface associated with the EC2 instance created previously, as shown in the following screenshot:

If you have many network interfaces in the same subnet, this means that you have multiple machines, and you need to go to the EC2 service and the **Network Interfaces** option, and locate the network interface using the **Instance ID** column, as shown in the following screenshot:

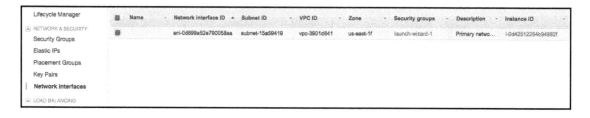

However, you will probably only have one network interface, so click on its name. In my case, this is `eni-0d899a52e790058aa-accept`.

There are many lines; to understand the details of each one, you can take a look at the record documentation at `https://docs.aws.amazon.com/AmazonVPC/latest/UserGuide/flow-logs.html#flow-log-records`:

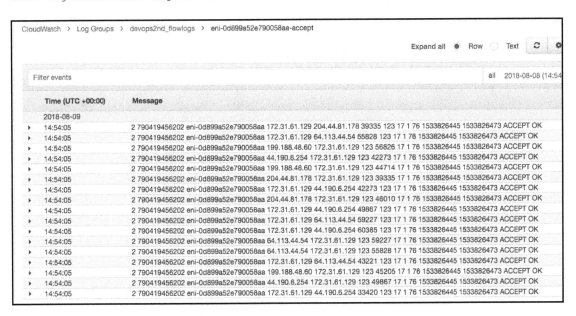

However, we want to find our SSH connection attempt, so it is necessary to recover our laptop's public IP with a service like the one at `http://www.whatsmyip.org/`, and put it in the filter, as follows:

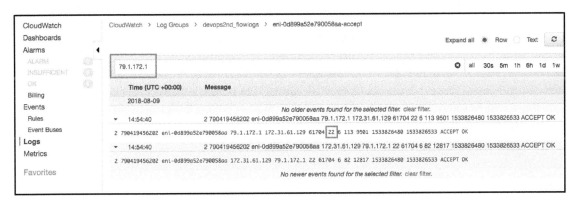

In the first line, you can see the following items:

- The public IP of my laptop is `79.1.172.1`
- The private IP of the EC2 instance is `172.31.61.129`
- The source port of my laptop is `61704`
- The destination port of the EC2 instance for the SSH service is port `22`

VPC Flow Log consideration

We have completed a tour of the VPC Flow Log service with a working **proof of concept (PoC)**. Of course, there are many other options available in the service, which you can find in the official AWS documentation. By visiting these, you can continue to explore the potential of the VPC Flow Log.

At this point, if you ever try to do the same task performed by the VPC Flow Log in an on-premise environment, it should be clear how easy it is to enable a full traffic monitor on the AWS cloud compared with doing do so in an on-premise environment.

Don't forget to delete the EC2 instance that was created previously, in order to avoid incurring any unnecessary extra charges. The other resource will not have any costs, unless you generate a very great amount of traffic in that subnet.

VPC subnets

In this section, we will look at how to organize our VPC subnets, following the least privileged principle. We have to expose and give access to our resources (EC2, ELB, and RDS) in the fewest possible circumstances, in order to limit security attacks and data leaks.

In each AWS region there is already a default VPC that has been created. If you want to know all of the details of this, I would recommend that you read the *Default VPC and Default Subnets* documentation at `https://docs.aws.amazon.com/AmazonVPC/latest/UserGuide/default-vpc.html`. However, in short, it is possible to say that everything you put there is potentially exposed to the public network if the security group that you configure allows that.

Routing and subnet types

In the official documentation
at `https://docs.aws.amazon.com/AmazonVPC/latest/UserGuide/VPC_Scenarios.html,` the
re are four scenarios described for your VPC configuration, and it will be useful to look into
that. It is important to understand that access to the resources that you place in your
subnets is determined by the three following factors:

- Routing
- The **Network Access Control** (**NAC**) list (a stateless firewall)
- The security group (a stateful firewall)

My advice is to not touch the NAC; leave the default one attached to each subnet, which
allows all of the inbound and outbound traffic, and use the security group as a firewall
instead. A subnet can be classified into three types, based on their security levels:

- Public subnets
- Private subnets with internet access
- Private subnets without internet access

Accessing private subnets

The resources in public subnets can be accessed by using the public IP and enabling the
security group to receive connections. For private subnets, you have at least three ways to
do this, as follows:

- Jump on a bastion host in one public subnet, and, from there, reach the private
  resources.
- Use site-to-site VPNs from the AWS VPN service, `https://docs.aws.amazon.`
  `com/AmazonVPC/latest/UserGuide/vpn-connections.html,` to the physical
  router/s in your office. You can connect two routers, for redundancy.
- Place a virtual VPN software in an EC2 machine and connect your device to it.
  There are countless solutions that do this, and many are in the AWS Marketplace,
  ready to be used in exchange for a monthly fee.

The preferred option, if you have an office with physical routers, is always the site-to-site
solution.

What to place in which subnet?

In my test VPC, I have six subnets—two for each type, as you can see in the following screenshot:

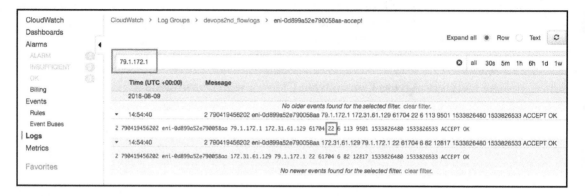

What should you insert in each kind of subnet? Consider the following points:

- **Public subnets**: This refers to all of the external **Elastic Load Balancing** (**ELB**) with public access, the bastion host (if you have one), the virtual VPN software in an EC2 machine, and any other resource that requires access from the internet, and cannot be accessed in any other way.
- **Private subnets with internet access**: This refers to all of the internal ELBs as well as all EC2 machines behind an ELB (internal or external), that have to download or upload something to the internet, and a database that is required to download or upload something to the internet
- **Private subnets without internet access**: This refers to all resources that don't need access to the internet for any reason, and also resources whose updates are downloaded from an internal repository

Identifying subnets from the web console

Keep the following points in mind :

- Every subnet can have one associated route table
- One route table can be associated with multiple subnets
- If you don't explicitly associate a route table to a subnet, the default route table is associated automatically

In the following screenshot, you can see three route tables, where the **Public Route** is the default route table:

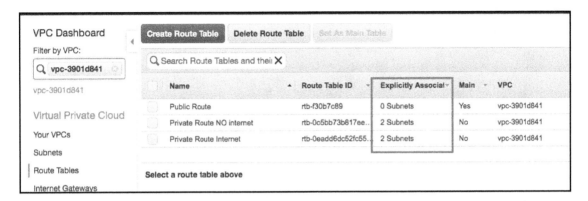

In the **Subnets** section, you can see the route table associated with that subnet and the single routes, but to change the content of a route table, you have to edit from the **Route Tables** section. What differentiate a private route from a public route table/subnet is the destination of the 0.0.0.0/0 route. If it's a forward internet gateway, igw-xxxxx means that this subnet is reachable from the outside world and can connect to the internet, as well (assuming that the security group allows for that):

If it points to an NAT gateway or another EC2 instance instead, this means that it is a private subnet with internet access, and it can access the internet in any way, and so it is reachable from the external world. First, you have to click on the **Create a NAT Gateway** button, as follows:

After that, you can change the routing table and have a situation like the one shown in the following screenshot:

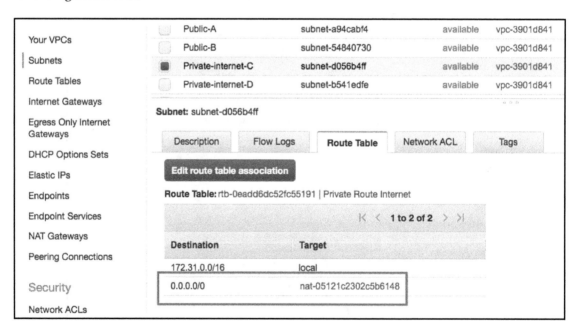

If the `0.0.0.0/0` isn't present, as shown in the preceding screenshot, it is a completely private subnet:

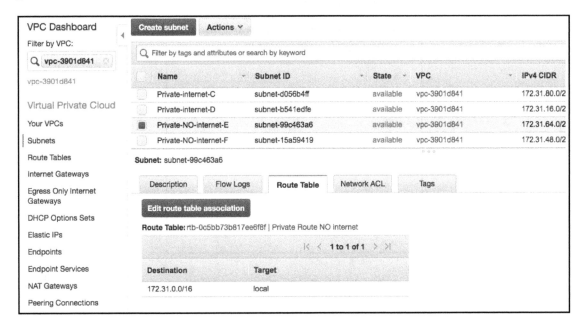

Endpoint routing

If a database has to upload a backup to a private S3 bucket in the same region, it should never use internet access, but should take a private, internal route. This is called a VPC endpoint. With this kind of route, you can avoid passing through the internet to reach an AWS service, such as S3, DynamoDB, or CloudWatch, and gain speed, security, and cost savings (internet traffic has a cost). To see all of the services with a VPC endpoint, you can take a look at the official documentation at `https://docs.aws.amazon.com/AmazonVPC/latest/UserGuide/vpc-endpoints.html`.

Here, we will configure the first VPC endpoint available for the S3 service, as follows:

1. Go to **VPC | Endpoints | Create Endpoint:**

2. Leave the default AWS service and select the S3 service, as seen in the following screenshot:

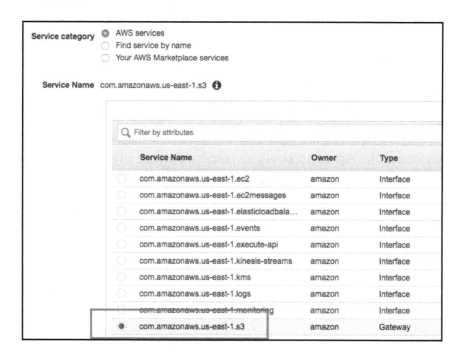

3. Select the VPC that you are working on, and all of the route tables to modify:

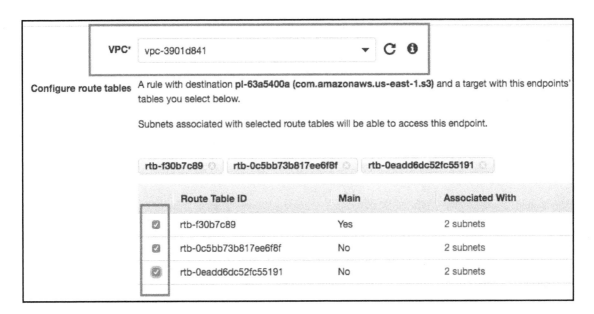

4. Now, you can see a new route rule, as shown in the following screenshot:

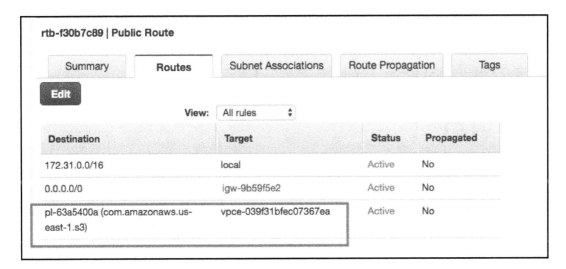

Keep in mind that this will work for all of the buckets created in the same VPC region. In this example, it is us-east-1, North Virginia.

In the AWS documentation for the *Endpoints for Amazon S3* at https://docs.aws.amazon.com/AmazonVPC/latest/UserGuide/vpc-endpoints-s3.html, there is an interesting hardening rule for the S3 bucket policy, as follows:

```
{
    "Version": "2012-10-17",
    "Id": "Policy1415115909152",
     "Statement": [
        {
            "Sid": "Access-to-specific-VPCE-only",
            "Principal": "*",
            "Action": "s3:*",
            "Effect": "Deny",
            "Resource": ["arn:aws:s3:::my_secure_bucket",
                        "arn:aws:s3:::my_secure_bucket/*"],
            "Condition": {
                "StringNotEquals": {
        "aws:sourceVpce": "vpce-039f31bfec07367ea"
                }
            }
        }
    ]
}
```

I have changed this by adding my VPC endpoint ID, vpce-039f31bfec07367ea instead of the one in the documentation. With this rule, the bucket my_secure_bucket will be only reachable from the VPCs that are associated with that endpoint.

AWS WAF

You restrict access by using security groups and private subnets for all your resources. All of the monitor logs, VPC Flow Logs, and CloudTrails are active. IAM policies are enforced, everything is correctly secured, and nothing is exposed. This is because you have the VPN service to access any resources. However, if you want to provide an internet service, you have to open at least one point of access to the external world. As we already discussed in the *VPC Subnets* section, you should expose as few resources in the public subnet as possible, with the 0.0.0.0/0 security group rule open. If possible, only an ELB should stay in this situation, passing connections to the EC2 machines in private subnets, since the EC2 machines communicate with the RDS databases with strict security rules.

This is the most classic AWS application, and it is not necessary to explain it in detail here. Instead, we want to focus on increasing the security of the ELB with the AWS WAF. For more information, refer to `https://aws.amazon.com/waf/`. AWS WAF is a firewall that works at the application level and can protect at level 7 of the TCP/IP stack protocol, rather than at level 4 of the TCP/IP stack, where the security groups work.

What can the WAF do that a security group can't? Consider the following answers to this question:

- Protect against SQL injection and cross-site scripting
- Block **denial-of-service (DoS)** and **distributed denial-of-service (DDoS)**
- Protect a part of the URL of your web application, such as `www.mywebsite/admin`

In this chapter, we will create two practical POCs with Terraform about DoS and a sub-URL. To do this, we are going to create a web application playground, apply the WAF, and test the rules to trigger its protection. Keep in mind that when this part of the book was being written, the WAF could only be applied to the **application load balancer (ALB)** and CloudFront, but AWS continuously updates its services, so there is no knowing what might be done in the near future.

Web application playground

Our test playground will be an ALB and an EC2 machine with an Apache2 web server installed. In this section, we will only create the environment and test it, without any WAF configuration. In the next section, however, we will add the WAF level on the ALB.

To create the following playground, we will use a Terraform module that is available on GitHub:

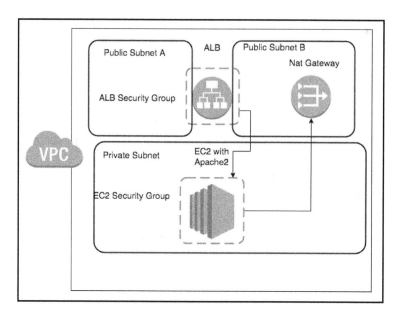

Start by adding the following code to your `main.tf` file:

```
module "webapp-playground" {
  source =
"github.com/giuseppeborgese/effective_devops_with_aws__second_edition//terr
aform-modules//webapp-playground"
  subnet_public_A = "subnet-a94cabf4"
  subnet_public_B = "subnet-54840730"
  subnet_private = "subnet-54840730"
  vpc_id = "vpc-3901d841"
  my_ami = "ami-b70554c8"
  pem_key_name = "effectivedevops"
}
```

Some things to keep in mind are as follows:

- The ALB must always live in at least two subnets, in two different availability zones.
- This ALB is reachable on port 80 and uses an HTTP listener that can be acceptable for a PoC. However, in your real environment, it is best to register a public domain with AWS Route 53, create an SSL certificate with AWS Certificate Manager, associate this certificate to the ALB, and use an HTTPS listener.

- The security group settings are very strict, and you can take a look at the module code to see that the ALB security group ingress is reachable only from port 80 to the whole internet, 0.0.0.0/0, and this can be reached in *egress* only from port 80 of the EC2 security group.

As usual, to create the resource you need to run the following commands:

```
terraform init -upgrade
terraform plan -out /tmp/tf11.out
Plan: 12 to add, 0 to change, 0 to destroy.
terraform apply /tmp/tf11.out
```

Find the DNS ALB name, as shown in the following screenshot, and copy it:

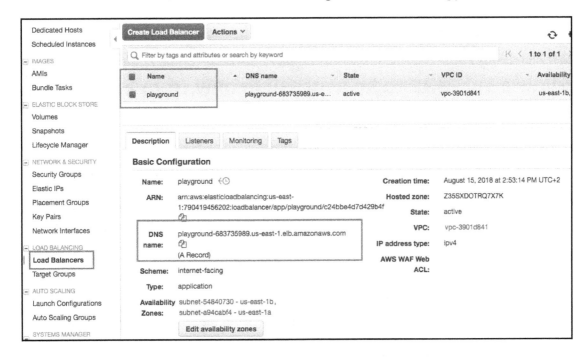

Open it from your browser, as follows:

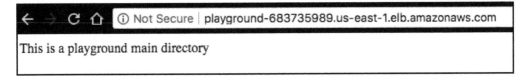

There is also a subdirectory that we can use to test our WAF later:

If you don't use it quickly enough, your playground will destroy it with the `terraform` command, to avoid incurring any unnecessary charges. If you want to destroy just the playground, but not the other resources that were created, you can use a selective `destroy` module, as follows:

```
terraform destroy -target module.webapp-playground
```

If you confirm with a `Yes`, then the 12 module resources will be destroyed.

Allow a sub-URL to be accessible only from an IP

Usually, in your web application, you have an admin area, and it could be the case that this part of your portal isn't accessible by everyone. Of course, you have a username and password, but an attacker can steal those credentials in many ways.

If it is a sensitive application, for the principle of least privilege to be followed, it is convenient to restrict access to the locations where this kind of admin access needs to be used; for example, from the office. If you can have different access for the admin section you can put this behind an internal load balancer and connect the VPC to your office by using a VPN service, as discussed in previous sections. The internal load balancer DNS name is converted with the private IPs of your VPC, and, in this way, you can assure that connections are only made from a trusted source, such as your office.

However, many times, you won't have this option, because the application is all in one bundle, and you cannot separate the admin sub-URL from the main part. In such cases, the only change available is to use an AWS WAF and apply a filter to the admin sub-URL only. We need to create a WAF and attach it to the ALB for our playground web app.

To do this, I have created a `terraform` module, and you can use it in your code with the following lines:

```
module "limit_admin_WAF" {
  source =
"github.com/giuseppeborgese/effective_devops_with_aws__second_edition//terr
aform-modules//limit-the-admin-area"
  alb_arn = "${module.webapp-playground.alb_arn}"
```

```
    my_office_ip = "146.241.179.87/32"
    admin_suburl = "/subdir"
}
```

Of course, don't forget to replace your office IP or home connection public IP in the `my_office_ip` field, and to use the subnet mask `/32` if it is a single IP, as in my case.

The commands are the usual ones, as follows:

```
terraform plan -out /tmp/tf11.out
terraform init -upgrade
terraform apply /tmp/tf11.out
```

To facilitate the test, I have added an `alb_url` output variable, as follows:

```
alb_url = playground-1940933132.us-east-1.elb.amazonaws.com
loggroup = arn:aws:logs:us-east-1:790419456202:log-
group:devops2nd_flowlogs:*
role = devops2nd_flowlogs
giuseppe@Giuseppes-MacBook-Air ~/p/effectivedevops>
```

Now, the WAF is associated to the ALB, and all of the requests will be filtered.

Testing with the command line

This time, we are going to test it using the command-line tool, `curl`. As you can see from my office IP, no issues arose when trying to reach both the root directory and the sub-URL:

```
giuseppe@Giuseppes-MacBook-Air ~> curl
http://playground-1940933132.us-east-1.elb.amazonaws.com/subdir/
  This is a sub directory
giuseppe@Giuseppes-MacBook-Air ~> curl
http://playground-1940933132.us-east-1.elb.amazonaws.com/
  This is a playground main directory
giuseppe@Giuseppes-MacBook-Air ~>
```

Instead, when I used a virtual machine with another public IP, I got back the following result:

```
[ec2-user@ip-172-31-6-204 ~]$ curl
http://playground-1940933132.us-east-1.elb.amazonaws.com/
  This is a playground main directory
  [ec2-user@ip-172-31-6-204 ~]$ curl
http://playground-1940933132.us-east-1.elb.amazonaws.com/subdir/
  <html>
  <head><title>403 Forbidden</title></head>
  <body bgcolor="white">
```

```
<center><h1>403 Forbidden</h1></center>
</body>
</html>
```

Identifying the WAF from the web console

Take a look at the resource created, that is, the service WAF, as follows:

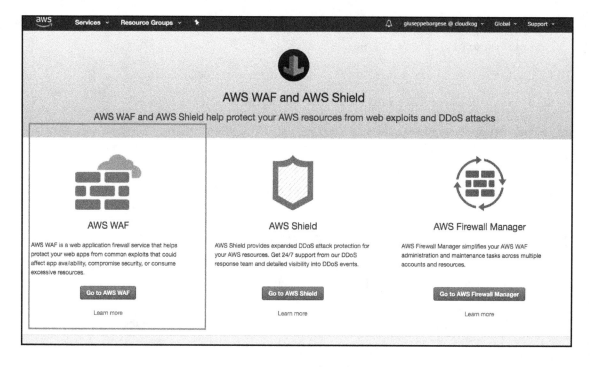

View the **Web ACLs** option, and select the region where you are working from the **Filter** menu. You can see what the Terraform module creates, as follows:

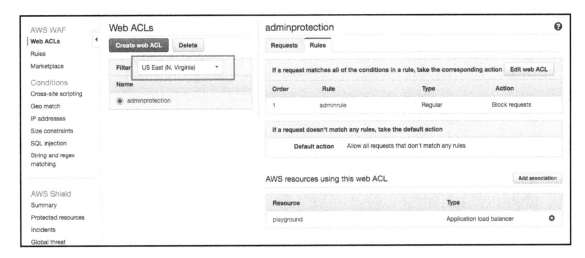

In the **Rules** section, it is possible to see the filter itself, and the IP that is allowed to access the restricted area:

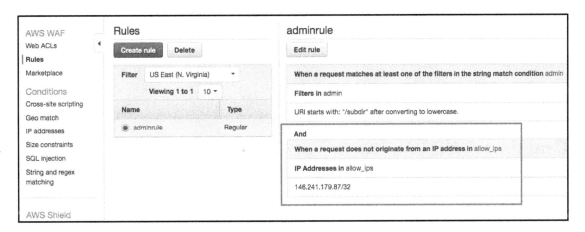

Blocking DoS/DDoS attacks

A DoS attack is an old problem for our applications, especially in their distributed versions, the DDoS, where multiple sources (usually hacked devices of many kinds, that form a botnet) try to run a DoS by running so many queries at the same time that a network becomes overloaded. In this case, to defend and continue to serve traffic to legitimate users, it is fundamental to identify and block malicious sources.

It is worth spending a little bit of time reading the official documentation on *Denial of Service Attack Mitigation on AWS*, at `https://aws.amazon.com/answers/networking/aws-ddos-attack-mitigation/`. What we want to do here is to focus on a practical example of using WAF.

The AWS WAF can block a single public IP that is sending too many requests. The question that should pop up in your mind is, *how many requests are too many?* This depends on your web application, so what you should do before applying any filter of this kind is measure the number of requests received from a single IP in a five-minute time range.

Keep in mind that the AWS WAF lower limit that it is 2,000 requests and also according to my tests, though request `2001` will be not blocked, after a while, you will see a number of subsequent requests blocked. As we did for the other examples, we will not trust what AWS declares, but we will test our PoC after its creation. To immediately see whether the system is working, we will set up the AWS limit for our sub-
URL: `http://playground-1940933132.us-east-1.elb.amazonaws.com/subdir/`.
We are not going to apply anything on the main page, at
`http://playground-1940933132.us-east-1.elb.amazonaws.com`.

Creating AWS WAF with Terraform

Destroy the `limit_admin_WAF` module to avoid conflicts. You can do so with the following command:

```
terraform destroy -target module.limit_admin_WAF
```

Next, comment on the module in your code, using `/* */`:

```
/* module "limit_admin_WAF" {
  source
  . . . . . . . . . . . .
} */
```

Create the new module with the following code:

```
module "limit_admin_WAF" {
source =
"github.com/giuseppeborgese/effective_devops_with_aws__second_edition//terr
aform-modules//ddos_protection"
alb_arn = "${module.webapp-playground.alb_arn}"
admin_suburl = "subdir"
}
```

As usual, include the following code snippet:

```
terraform init --upgrade
terraform plan -out /tmp/tf11.out
terraform apply /tmp/tf11.out
 Outputs:
alb_url = playground-1757904639.us-east-1.elb.amazonaws.com
```

Take the DNS name from the output and test that everything is working with the `curl` command, as follows:

```
curl playground-1757904639.us-east-1.elb.amazonaws.com
```

The following is a `playground` main directory:

```
curl playground-1757904639.us-east-1.elb.amazonaws.com/subdir/
```

This is a subdirectory. Log in to the web console, go to the WAF service, select the Virginia region, and note the `subdir` rule of the **Rate-based** type, as shown in the following screenshot:

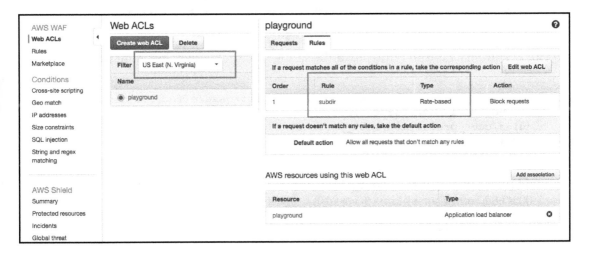

Also, in the **Rules** section, you will notice that right now, there aren't any IPs blocked:

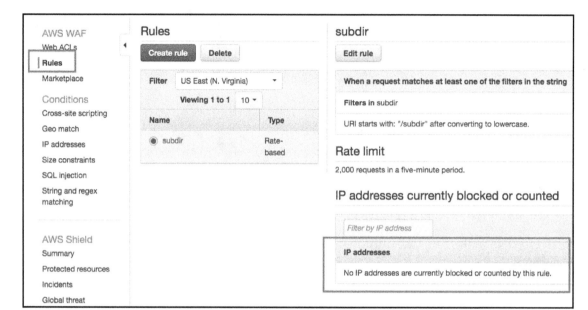

Keep in mind that any kind of DoS test is forbidden by AWS by default, and it can be blocked, because it violates the terms and conditions. For more information on the *AWS Service Terms*, refer to https://aws.amazon.com/service-terms/. In our case, we are going to run 2,000/4,000 requests from a single IP in a short period of time. It is not so large an amount that it will trigger the AWS alarm. If you have a very good internet connection, you can run this script from your laptop, but my advice is to use an Amazon Linux EC2 machine in a public subnet directly exposed to the internet, so that we have the same conditions of experimentation.

Log in on your machine and download the script with the following command:

```
curl -O
https://raw.githubusercontent.com/giuseppeborgese/effective_devops_with_aws
__second_edition/master/terraform-
modules/ddos_protection/test_protection.sh
chmod +x test_protection.sh
./test_protection.sh ...
```

This will run 4,000 requests to your ALB playground. From the output, you can see that the first 2,000/3,000 requests will be successful:

```
This is a subdirectory
538
```

```
This is a subdirectory
 539
This is a subdirectory
 540
This is a subdirectory
 541
This is a subdirectory
```

However, you will then start to receive rejected requests like the following:

```
259
<html>
<head><title>403 Forbidden</title></head>
<body bgcolor="white">
<center><h1>403 Forbidden</h1></center>
</body>
</html>
260
<html>
<head><title>403 Forbidden</title></head>
<body bgcolor="white">
<center><h1>403 Forbidden</h1></center>
</body>
</html>
```

If you don't see this during the first run, you will have to run the script again to trigger the requests. You can log in with the web console in the WAF service, and you will see the public IP of your EC machine in the **Rules** section:

Still, if you run a `curl` to the root directory, you will see that it is still accessible from your EC2 machine. If you try to access it from your laptop, the `subdir` URL will still be accessible. If you don't send any more requests for a while, the public IP of your EC2 machine will be removed from the blacklist, and this is correct, because that IP is not a threat if it returns to transmitting normal traffic amounts.

DDoS attach consideration

AWS WAF can be a very useful tool for mitigating DOS and DDOS attacks, but before starting to use it, it's convenient to do the following:

- Read and observe how to implement the DoS attack mitigation on AWS
- Know your application, and set up a good limit for concurrent connections, to avoid blocking valid traffic and getting false positive responses
- Build a scalable web application, to respond to requests until the WAF understands that it is under attack and triggers its filters

WAF for SQL Injection (SQLi)

We created and tested the WAF features for rate rules and sub-URL limits. As we said at the beginning, there is also the SQLi feature, and it is possible to find some CloudFormation templates related to this on the official AWS website at `https://github.com/aws-samples/aws-waf-sample` GitHub repository.

Summary

In this chapter, we applied the least privilege principle at different level. In the IAM section, you learned how to lock in your root account and pass control to IAM users, by configuring a password policy and setting up permissions and groups. Enabling CloudTrail, we tracked and monitored every action performed on our infrastructure by an IAM user or by a service, in our environment. With VPC Flow Logs, we observed a powerful network monitor applicable at any point of our VPC, and we also created our prerequisites using Terraform, a wonderful tool for growing our practice. . We also covered the concept of the Terraform module. In the *VPC subnets* section, we looked at the three kinds of subnet that we can use in our AWS cloud, and where to place the different kinds of resources available in our infrastructure, exposing it to the internet as little as possible and keeping as much as possible in private zones.

While discussing the WAF service, we explored one of the most powerful services for security available in the AWS world. Protecting some sensitive parts of your web application can be useful. DoS protection is something that should always be present in professional web service. Configuring WAF is not always easy, but thanks to the power of Terraform automation and to the PoC modules available in this book, understanding the principles and configuring accordingly is only some `terraform` and `git` commands away.

Questions

1. Suppose that I have just registered to the AWS cloud and received my password by email. Can I start to build my infrastructure, or do I have to follow some best practice beforehand?
2. What type of logging in should I enable in my AWS account?
3. Are security groups and NACL the only firewalls available in AWS?
4. How can I protect my web application from DDoS attacks by using AWS?
5. Can I put all of my resources in one subnet?

Further reading

Security is a very wide field and one chapter cannot be exhaustive. Further resources are available at `https://aws.amazon.com/whitepapers/aws-security-best-practices/`.

The **Center for Internet Security (CIS)** Benchmark for AWS Foundation is a security hardening guideline for securing AWS accounts/environments. Refer to the following links:

- *CIS Amazon Web Services Foundations* at `https://d0.awsstatic.com/whitepapers/compliance/AWS_CIS_Foundations_Benchmark.pdf`
- *CIS Script to check benchmark against the AWS API* at `https://github.com/awslabs/aws-security-benchmark`

For more information on *AWS Certified Security - Specialty*, refer to `https://aws.amazon.com/certification/certified-security-specialty/`.

Assessment

Chapter 1: The Cloud and DevOps Revolution

1. DevOps is a framework and a methodology concerned with adopting the right culture for developers and the operations team to work together.
2. DevOps – IaC stands for **DevOps – Infrastructure as Code**, where we should treat and manage our vertical infrastructure in the form of code, helping us with repeatable, scalable, and manageable infrastructure.
3. The key characteristics of a DevOps culture
   - Source controlling everything
   - Automated testing
   - Automated provisioning
   - Configuration management
   - Automated deployment
   - Measuring
   - Adaptation to virtualization (public/private cloud)
4. The three major service models in the cloud:
   - **Infrastructure as a Service (IaaS)**
   - **Platform as a Service (PaaS)**
   - **Software as a Service (SaaS)**
5. AWS is the largest public cloud service platform available today. AWS offers multiple services, from computing and storage to machine learning and analytics, all of which are highly scalable and reliable. The most important part of using AWS is the *pay-per-use model*. You need not invest in any hardware. Instead, deploy the services, and pay for them until you are using the services. The day you shut down and remove the services, no charges will be applicable - which is great.

Chapter 2: Deploying Your First Web Application

1. If you don't have an AWS cloud account, go to `www.aws.amazon.com` and create a free-tier account. Follow the step-by-step instructions at `https://aws.amazon.com/`. You need to provide your credit or debit card details in order to create an AWS account.

2. Go to `console.aws.amazon.com` and choose **AWS compute services** to create your first EC2 instance. Click on the **Launch Instance** button on the console and follow the steps to select an AMI, instance type (select free-tier in this case), followed by instance details, storage details, tags, and security group. For this exercise, you can select default options as our AIM is just to get familiar with the console portal so that we can automate this process using DevOps practices.

3. Follow the step-by-step instructions provided under the *Creating our first web server* section in the chapter to create your first AWS instance using AWS CLI.

4. Follow the steps mentioned in the *Creating a simple Hello World web application* section in the chapter. You can download the sample code of the application from the following links:
    - `https://raw.githubusercontent.com/yogeshraheja/Effective-DevOps-with-AWS/master/Chapter02/helloworld.js`.
    - `https://raw.githubusercontent.com/yogeshraheja/Effective-DevOps-with-AWS/master/Chapter02/helloworld.conf`.

5. Find the instance ID of your AWS instance using `ec2-metadata --instance-id` and then execute the mentioned command by amending your instance ID: `aws ec2 terminate-instances --instance-ids <YOUR AWS INSTANCE ID>`.

Chapter 3: Treating Your Infrastructure as Code

1. IaC stands for Infrastructure as Code. This is a process of treating your infrastructure objects, such as EC2 instances, VPC network, subnets, load balancers, storage, application deployment and orchestration, and in the form of infrastructure codes. IaC allows the infrastructure vertical to change, replicate, and roll back changes in the entire environment in a very short space of time.

2. Open the CloudFormation template at `https://console.aws.amazon.com/cloudformation` and click on **Create Stack** button. Now create a `helloworld-cf.template` template file, using the Python file located at `https://raw.githubusercontent.com/yogeshraheja/Effective-DevOps-with-AWS/master/Chapter03/EffectiveDevOpsTemplates/helloworld-cf-template-part-1.py`. After doing this, upload a template to Amazon S3. Provide a name to your stack, followed by an SSH key-pair, and other additional information that can be taken as default here. Now review the information and click on **Create**. When the creation of the template is complete, click on the **Outputs** tab and click on **Weburl**, which will take you to the application home page.

   Hint: Generate the CloudFormation template by saving the output of the script in the `python helloworld-cf-template.py > helloworld-cf.template` file.

3. There are multiple SCM offerings available on the market, including GitLab, BitBucket, GitHub, and even SCM offerings by public clouds. Here, we will use one of the most popular SCM offerings: GitHub. Create your free account on Github at `https://github.com`. Once you have done this, log into your GitHub account and create your first public repository with the name `helloworld`.

4. Install a Git package for your supported platform and clone the previously created GitHub repository here using `git clone <github repository URL>`, which you can find from the GitHub console for your repository. Now copy your `helloworld-cf.template` in the repository followed by the `git add` and `git commit` operations. Now you are in a position to push your local repository file to your GitHub account. To do this, execute `git push` to push your committed file and confirm this by checking your GitHub repository.

5. Ansible is a simple, powerful, and easy-to-learn configuration management tool used by the system/cloud engineers and DevOps engineers to automate their regular repetitive tasks. The installation of Ansible is very simple and works as an agentless model.

   In Ansible, modules are the fundamental building blocks for creating Ansible code files written in YAML. These files, written in YAML, are called Ansible Playbooks. Multiple Ansible playbooks are arranged in well defined directory structures, called `roles` in Ansible, where roles are the structure directories for Ansible codes that contain Ansible playbooks, variables, static/dynamic files, and so on. There are also a number of other objects in Ansible, including Ansible Vault, Ansible Galaxy, and a GUI for Ansible called **Ansible Tower**. You can further explore these objects at `https://docs.ansible.com`.

Chapter 4: Infrastructure as Code with Terraform

1. Terraform is a high level infrastructure tool that is primarily used for building, changing, and versioning infrastructure safely and efficiently. Terraform is not a configuration management tool as it focuses on the infrastructure layer and allows tools such as Puppet, Chef, Ansible, and Salt to perform application deployment and orchestration.

2. HashiCorp does not provide native packages for operating systems. Terraform is distributed as a single binary, packaged inside a ZIP archive, which can be downloaded from `https://www.terraform.io/downloads.html`. Once downloaded, extract the `.zip` file and place it under the `/usr/bin` Linux binary path. Once this is done, run `terraform -v` to confirm the installed Terraform version.

3. In order to provision AWS instances using Terraform, you need to initialize the AWS provider by creating a `provider` block inside the `.tf` file. You then have to run `terraform init`. Upon successful initialization, you need to proceed by developing a Terraform template with `resources`. In this case, you need to use the `aws_instance` resource type with the appropriate attribute. Once this is done, validated, and planned, apply your Terraform template to create your first AWS instance.

4. In order to configure Terraform with Ansible, you need to use a **provider**, to initialize the platform; **resources**, to create the platform-related services; and finally **provisioner**, to establish a connection with the created service to install Ansible and to run `ansible-pull` to run Ansible code on the system. You may refer to the following link for a sample Terraform template: `https://raw.githubusercontent.com/yogeshraheja/EffectiveDevOpsTerraform/master/fourthproject/helloworldansiblepull.tf`.

Chapter 5: Adding Continuous Integration and Continuous Deployment

1. The terms CI, CD and continuous delivery can be defined as follows:
    - **Continuous Integration**: A CI pipeline will allow us to test proposed code changes automatically and continuously. This will free up the time of developers and QAs who no longer have to carry out as much manual testing. It also makes the integration of code changes much easier.
    - **Continuous Deployment**: In CD, you drastically accelerate the feedback loop process that DevOps provides. Releasing new code to production at high speed lets you collect real customer metrics, which often leads to exposing new and unexpected issues.
    - **Continuous Delivery**: In order to build our continuous delivery pipeline, we are first going to create a CloudFormation stack for a production environment. We will then add a new deployment group in CodeDeploy, which will provide us with the ability to deploy code to the new CloudFormation stack. Finally, we will upgrade the pipeline to include an approval process to deploy our code to production and the production deployment stage itself.

2. Jenkins is one of the most widely used integration tools to run our CI pipeline. With over 10 years of development, Jenkins has been the leading open-source solution to practice continuous integration for a long time. Famous for its rich plugin ecosystem, Jenkins has gone through a major new release (Jenkins 2.x), which has put the spotlight on a number of very DevOps centric features, including the ability to create native delivery pipelines that can be checked in and version-controlled. It also provides better integration with source control systems such as GitHub

3. In order to implement our continuous deployment pipeline, we are going to look at two new AWS services—CodePipeline and CodeDeploy:
    - **CodePipeline** lets create our deployment pipeline. We will tell it to take our code from GitHub, like we did before, and send it to Jenkins to run CI testing on it. Instead of simply returning the result to GitHub, however, we will then take the code and deploy it to our EC2 instance with the help of AWS CodeDeploy.

- **CodeDeploy** is a service that lets us properly deploy code to our EC2 instances. By adding a certain number of configuration files and scripts, we can use CodeDeploy to deploy and test our code reliably. Thanks to CodeDeploy, we don't have to worry about any kind of complicated logic when it comes to sequencing our deployment. It is tightly integrated with EC2 and knows how to perform rolling updates across multiple instances and, if needed, perform a rollback.

For more details, please refer to *Building a continuous deployment pipeline* section of this chapter

Chapter 6: Scaling Your Infrastructure

1. No, it is not always the best choice because a multi-level application means more components to manage. If your application works well as a monolith, you can accept a short period of downtime and the traffic will not increase over time. You can also consider letting it run as it is.
2. In the multi-level approach used in this book, all software is in one ZIP file, instead in a microservices and more in the serverless approach it is broken in multiple parts. For example, in an e-commerce software (the software used to show the content to the users in one service), the part to manage the backend to place a new product is in one service, while the part to manage the payment is in another service, and so on.
3. If you are not familiar with the service, it can be difficult. However, AWS is full of documentation and video. Furthermore, in this book we demonstrated how to use a set of basic services to break the classic monolith approach in multi-level.
4. This is true for an NLB but you need to pre-warm it if you use an ALB or a CLB. You must also do this if your traffic goes up to more than 50 percent every five minutes.
5. Using the Certificate Manager is free unless you want to **Request a private certificate**, a classic SSL * certificate can also cost 500 dollars a year.
6. Each AWS Region is organized in AZs and each zone is a separate datacenter. Consequently, it is rare that there are issues in one zone but it is not likely multiple issues in the same moment. Each subnet can belong to only one zone so it is convenient to place each component in at least two, or preferably three, zones.

Chapter 7: Running Containers in AWS

1. Docker is a container platform to build, ship and run containerized applications. The four important components of Docker Engine are as follows:

   - **Containers**: A read write template
   - **Images**: A read only template
   - **Network**: A virtual network for containers
   - **Volumes**: A persistent storage for containers

2. Docker CE can be installed on many platforms including Linux, Windows, and MacOS. Refer to `https://docs.docker.com/install/`, the official Docker link, click on your choice of platform, and follow the instructions to install and configure the latest version of Docker CE on your system.

   Confirm the installed Docker CE version by running `docker --version` command.

3. Use a Dockerfile `https://github.com/yogeshraheja/helloworld/blob/master/Dockerfile` and create an image using `docker build` command. This newly created image is an image for Hello World application. Create a container by exposing the port outside using `docker run -d -p 3000:3000 <image-name>`. Once done, check and confirm the webserver outputs either using `curl` or using your public IP with port `3000` from the web browser.

4. Login to your AWS account using your credentials and select **ECS service** from the services tab. There you will find options to Create Amazon ECS Cluster and Amazon ECR repository. At this point, click on **Repository** and create your first ECR repository. The screen will also display some of the commands that you can use to perform an operation on ECR. Similarly, click on the **Cluster** tab followed by **create cluster** on the ECS screen. From here, select your choice of cluster for Windows or Linux or Network only, click 'next step', and fill in the details of your choice. These details include cluster name, provisioning model, EC2 instance type, number of instance, and so on. To complete the process, click **Create**. Once a few minutes have passed, your ECS cluster will be ready to use. In this chapter, we have demonstrated this using CloudFormation. If you are interested in setting up an ECS cluster using the same process, feel free to follow the steps provided in the chapter in *Creating an ECS cluster* section.

Chapter 8: Hardening the Security of Your AWS Environment

1. Before starting to build your infrastructure, it is strongly recommended that you *lock in* your root account (that is, the account bound to your registration email). Then, create IAM users and groups with the necessary privileges, and use MFA (instead of just usernames and passwords) for root and IAM users.

2. You should enable CloudTrail for registering IAM users and role actions, and VPC Flow Logs for monitoring and logging network traffic.

3. No; there is also WAF, an application firewall that works at level 7 of the TPC/IP protocol.

4. You have to follow some best practices to configure your application, expose the least possible surface of the app to the internet and scale up and down. There are also WAF rate rules that help to limit malicious DDoS attacks.

5. In theory, you can, but it is convenient to split them between private and public subnets, to expose only the necessary resources to the internet. Anything else should stay private. Also, it is a best practice to spread parts of your application over multiple availability zones. This means, in practice, using multiple data centers. For these reasons, and also because one subnet can be in a single AZ, you have to use multiple subnets.

Other Books You May Enjoy

If you enjoyed this book, you may be interested in these other books by Packt:

Hands-On Security in DevOps

Tony Hsu

ISBN: 978-1-78899-550-4

- Understand DevSecOps culture and organization
- Learn security requirements, management, and metrics
- Secure your architecture design by looking at threat modeling, coding tools and practices
- Handle most common security issues and explore black and white-box testing tools and practices
- Work with security monitoring toolkits and online fraud detection rules
- Explore GDPR and PII handling case studies to understand the DevSecOps lifecycle

Expert AWS Development
Atul V. Mistry

ISBN: 978-1-78847-758-1

- Learn how to get up and running with AWS Developer Tools.
- Integrate the four major phases in the Release Processes. Source, Build, Test and Production.
- Learn how to integrate Continuous Integration, Continuous Delivery, and Continuous Deployment in AWS.
- Make secure, scalable and fault tolerant applications.
- Understand different architectures and deploy complex architectures within minutes

Leave a review - let other readers know what you think

Please share your thoughts on this book with others by leaving a review on the site that you bought it from. If you purchased the book from Amazon, please leave us an honest review on this book's Amazon page. This is vital so that other potential readers can see and use your unbiased opinion to make purchasing decisions, we can understand what our customers think about our products, and our authors can see your feedback on the title that they have worked with Packt to create. It will only take a few minutes of your time, but is valuable to other potential customers, our authors, and Packt. Thank you!

Index

CPSIA information can be obtained
at www.ICGtesting.com
Printed in the USA
LVHW102155270819
629195LV00012B/739/P

9 781789 539974